Expanding Our Vision

Insights for Language Teachers

Edited by
David J. Mendelsohn

Toronto
Oxford University Press
1999

Oxford University Press
70 Wynford Drive, Don Mills, Ontario M3C 1J9
http:\\ www.oupcan.com

Oxford   New York
Athens Auckland Bangkok   Bogota Buenos Aires
Calcutta   Cape Town   Chennai Dar es Salaam   Delhi
Florence   Hong Kong   Istanbul   Karachi
Kuala Lumpur   Madras   Madrid   Melbourne
Mexico City   Mumbai Nairobi   Paris São Paulo Singapore
Taipei   Tokyo   Toronto Warsaw

and associated companies in
Berlin   Ibadan

Oxford is a trademark of Oxford University Press

This book is printed on permanent (acid-free) paper.

Copyright © Oxford University Press (Canada) 1999. All rights reserved. No part of this book may be reproduced in any form without the written permission of the publisher. Photocopying or reproducing mechanically in any other way parts of this book without the written permission of the publisher is an infringement of the copyright law.

Canadian Cataloguing in Publication Data

Main entry under title:
Expanding our vision

Includes bibliographical references.
ISBN 0-19-541398-9

1. English language—Study and teaching as a second language.*
I. Mendelsohn, David.

PE1128.A2E96 1998   428'.0071   C98-932447-8

Cover and text design by Brett Miller

Photo credits: page 5 UPI/Corbis-Bettmann; page 17 Courtesy of Joseph Bogen, MD; page 41 Linda Fox/Toronto Sun; page 60 Archive Photos; page 74 Courtesy Tom Scovel; page 93 Courtesy of ICELP. Photo by Ami Shitreet; page 110 Courtesy Louise Rosenblatt; page 130 Courtesy Sidney Simon; page 155 McHenry Library, University of Santa Cruz; page 173 Janusz Korczak International Society, courtesy of USHMM Photo Archives.

Printed and bound in Canada
1 2 3 4   99 00 01 02

Contents

Introduction	The Philosophy that Underlies *Expanding Our Vision* by David J. Mendelsohn	1
Chapter One	Joseph Campbell: An Inspiration and Role Model for Language Teachers by Adrian Palmer	5
Chapter Two	Joseph E. Bogen: Clarifying the Wine by Judy B. Gilbert	17
Chapter Three	Jane Jacobs: Eyes on the City by Robert Oprandy	41
Chapter Four	Gabriela Mistral: A Life of Service and Passion by Mary Ann Christison	60
Chapter Five	Myra Scovel: A Woman of Spirit by Thomas Scovel	74
Chapter Six	Reuven Feuerstein: Releasing Unlimited Learning Potential by Marion Williams and Robert Burden	93
Chapter Seven	Louise Rosenblatt: A Voice That Would Not Be Silenced by Carol Hosenfeld	110
Chapter Eight	Sidney Simon: Prizing Our Personal and Cultural Values by Sharron Bassano	130
Chapter Nine	Gregory Bateson Communication and Context: An Ecological Perspective of Language Teaching by Mark A. Clarke	155
Chapter Ten	Janusz Korczak Untunnelling Our Vision: Lessons From a Great Educator by David J. Mendelsohn	173
Notes on Contributors		187

DEDICATION

This book is dedicated to my beloved wife, Jenny,
and my children Lee, Roberto, Noa, and Jon,
whose love and support for me is unconditional.

INTRODUCTION

THE PHILOSOPHY THAT UNDERLIES
EXPANDING OUR VISION

David J. Mendelsohn
York University, Toronto

WE HAVE ALL, AT SOME POINT in our lives, met or read about an individual whose ideas, behaviour, or values have had a profound effect on us—a person we would call "inspirational" or a "role model." These people have moved us, perhaps inspired us to try new things, or empowered us to take bolder steps than we would normally take.

I myself was deeply moved and greatly inspired by the life and ideas of Janusz Korczak (see Chapter 10 in this volume). I first learned about Korczak in the 1960s when I was studying to be a TESOL teacher, and his ideas have guided me all of my professional life. Recently I went back and studied his life and works in more detail. While doing the research on Korczak, I was inspired and captivated in a way that I have never been before, and it struck me that there must be a large number of eminent professionals who have role models as I do. What is more, these role models, who may not be from our own field, have important things to tell us about language education. We tend to think that knowledge and ideas in our field reside in its scholarly literature, and in the main that is true. However, the basic philosophical thinking of each of us, and indeed our greatest inspiration, may well come from elsewhere. We need to keep our eyes open to these ideas and values in other areas and disciplines, as they may have tremendous impact on how we think and function as professionals. These thoughts about the importance of "untunnelling" our vision were the genesis of this book.

I approached nine prominent professionals whose ideas I particularly admire, and who are themselves inspirational teachers, researchers, writers, and speakers very highly regarded in our profession and very well known around the world. I asked them whether they had a role model *outside* of the domain of TESOL or Linguistics who had had a decisive influence on their thinking, and whether they might like to write a chapter for this volume. The response was overwhelming! All nine jumped at the opportunity, and the result is this inspirational volume, *Expanding Our Vision: Insights For Language Teachers*.

The chapters describe the lives and ideas of 10 unique individuals, each of whom has touched the life of the author and inspired changes in his or her thinking and professional work. The range of backgrounds, fields, and ideas represented by these individuals is remarkably broad, yet each and every one has something to say to language teachers. The 10 individuals written about are a comparative mythologist (Campbell), a neurosurgeon and neuroscientist (Bogen), a city planner (Jacobs), a teacher/poet (Mistral), a mother/nurse/writer/teacher (Scovel), a psychologist/educator (Feuerstein), a researcher on reading (Rosenblatt), an expert on peer counselling and values clarification (Simon), an anthropologist/biologist/ecologist (Bateson), and a director of orphanages (Korczak).

Expanding Our Vision, then, is not intended to be a methods book or a book of practical recipes for use in the classroom next day. It is a collection of essays on 10 great women and men whose ideas and beliefs have enormous value and poignancy for us as language teachers and educators. It opens channels to extra-disciplinary ideas and thus "expands our vision" beyond the research world of linguistics and language education. To this end, each author has carefully and explicitly described the insights that the ideas they are discussing offer to language educators.

It is common practice in edited scholarly volumes for the editor in his or her introductory chapter to group the papers into sections and to explain the rationale for the grouping. After much thought, it became evident to me that the very uniqueness of the individuals being described, and the variety of their fields, make such grouping impossible. Moreover, to do so would run counter to the very spirit of this book. I therefore offer a brief summary of each chapter and trust that the value of each one, and the essential connection among them, will clearly present themselves.

In Chapter One, Adrian Palmer discusses Joseph Campbell, the famous teacher and writer on comparative mythologies. Palmer describes Campbell's ideas about the nature of the human experience and the common themes and lessons he drew from cultures around the world. The chapter then focuses on the major themes addressed by Campbell that directly impact on our effectiveness as teachers, on the satisfaction that we derive from the experience, and on the quality of the transformational experience teaching can have on our lives.

In Chapter Two, Judy Gilbert writes about Joseph E. Bogen, a distinguished neurosurgeon, who has devoted a lifetime to studying the cognitive differences between the two hemispheres of the human cerebrum, specifically the idea that the brain has two complementary, but different aptitudes. Gilbert describes the practical relevance of this research for language teachers. Bogen's work on "hemispheric complementarity" explains why we need to teach to exploit the potential power of *both* sides of the brain, rather than rely on the traditional analytic methods that focus primarily on the left hemisphere. This work shows why language learning can be enhanced by visual and kinesthetic techniques.

Robert Oprandy's chapter (Chapter Three) describes the ideas and philosophy of Jane Jacobs, a famous city planner. It is indeed a tribute to Jacobs that her writing on the nature of cities and how they should be planned has clear and very important implications for how we can create more lively and varied school and classroom environments. Oprandy draws fascinating parallels between Jacobs' view of "how to do cities" and how to make them more vital, and the practices of sensitive and creative teachers.

In Chapter Four, Mary Ann Christison writes about the Chilean poet/educator, Gabriela Mistral, recipient of the 1945 Nobel Prize for Literature. In spite of her fame as a writer, Mistral always insisted that she was a teacher first. Teaching was her true vocation. She considered teaching a "spiritual maternity." Christison describes four inspirational themes from Mistral's life and work—themes governed by notions of commitment, service, and love for her students.

Chapter Five, by Tom Scovel, is about Myra Scovel, his mother, a missionary nurse, a person of faith, and someone often caught in international conflicts. Although also a published author, Myra Scovel was never very famous in any conventional sense of the word. Nevertheless, she inspired many in her lifetime with her publications and her personal story. Her lifestory and in particular her experiences with different cultures, often in very difficult circumstances, provide an alternative and inspiring perspective for language teachers today.

Chapter Six is written by Marion Williams and Robert Burden about Reuven Feuerstein, a remarkable psychologist and educator. The chapter focuses on Feuerstein's "Instrumental Enrichment" learning-to-learn program and his dynamic approach to assessment. Feuerstein's basic philosophy is that anyone can be helped to become a fully effective learner. Williams and Burden describe the importance of Feuerstein's theories to language educators in particular, and show how they can inform and help to develop practices and methodologies in teaching a second/foreign language.

Chapter Seven by Carol Hosenfeld is about the work of Louise Rosenblatt, a pioneer in the field of reading research and instruction. Rosenblatt offers a "transactional" view of reading, contesting the more commonly accepted "interactional" view. She also places great importance on readers as "agents" of their own reading and writing. Hosenfeld shows how Rosenblatt's ideas can open up new ways of reviewing how ESL/EFL learners experience texts and how they, as teachers, can facilitate their own transactions with texts.

Sharron Bassano's chapter (Chapter Eight) is about Sidney Simon, a founder of the Values Clarification Movement. Bassano describes how Simon's ideas have altered counselling practice, education, parenting practice, medical care, and social work in the United States and abroad. She emphasizes the special value of Simon's ideas for TESOL professionals, and provides examples of practical TESOL classroom strategies which have been inspired by, and adapted from, Simon's writings.

In Chapter Nine, Mark Clarke focuses on the work of Gregory Bateson, the anthropologist, biologist, and ecologist. The basis of the chapter is Bateson's "systems thinking" and his ideas about the patterns that connect seemingly unconnected phenomena. Clarke applies Bateson's ideas to language education and describes how the main role of the second/foreign language teacher is to create the conditions for people to change themselves. He describes how this calls for flexibility on the part of the teacher and creative use of the learners' experiences in the language classroom. "The basis of such teaching," says Clarke, " is relationship, not method or materials, much less curriculum."

The final chapter, Chapter Ten, by David Mendelsohn is about the life and works of Janusz Korczak. Korczak was an author and a pediatrician-turned-educator who devoted his life to running orphanages in Poland. His work with these disadvantaged children, even in the face of unspeakable cruelty during World War II, is a living testament to his beliefs as to how we should love the people whom we are entrusted to educate. His writings, both fictional and educational, are a beacon of light for all of us.

CHAPTER ONE

Joseph Campbell

An Inspiration and Role Model for Language Teachers

Adrian Palmer
University of Utah

Introduction

A chance childhood visit to Buffalo Bill's *Wild West Show* ignited Joseph Campbell's lifelong fascination with the stories of mythic heroes."Following his bliss" took Campbell to Paris and Germany in the 1920s, and then to Sarah Lawrence College for 38 years. His life and work also led him into meetings with an amazing range of world-famous teachers, artists, and spiritual leaders. Informed by his personal contacts with these individuals and his lifelong love of the printed word, Campbell passed on his own perspectives in 18 books including *The Hero With a Thousand Faces* (1973) and *The Masks of God* (4 vols: 1959, 1962, 1964, 1968), as well as in the videotaped conversations with Bill Moyers, *The Power of Myth* (1992). Transcripts of a series of edited interviews hosted by Michael Toms appear in *An Open Life* (Maher and Briggs 1988). The life of Joseph Campbell is also described in a highly readable biography by Stephen and Robin Larsen, *A Fire in the Mind* (1991).

Discovering Joseph Campbell

Just prior to discovering Joseph Campbell, I had gone through a significant shift in how I perceived teaching and fulfillment in my life. Whereas I had previously thought of teaching as a rather compartmentalized skill to be learned, as if I could master the mechanics of sailing a boat without knowing much about the sea, I was now starting to see teaching as a slice of life, so that the more I knew about life, the better I would be able to teach.

I first encountered Joseph Campbell in a Public Broadcasting Service airing of his videotaped conversations with Bill Moyers, *The Power of Myth* (1992). In these conversations, Campbell spoke to me about the nature of the human experience and the common themes and lessons drawn from it in cultures around the world. Expressed in the myths of these cultures, these themes seemed as relevant to me as they must have been to the people and cultures in which they originated. I immediately ordered audiotapes of the Moyers series, as well as a three-volume set of audiotaped lectures taken from Campbell's final lecture series, *The World of Joseph Campbell: Transformations of Myth Through Time* (1989).

On my frequent car trips through Utah's deserts and national parks, I listened to Campbell tell stories of how Europeans, West and East Indians, Africans, Asians, and peoples from a variety of aboriginal cultures made sense of their lives. Although the meanings they constructed were influenced by the different environments in which they lived, common themes emerged. I found myself drawn to what Joseph Campbell calls "elementary ideas," perspectives more general than those of any particular culture or set of traditions, and I began to explore the elementary ideas as they might relate to my teaching.

ELEMENTARY IDEAS

According to Campbell, all of the mythologies and religions of the world share elementary ideas—common ways of relating to ourselves and to the world around us—and it is these ideas (and not the specific symbols or stories used in any particular religion or mythology) that are of the greatest interest. In fact, Campbell cautions against losing the underlying message through concreticization of the symbol:

> One such symbolic theme ... is the virgin birth which occurs throughout American Indian mythology. This is what awakened me to the realization that these things had nothing to do with historical events. The mythic image of the virgin birth refers to the birth of the spiritual life in the human anima. We can live with the same interests as animals: clinging to life, begetting future generations, and winning our place in the world. But there can open the sense of the spiritual quest and realization—the birth of the spiritual life. And this essentially is the virgin birth (Maher and Briggs 1988: 23).

Of course, for many people, the details of events reported in religions and mythologies do not get in the way of appreciating the underlying messages, but for me the specifics of one story or another have often been distracting enough that I've missed the real lessons. I regret this because I've surely passed over many a valuable insight over the years. According to Campbell:

> We know that there was no Garden of Eden; we know that there was no Universal Flood. So we have to ask, what was the spiritual meaning of the Garden of Eden? What was the spiritual meaning of the Flood? Interpreting Biblical texts literally reduces their value; it turns them into newspaper reports. So there was a flood thousands of years ago? So what? But if you understand what the Flood means in terms of a reference to spiritual circumstances—the coming of chaos, the loss of balance, the end of an age, the end of a psychological posture—then it begins to talk to you again (Maher and Briggs 1988: 67-68).

Campbell taught me that I had a choice. Reading the story of a hero such as Moses, I could preoccupy myself with whether or not the Red Sea actually parted for him and how such an event could be seismologically accounted for, or I could look for a more general underlying principle, such as that with enough faith, conviction, or intention, heroes can, as it were, move heaven and earth to get things done. As a teacher, I have found many occasions where heroic behaviour of one sort or another is called for. For example, giving a deserved low grade and facing a student's anger used to be a frightening experience, and admitting that I was confused, embarrassed, or had made a mistake required a lot of intention and personal courage. And when nothing would have felt better than to put down a student by whom I felt offended, heroic behaviour for me sometimes meant setting my anger aside and doing my best to see the student's point of view.

Reading the stories of religious heroes and their teachings, I realized that I could obsess about whether I would literally "go" to heaven or hell after I die, or whether I would literally be "reborn" as another being after I die, or I could spend some time reflecting on the immediate, here-and-now experiences of heaven, hell, or limbo. I could walk out of a class feeling "like hell," and depending on whether I owned up to the experience and learned from it or whether I simply looked for someone else to blame, I could see that I had a good bit of control of how I would feel when "reborn" the next moment or day.

When I listened to or read about discussions of faith in various cultures and traditions, I also realized that I could spend a lot of energy trying to decide whether specific acts of faith made sense to me or not, or I could look at how the use of faith in general could help me in my life and in my teaching. In fact, I found that some acts of faith, such as adopting a belief that I could always learn something positive from any experience, helped me through difficult times in my teaching and life (if, for no other reason, than focusing on something positive felt better than dwelling on negatives).

UNIVERSAL ENERGIES

Campbell believed the common themes of the mythologies and religions of the world to be expressions of the basic "energies" of the organs of the human body in competition.

> Heaven and hell are within us, and all the gods are within us ... They are magnified dreams, and dreams are manifestations in image form of the energies of the body in conflict with each other ... This organ wants this, that organ wants that. The brain is one of the organs (Campbell 1988: 39).

While he basically offered this observation as a "one-liner" on one of his tapes without much elaboration, his statement caught my attention because of the way it brought spirituality down to earth: our spirituality could be seen as a projection of our physicality. Not only did I appreciate this demystified explanation of the origins of things mystical (gods, deified human beings, spirits, their struggles, and so on), but I also began to look at teaching from this physical perspective.

I practised expecting and anticipating a full range of "energies" from my students, a range encompassing the energies of our physical organs. I tried to plan on encountering students who digested everything I gave them, students who liked heart-to-heart talks, mindful students who loved to ponder, and students who always saw the point and heard me, no matter what. When I was successful in anticipating energies such as these, I felt less judgmental of so-called "negative" energies and seemed able to respond to them more effectively. I also began to enjoy this variety of energies as an expression of the richness of life, and of teaching as a part of life. And relating to these energies in others as expressions of the very energies of my own body helped reduce the distance or separation I felt between myself and my students or colleagues. When someone got on my case, I could always remember that my spleen also produced bile.

RITUALS, RULES, AND LAWS

Campbell taught that one of the major themes of Eastern and pre-12th century Western traditions is that of group psychology. In this view, each of us is an organ in an organism (that is, each of us is a member of society), and the emphasis is on rituals, rules, and laws. Now over the years, rules and rituals have helped me enormously. They have helped me organize my thinking and provide my students with the security of knowing what kinds of instruction to expect in class and what material they are expected to understand. Some of the explicit theories that I have found useful over the years include Rivers' (1964) assumptions underlying audiolingual language teaching, Stevick's (1976) principles underlying memory and meaning, Schumann's (1978) acculturation model for second language acquisition, Krashen's (1985) input hypothesis, Richards' and Rodgers' (1986) principles underlying approaches and methods in language teaching, and Spolsky's (1989) conditions for second language learning.

Campbell described a wide range of specific rituals, rules, and laws that have guided individuals in societies around the world, but I think he was a particular fan of the Buddha, for he spoke at length of Buddhist principles and practices. The following three examples of Buddhist rules have particularly impacted my teaching:

1. *Life is unsatisfactory or imperfect and involves suffering.* When I first heard this principle, I thought it was overly negative and pessimistic, but Campbell thought it was simply realistic. In Campbell's words:

> One of the main problems of mythology is reconciling the mind to this brutal precondition of all life, which lives by the killing and eating of lives. You don't kid yourself by eating only vegetables either, for they, too, are alive. So the essence of life is this eating of itself! (Campbell 1988: 42).

Applied to teaching, this principle helped me to let go of expectations of perfection and focus instead on the steady development and improvement of what will always be imperfect instruction. It also helped me learn to expect inevitable problems. In fact, Sharron Bassano, a contributor to this volume, recently told me, "No matter how hard you try to teach well, there's always someone in the class who hates your guts."

2. All things change. While this second principle seemed reasonable to me when I first heard it, there were (and still are) many teaching situations in which I don't act like it's true. When I've gotten used to a spirited and enthusiastic class, I tend to think that I've finally found the secret to teaching, and from now on my classes will always be lively. After getting several excellent course evaluations in a row, I start expecting this to continue and get upset when it doesn't. After several years of harmony among the members of my department, I feel upset when a new teacher decides not to go along with the group. In circumstances like these, it often takes me quite a time to stop focusing on why the new situation is so messed up and start focusing on how my own expectations of consistency are creating my problem with the situation. I've also found that encouraging new teachers to expect change helps them relax and act more flexibly.

3. The "self" is an illusion. According to Campbell, this principle is more specifically associated with Eastern than Western thought, so for me as a Westerner it seemed quite foreign at first. But people who spend some time trying to locate the "self" within them often report that what they had thought of as the "self" starts to look like merely a string of experiences—thoughts and sensory perceptions of various sorts. They often have trouble finding a consistent glue that holds them together. I've practiced this myself from time to time and found that as long as I am paying attention and staying reasonably focused on the present moment, I also have had trouble finding anything consistent. The thought "I am experiencing all this," however, often seems particularly hard to recognize as a thought (and thus seems relatively permanent). So when I start to daydream and get lost in my thoughts, or when I am either upset about something or in some kind of rapture, the "self" seems very real to me.

In any case, regardless of whether or not the "self" is real, I've found that the more of an investment I have had in my self-image, the more trouble I've made for myself in teaching. These self-image created problems include behaving inflexibly by not listening to student requests with an open mind before making a decision, allowing my current pet ideas, beliefs, and interests to replace what students could rightfully expect to be the main focus of the class, or feeling threatened when students challenge my deeply held beliefs.

INDIVIDUALISM AND THE ADVENTURE

Many organized spiritual traditions emphasize the roles of the spiritual leader and specific kinds of practices for learning life's lessons. According to Campbell, in many of these traditions the teacher or guru has experienced the truth of these principles for himself or herself, knows the path by which one learns to experience the principles, and knows when the student is on the path.

In most of my own search for principles of universal life and teaching, I have focused on the elementary ideas common to mythological and religious traditions of ancient India, ancient Greece, and early Christianity. In fact, I was so taken by these ideas that I listened to Campbell's earlier tapes over and over and didn't really want to leave the sources of ancient wisdom which had always held a particular fascination for me. Then, two thirds of the way through the audiotapes of *The World of Joseph Campbell: Transformations of Myth Through Time* (1989), I first heard Campbell speak of the "Arthurian Legends and the Western Way."

According to Campbell, with the unique tales of the Arthurian romances in the middle of the 12th century emerged the central theme of modern Western civilization, which distinguishes it from earlier Christian traditions, as well as from the traditions of the Orient. That central theme is respect for the individual and the individual way. According to Campbell (1989, vol. 3, program 1), that which we intend, that which is the journey or the goal, is the fulfillment of something that never was on the earth before, namely one's own potentialities. In searching for the Holy Grail, we find that transcendent power within us, our own potentiality: "every human being enters the forest of the adventure at a point that [one] has chosen, where it was darkest, and there is no path." In this new tradition, Christ became a symbol, a metaphor for that transcendent power which is the support and being of one's own life.

While I always sensed Joseph Campbell's profound respect for ancient traditions, it was here that I first heard him speak with passion for an idea that seemed to resonate with his own heart, as it did with mine. I'm not entirely sure why, but perhaps it was because after years of trying out others' principles and procedures for living and teaching I had begun to wear out most of my illusions, my hopes that someone else would provide me with my answers and my sense of direction. Not that others' paths and principles were not useful—of course, they were. But at some point the principles and procedures of others seemed to stop working for me, or they seemed inappropriate or somewhat irrelevant given where I was at. In any case, I was fascinated to find out that an entire cultural tradition had come to the same conclusion, that ultimately we need to work things out for ourselves. I was also intrigued with the parallel between the late emergence of this cultural tradition and the rather late emergence of self-reliance in the lives of "seekers-of-truth" people like me. I also found there to be an interesting parallel within our own profession, as indicated by the relatively late emergence of focus on individual differences in second language learning (Schumann 1997, Skehan 1989).

So what is the role of the teacher and rules in this tradition? According to Campbell, individuals can get clues from people who have followed their own paths, but we then have to bounce off their experiences and translate them into our own decisions. There is no book of rules, and we fail on the adventure when we do what we are supposed to do, rather than what we want to be doing. On this quest, when we come upon the path of another and think, "Oh, he's getting there" and begin to follow that, we go astray totally, even though the other person may get there. In Campbell's frequently quoted words, "If there is a path, it is someone else's path, and you are not on the adventure."

Well, how do you know you are on your own path? Campbell says you're on your own path when you're "following your bliss, going where your heart leads you, living an authentic life instead of doing what you're supposed to do."

> If you have the guts to follow the risk, however, life opens, opens, opens up all along the line. I'm not superstitious, but I do believe in spiritual magic, you might say. I feel that if one follows what I call one's 'bliss'—the thing that really gets you deep in the gut and that you feel is your life—doors will open up. They do! They have in my life and they have in many lives that I know of (Maher and Briggs 1988: 24).

All around us in TESOL are colleagues and friends who are following their own paths, their bliss. Carolyn Graham developed *Jazz Chants* because she loved performing as a jazz pianist in nightclubs. Tom Scovel, a contributor to this volume, loves language, loves puns, and loves to give talks which I appreciate as much for his wit as for his message. Ted Rodgers, among whose many passions are singing and performing, presents entire plenary convention addresses in song, or in dialogue with a mechanical parrot against a pyrotechnic background. On a somewhat quieter but no less personally rewarding note, Stephen Krashen talks about how much he enjoys, among other things, going to the library with a roll of nickels and plenty of time to read, photocopy, and then synthesize.

Recently I met Millie Grenough, a long-time ESL teacher and materials developer, at a convention for ESL teachers in Monterey, Mexico. Millie gave several spirited presentations on the use of song in language teaching, using materials from *Sing It! Learn English Through Songs* (1995)—books and cassettes she had created to encourage other teachers to use songs to help people learn language and self-expression. One morning at breakfast, I asked Millie to tell me about how she got into teaching through music. Here's her story:

> When I was 29 years old and had been a Catholic missionary nun for eight years, I realized that that was no longer the life for me. The realization did not come instantly. I had been raised in a very Catholic family, and the highest aspiration for a Catholic girl at that time was to be a nun, and even better, to be a missionary nun. I did that, thoroughly, and learned immeasurably about other people and myself, especially in my years working in Bolivia and Peru.
>
> It was these experiences in Latin America which cracked my head open, jolting the Kentucky Catholic values which had led me to this life. Abandoning this commitment was not easy. After several years of wrestling with 'shoulds,' 'what I was meant to do in this life,' 'the needs of the people,' 'my calling,' etc., I knew that I had to make a clear decision to stay or to go. Once I faced the either/or choice, the matter seemed simpler. I felt that if I stayed, I would die, and the

God that the Latin American people had helped me to meet in a new way would certainly not want me to kill the spirit that was given me.

I went to the Sisters Motherhouse to clarify my decision. After a month of soul-searching and prayer, I knocked on the door of Sister Grace Mary, the Superior, to ask to speak with her. She was busy then and asked me to come back the next afternoon. Next afternoon, I went in. Sister Grace Mary asked, 'What is it, Sister?' I said immediately, 'I have to leave.' She listened calmly and, to her everlasting credit, did not try to convince me to stay. After listening to me a while, she asked matter-of-factly, 'What will you do, Sister?' Her question stunned me. I had not a clue about what I would do instead. I just knew that I needed to be out. She noticed my shock and then asked, 'What has ever made you happy in your life?' That question also shocked me. I had no answer. She said, 'Why don't you think about that and come back and talk with me when you have an answer.'

For the better part of two weeks I searched to come up with something that had really made me happy. Even though my life had been filled with many 'wonderful' things, at least to the eyes of others, none of them answered that question in a way that truly mattered. At last I got a few glimmers: it had to be something with music, and more, something about doing music with others. Some clear memories began coming through—singing with my family on car trips and making up harmonies as we did the dishes ... learning guitar from my Chicana friend Graciela when we were in the novitiate together ... fighting my way through Spanish grammar by memorizing Mexican and Bolivian songs given to me by my teachers ... trading spirituals for Peruvian valses as I learned more guitar from [disabled] guitarist Eduardo in Lima ... singing with the children and adults in Caja de Agua ... So at last I knocked on her door to tell her: 'I've got to find a way to do music and do it with other people.' That was the thread.

After that, when I was in my first ESL class with students from 15 different countries and I asked what they knew in common, a guy from Peru knew 15 Beatles sounds, a guy from Chile knew 40-50 Beatles songs by heart, a Slovak dentist loved 'Clementine.' And a businessman from Korea, who I thought would never talk, when I said my name was Millie and I was from Kentucky, his eyes lit up, and he started singing 'Oh Susanah.' Within that first week I began gathering a list of songs that either I knew they liked or I knew would be useful, and began using them immediately.

Three years later, I was teaching at an institute of North American studies in Barcelona, but I was not using my music. Then flying back over the Atlantic I was talking with my seatmate and I said, 'I'm really bored. I wish I could do more music.' My seatmate fell asleep.

In the hours during which she slept, I cooked up this scheme for my boss, Robert Ramsey, that he would let me be the wandering minstrel and go to various classes. Teachers would give me one week's notice of what they were teaching, and I would find a song or songs that would illustrate that teaching point and work up activities to go with it. Robert suggested that I bring it up with the teachers at the next meeting, and that's where *Sing It* began, way back in 1972 (Grenough personal communication).

Over the years, I've seen languages taught through art by teachers who love to draw, through drama by actors, through computers by hackers, through storytelling by talkers, through literature by deconstructionists, through poetry by teachers who love to rhyme, and by the structural approach by teachers who live by their day planners. Their enthusiasm for what they do is contagious—and inspiring. So when students beginning to study TESOL ask me what they ought to be doing, or when I start worrying about where what I am doing will lead, I try to encourage them to follow their bliss, to become aware of what it is they really enjoy, to find some way to express their personal variety of joy in their professional lives, and then trust that in its own mysterious way, teaching as an expression of who we are can provide us with the opportunities we need.

CONCLUSION

Far from being a guru with all of the answers, Joseph Campbell believed that life is ultimately a mystery to be lived rather than figured out, that we cannot be in another person's experience, and that we surely cannot experience life outside of the limits of our own senses, those of our species. And who's to say that the human species has cornered the market on ultimate reality? While some might understandably say that this mystical orientation has little to do with our lives as teachers, I have found that viewing life as ultimately a mystery helps me share my own experience freely with my students without taking myself or my ideas too seriously.

Campbell understood and appreciated a huge variety of traditions and ways of understanding the human experience. He honoured the history, traditions, and principles of seekers before him while also respecting the uniqueness of each human being's experience. In my life, both professional and personal, when I think of Joseph Campbell, I ask: "How can I engage enthusiastically in my own life and teaching without imposing my values on others? How can I learn from others without giving up my individuality? How can I live and teach as Campbell did, participating joyfully in an imperfect world and experiencing the magnificence of it all?"

REFERENCES CITED

Campbell, J. 1959, 1962, 1964, 1968. *The Masks of God*, 4 vols. New York: Viking.

———. 1973. *The Hero With a Thousand Faces*. Bollingen Series XVII. Princeton, NJ: Princeton University Press.

———. 1988. *The Power of Myth. With Bill Moyers*. New York: Doubleday.

———. 1989. *The World of Joseph Campbell: Transformations of Myth Through Time*, 3 vols. St. Paul, MN: HighBridge Productions.

———. 1992. *The Power of Myth*. New York: Mystic Fire Video.

Grenough, M. 1995. *Sing It! Learn English Through Songs*. Blacklick, OH: McGraw-Hill.

Krashen, S. ed. 1985. *The Input Hypothesis: Issues and Implications*. Essex, England: Longman.

Larsen, S. and R. Larsen. 1991. *A Fire in the Mind: The Life of Joseph Campbell*. New York: Doubleday.

Maher, J. and D. Briggs. 1988. *An Open Life: Joseph Campbell in Conversation with Michael Toms*. Burdett, New York: Larson Publications.

Richards, J. and T. Rodgers. 1986. *Approaches and Methods in Language Teaching*. Cambridge: Cambridge University Press.

Rivers, W. 1964. *The Psychologist and the Foreign Language Teacher*. Chicago: University of Chicago Press.

Schumann, J. 1997. *The Neurobiology of Affect in Language*. Language Learning Monograph Series. Malden, MA: Blackwell Publishers.

———. 1978. *The Pidginization Process: A Model for Second Language Acquisition*, ch. 7. Rowley, MA: Newbury House.

Skehan, P. 1989. *Individual Differences in Second-Language Learning*. London: Edward Arnold.

Spolsky, B. 1989. *Conditions for Second Language Learning*. Oxford: Oxford University Press.

Stevick, E. 1976. *Memory, Meaning, and Method*, chs. 1-3. Rowley, MA: Newbury House.

Additional Bibliography

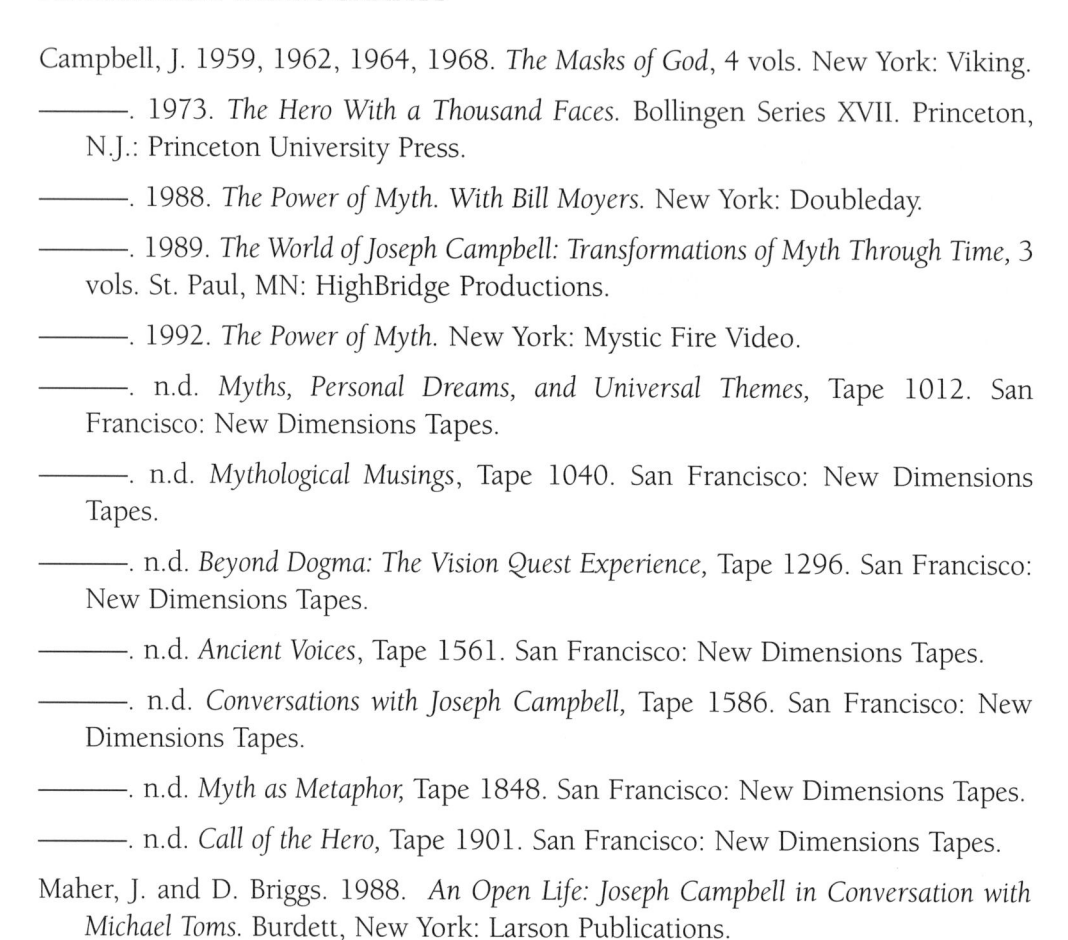

Campbell, J. 1959, 1962, 1964, 1968. *The Masks of God*, 4 vols. New York: Viking.

———. 1973. *The Hero With a Thousand Faces.* Bollingen Series XVII. Princeton, N.J.: Princeton University Press.

———. 1988. *The Power of Myth.* With Bill Moyers. New York: Doubleday.

———. 1989. *The World of Joseph Campbell: Transformations of Myth Through Time*, 3 vols. St. Paul, MN: HighBridge Productions.

———. 1992. *The Power of Myth.* New York: Mystic Fire Video.

———. n.d. *Myths, Personal Dreams, and Universal Themes*, Tape 1012. San Francisco: New Dimensions Tapes.

———. n.d. *Mythological Musings*, Tape 1040. San Francisco: New Dimensions Tapes.

———. n.d. *Beyond Dogma: The Vision Quest Experience*, Tape 1296. San Francisco: New Dimensions Tapes.

———. n.d. *Ancient Voices*, Tape 1561. San Francisco: New Dimensions Tapes.

———. n.d. *Conversations with Joseph Campbell*, Tape 1586. San Francisco: New Dimensions Tapes.

———. n.d. *Myth as Metaphor*, Tape 1848. San Francisco: New Dimensions Tapes.

———. n.d. *Call of the Hero*, Tape 1901. San Francisco: New Dimensions Tapes.

Maher, J. and D. Briggs. 1988. *An Open Life: Joseph Campbell in Conversation with Michael Toms.* Burdett, New York: Larson Publications.

CHAPTER TWO

Joseph E. Bogen

Clarifying the Wine

Judy B. Gilbert
University of California, Berkeley

Hay que sedimentarlo.
In thought, as in wine, clarity takes time.
— Spanish proverb

Introduction

> Something I owe to the soil that grew—
> More to the life that fed—
> But most to Allah Who gave me two
> Separate sides to my head.
>
> I would go without shirts or shoes
> Friends, tobacco, or bread
> Sooner than for an instant lose
> Either side of my head.
> (Rudyard Kipling 1901, 1987:179)

The natural history of a scientific idea often shows a pattern of pendulum swings of fashion. This article is about such an idea, *complementary hemispheric specialization*, meaning that each hemisphere in a human brain has different but complementary special capacities. The article is also about an individual, Joseph Bogen, MD, who refused to look at the world in the prescribed narrow way, saw new possibilities, and continued to pursue those possibilities despite storms of controversy. In effect, this is an article about the human benefits of a broader vision.

The Physical Setting

In order to understand the cognitive issues involved in this article, it helps to have a mental picture of the brain and a few technical terms:

> The brain looks something like a mushroom. It has a stem with the overhanging *cerebrum*, which doesn't look like the canopy of an ordinary mushroom but actually more like a walnut. The cerebrum looks like a walnut because it's all wrinkled and because it has two halves called the *cerebral hemispheres*. Like the two halves of a walnut, the two cerebral halves are joined together by the *corpus callosum*, which is a bundle of millions of nerve fibres. If the corpus callosum is cut, in an operation called a *callosotomy*, then we have what is called the *split brain* (Bogen interview: 10/5/96).

In this article, I will present the history of the concept of "Right Brain/Left Brain Thinking" as seen through the work of Joseph Bogen, "a pioneering surgeon and brain researcher" (Wittrock 1975:1). Then I will suggest why these ideas, shorn of a popularization which has led to much misinterpretation, have useful implications for today's communicative classroom. They are useful both as a rationale for increasing the use of visual and kinesthetic (physical) aids in language teaching, and as a reason to balance the usual attention to details of grammar and individual sounds with a complementary attention to discourse-level communication.

Sometimes it takes a long time for a story to settle out to the point that reasonable conclusions can be reached. In this article, I hope to clarify some of the issues and separate the sediment from the wine.

Historical Background

Since the beginning of recorded time, literature and myth, oral tradition, poetry and dreams, have all repeated the same concept of two natures living in the same body. Popular images easily come to mind: for instance, Dr. Jekyl and Mr. Hyde. This duality, doubled but not the same, has recurred in such a persistent way that religious thinkers, philosophers, and more recently psychologists, have long tried to divine the underlying duality which drives human beings to create these contrasting images. Why has this been such a persistent theme of art, philosophy, and psychology?

19th Century

From early in the 19th century, medical authors debated and wrote about the possible locations of various aspects of thought in the brain, and the possibility that the two cerebral hemispheres, although appearing identical, could function independently to some degree. As the century moved on, interest in the duality of the two hemispheres was eclipsed by a more observable phenomenon: that injury to the left hemisphere interfered with language, while injury to the right hemisphere hardly interfered with language at all. This fact was established by a number of 19th century physicians. The left hemisphere became known as the "Dominant Hemisphere" because of preoccupation with language loss. The right hemisphere was called the "Minor Hemisphere" and was generally seen as having an automatic, or possibly, a reserve function.

The left hemisphere was considered dominant because it governed language, but it seems also that 19th century medical men were uneasy about the possible functions of the right hemisphere. Science historian Anne Harrington (1987) constructed a table of the most commonly assigned "left/right polarities of mind and brain" (Table 1). It is striking how these two columns seem to line up as good and bad attributes. Oddly enough, 100 years later, when the "Split Brain Dichotomania" was in full flood, many authors would reverse these attributes in terms of good and bad. Neither set of opposite polarities was sound scientifically, but in both the 19th and 20th centuries, some zealous educators proposed them as justification for radical curricular innovations.

Table 1
Left/Right Polarities of Mind and Brain, Posited by 19th Century Medical Writers

Left Hemisphere	Right Hemisphere
humanness	animality
volition	instinct
motor activity	sensory activity
intelligence	passion/emotion
male	female
white superiority	nonwhite inferiority
consciousness	unconsciousness
reason	madness

(Harrington 1987:100)

20th Century

In the first half of the 20th century, while medical interest remained focused on the left hemisphere, researchers began to realize that patients with injuries only on the right side of the brain tended to show more severe spatial and perceptual disorders than those with injury or disease on the left side (Zangwill 1961). Wider recognition followed Brenda Milner's (1971) summary of the accumulated evidence for this finding. Other researchers have come to realize that the "Minor Hemisphere" might well have equally important cognitive and communicative functions as the "Dominant Hemisphere" (Van Lancker 1997).

The Split-Brain Cats

The importance of the split-brain humans, to be described below, can be understood more easily with some knowledge of previous work with animals and a few technical terms.

During the first half of this century, there were two independent, unrelated lines of research. One line of research had demonstrated *hemispheric specialization* in humans on the basis of studying the effects of brain damage (Milner 1971; Zangwill 1961). Meanwhile, in an entirely different line of study, researchers at the California Institute of Technology were splitting cats' brains, and seeing that after this surgery these cats had *hemispheric independence*. That is, each hemisphere could function without any transfer of information from the other half. At that time, nobody connected these two lines of research.

Early in the 1950s, Roger Sperry of the California Institute of Technology demonstrated that cutting the *corpus callosum* (the connecting tissue of the two hemispheres) in animals largely abolishes interhemispheric transfer of sensory and learned information. He cut both the corpus callosum and the optic nerve crossing in a cat so that visual information from the animal's left eye made its way to only the left hemisphere, and information from the right eye to only the right hemisphere. In a normal animal, information seen by either eye is readily shared by both sides of the brain, but these cats were different. In its everyday behaviour, the split-brain cat appeared relatively unaffected by this surgery. However, specially designed tests for unilateral learning capacity showed a remarkable change. Working on a problem with one eye, the animal learned to solve a problem. When, however, that eye was covered and the same problem was presented to the other eye, the cat did not understand what it had to do and had to learn the task all over again with the other hemisphere. Sperry concluded from this that "splitting" the cat's brain had shown that there were two independent minds, each capable of learning separately. This is the work which contributed to Sperry's sharing the Nobel Prize in 1981.

Joseph Bogen, a medical student at the time, and spending the summer of 1955 as a graduate research assistant at the California Institute of Technology, met Sperry and observed the split-brain cats. Bogen later wrote about this event, "It was for me the most influential scientific experiment that I have ever seen or known about. It set the course of my life" (Bogen in press).

The Split-Brain Humans

In 1958, following two years in general surgery, Bogen returned to the California Institute of Technology to study neurophysiology. By this time, Sperry was working with split-brain monkeys; like the cats, they seemed quite normal in everyday behaviour. As Bogen continued to think about Sperry's work, his moment of insight occurred. He considered that maybe, when you had *human* subjects in which the hemispheres were functioning independently, with no cross transfer of information, it would be possible to get direct evidence for hemispheric specialization. That is to say, it occurred to him that there could be a connection between Sperry's work with hemispheric independence, and the possibility of testing separately what each hemisphere could actually do alone. In other words, for the first time someone had connected the two long lines of research: *hemispheric independence* and *complementary hemispheric specialization*.

At that time, Bogen's medical interest was intractable epilepsy, and he came to the clinical literature of partial *callosotomy* (cutting the callosal connection between the hemispheres) in order to stop the transfer of "electrical storms" from one side of the brain to the other. Callosotomies had been performed previously, with limited and diverse results. However, Bogen reasoned that the follow-up studies were deficient, both for lack of the tests developed by Sperry and because the operations had often been incomplete. This suggested that a complete callosotomy could more likely stop the epileptic seizure from involving the entire brain. The question then arose: Who would be a suitable candidate? Bogen described how he met the world's first complete callosotomy patient:

> I first met Bill Jenkins in the summer of 1960 when he was brought to the emergency room in *status epilepticus*; I was the neurology resident then on call. [Bogen describes how severe and intractable this man's condition was, and how he arranged for Jenkins to spend six weeks at the National Institute of Health Epilepsy Service.] Bill was sent home in the spring of 1961, having been informed that there was no treatment, standard or innovative, available for his problem.
>
> Bill and his wife Fern were then told of [previous results with partial cutting of the corpus callosum]. I suggested that a complete section [cutting] might help. Their enthusiasm encouraged me to approach Vogel [the Chief of Neurosurgery], who suggested that we practise a half-dozen times in the morgue. By the end of the summer, the procedure seemed reasonably in hand. During the period of preoperative testing, Bill said, 'You know, even if it doesn't help my seizures, if you learn something it will be more worthwhile than anything I've been able to do for years.' He was operated on in February 1962 (Bogen 1997:24-8).

The operation was successful: Jenkins' seizures almost entirely disappeared. The surgery was followed by others, with similar good results, and modifications of this operation have since become standard procedure for certain types of cases.

As soon as the original operation had been approved, Bogen had turned to Sperry at the California Institute of Technology to design an experimental study of the cognitive effects of the operation, since when Jenkins recovered, this would mark the first time in history that it would be possible to study the independent workings of the two hemispheres in a human brain.

Aaron Smith, Emeritus Professor of Neuropsychology, University of Michigan, has commented:

> First, while it is not widely known, although Roger Sperry was awarded the Nobel prize largely because of his studies of Dr. Bogen's and Dr. Vogel's patients with commissurotomy [callosotomy] for intractable seizures, the enormous research that was developed in studies of these patients [began with] Dr. Bogen, who succeeded in persuading Sperry about the unique opportunities that commissurotomy afforded for studying the functions of each of the two hemispheres before and after the sectioning of the forebrain commissures. Not only did he provide the patients and neurosurgical clinical background, but he also collaborated with Dr. Sperry in designing and developing unique approaches in experimental and clinical research studies of these remarkable patients (Smith personal communication: 10/18/96).

The split-brain patients appeared, after recovery from the operation, to be unchanged in temperament, personality, and general intelligence. However, it could be assumed that, like the split-brain cats and monkeys, they would have defects in interhemispheric transfer of information. Sperry's group developed tests to demonstrate similar transfer deficits with these humans. Initial testing of the split-brain patients quickly demonstrated a dramatic "disconnection syndrome," such that information put into one hemisphere was not available to the other. This made it possible, for the first time in history, to test each hemisphere of a human being for the specialization of each side, rather than only inferring specialization from the disabilities due to damage restricted to one or the other hemisphere. What specializations were found?

In a famous article, Sperry said:

> Though predominantly mute and generally inferior in all performances involving language or linguistic or mathematical reasoning, the minor hemisphere is nevertheless clearly the superior cerebral member for certain types of tasks .... Largely they involve the apprehension and processing of spatial patterns, relations, and transformations. They seem to be holistic and unitary rather than analytic and fragmentary, and orientational more than focal, and to involve concrete perceptual insight rather than abstract, symbolic, sequential reasoning (Sperry 1974:11).

Robert Ornstein, educational psychologist [discussing the older ideas calling the left hemisphere the "Major Hemisphere"], said:

> However, the conception of the function of the two hemispheres is changing, largely because of the superb work of Roger Sperry and Joseph Bogen and the increasing evidence, from thousands of new articles, of the brain's lateral specialization (Ornstein 1986:92).

In summary, the split-brain studies added to the body of research literature in confirming the principle of *complementary hemispheric specialization*, utilizing the phenomenon of *hemispheric independence*. *Complementary specialization* means that each hemisphere specializes in something different, so that what one lacks, the other can provide.

THE PENDULUM EFFECT

By an accident of history, the split-brain reports came to the public attention in the 1960s, popularly known as "The Age of Aquarius." This was a social period favouring dichotomies between Eastern Philosophy and Western Rationalism. Perhaps because of this coincidence of science and culture, the Left Brain/Right Brain dichotomy reached a near tidal wave of enthusiasm, especially marked in the educational community. Harrington described the context in which this hyperenthusiasm thrived:

> The rediscovery of the double brain in the 1960s coincided with a period in the English-speaking world marked by extreme ambivalence toward science and technology and, by extension, toward rational, analytic thinking in general ... [this] led to the rise of alternative value systems that stressed the virtues of other ways of knowing. The emerging notion of the brain's "bimodal consciousness" was to prove itself admirably suited to the ideological needs of this counterculture movement .... one finds a growing tendency to equate the left hemisphere with the evils of modern, technological society (Harrington 1987:283).

In other words, the good/bad polarity scheme was more or less a simple reversal of the 19th century conception of the two sides of human nature, due to social and historical factors at the time. Unfortunately, this enthusiastic "dichotomania" produced an extravagance of exaggeration. Some educational writers suggested altering the curriculum to suit hemispheric preferences, in one case suggesting that teachers should watch to see which direction students' eyes moved as an indication of the "right or left brain dominance" of the individual, upon which the teacher should base a curricular approach suited to the individual needs. Aside from being flawed scientifically, the practical demands this would make on a teacher would be considerable. A few schemes went to truly bizarre lengths, as in this proposal: "a system of mind development that involved binding the right arm in a cast and sling so as to prod the right hemisphere into action and thereby stimulate the intuitive faculties" (Weil, as quoted in Harrington 1987:283). Harrington also points to a 1985 article that proposed "ten ways to develop your right brain," including such exercises as "one day a week, make it a rule that no one in the office or plant can use the word *no*, because the right hemisphere has no equivalent of *no*" (Harrington 1987:284).

This kind of nonsense naturally produced a matching reaction, causing some educators to publish doubts that there might be *any* relevant applications to teaching. The pendulum effect grew in momentum, ultimately producing career-enhancing books and papers debunking the entire notion that the two hemispheres might have different cognitive functions (Hardyck 1979; Levy 1985; Efron 1990).

In spite of the pendulum of fashion, some of the original researchers, including Bogen, continued carefully to build the case for complementary hemispheric specialization. Benson described what happened:

> Following an initial period of exuberant and rather fanciful postulations concerning the activities of the two hemispheres, a considerable retraction to more solid observations has occurred .... The observations of the 1950s and 1960s emanated from neurosurgical procedures ... they clearly demonstrated that each cerebral hemisphere was capable of a mental life, even when the other hemisphere was absent, and that when the two hemispheres were both present but anatomically separated, significant differences in the function of the two hemispheres could be demonstrated (Benson 1985:385).

Now that there is a subsidence of the hoopla and its subsequent backlash, the patient work of Bogen and his colleagues from various fields seems to me worth a review at this time, when our field is focused on teaching language for communicative purposes. Perhaps it has taken the full 30 years for these concepts to clarify and mature into a usable form.

WHAT MAKES AN INNOVATIVE MIND?

Victoria Fromkin, Professor of Linguistics, UCLA, wrote:

> Would like to hear more about your work re Joe Bogen who is a great hero of mine ... I always thought he was a frustrated philosopher. Well, he is really a philosopher but I think he would have liked to be recognized as one rather than as a brain surgeon (Fromkin personal communication: 10/1/96).

Joseph Bogen was raised in a family with unusually wide-ranging interests. His mother, an MD, was also a PhD in Biochemistry and she combined laboratory research with her psychiatric practice. His father, a constitutional lawyer, was an Honorary Nisei Veteran because of his work on behalf of Japanese-American internees during World War II.

Bogen graduated from high school at age 16 in 1942, studied chemical engineering at the California Institute of Technology, served two years in the navy as a radar technician, and then earned a BA in economics at Whittier College. At this point he turned to medicine, which meant taking all the pre-med science courses he had not been interested in previously. Two unusual events marked Bogen's time in medical school. First, he published an article (1956) expressing doubt about an aspect of received medical wisdom, which so offended some of the faculty that he was nearly expelled. More thoughtful members of the Dean's Committee recognized his serious intent and he was allowed to graduate. The other distraction occurred when he took time from medical study to help his father write a brief for the US Supreme Court, which resulted in a landmark decision concerning conscientious objection to military service. His subsequent career has shown a similar wide range of interests.

I had two opportunities to interview Bogen, in August and October of 1996. Following are excerpts from these interviews, demonstrating how his lectures to teachers presented complicated issues in an accessible way by using metaphors to illustrate abstract concepts.

How did you get involved with split brains?
> When I was in medical school, I spent every summer in neurophysiology labs. In 1955, that summer, I was at the California Institute of Technology with Van Harreveld and down the hall was Roger Sperry and his split-brain cats. Unless you know the story about the split-brain cats, what I am about to say isn't going

to make much sense. Let me just summarize it all by saying that it *boggled my mind* when I saw these split-brain cats and it changed the course of my life.

[Later he was discussing *hemispherectomy*—removal of one of the hemispheres—which he described as a common operation.]

What is the purpose of such an operation?
> To control epilepsy. Turns out, surprising as it may seem, that when people get brain damage in early childhood or at birth, of the kind that causes epilepsy, the damage is quite often just in one hemisphere and not both. So if you take out the injured one, they do better because then it's not interfering with the function of the good one.

Can they live normally with just half a brain?
> That's a great lesson. That's Lesson Number Two. Let me back up and tell you about Lesson Number One. Everything in the cerebrum, except for a couple of glands, is double. They're in duplicate. Is it in duplicate like the runners of a sleigh? Or, is it in duplicate like a team of horses pulling the sleigh? If you take one runner off the sleigh it won't go. But if you take one horse away, the other horse can still pull the sleigh. Not as fast, not as far, but adequately. So how well somebody with one hemisphere does depends on how good the residual hemisphere is. One of these patients had a verbal IQ of 126. An IQ of 100 is average, right? Standard deviation is about 15. So if you had an IQ of 130, you would be smarter than 95% of the population. This person, with only one cerebral hemisphere, has a verbal IQ of 126. He's smarter than the majority of the people you've met in your whole life.

With one hemisphere? Can you imagine if he'd had two?
> Yeah, well. Maybe. We don't know that.

Wouldn't he be smarter with two?
> That's not altogether clear. If you've got two hemispheres, one is probably butting in to the function of the other one from time to time, even if you don't have epilepsy. So it's not that clear that he'd be twice as good if he had two of them. Anyway, Lesson Number One is that the anatomy is double. Lesson Number Two is that the function is double—like a team of horses. It's not like the runners on a sleigh. Hemispherectomy demonstrates that very clearly. You know, if you've got a lame horse, it keeps getting in the way all the time and you'd be better off to get that horse out of there and just get the one good one to pull the thing. Now, suppose you don't take out a hemisphere, suppose you just go in and cut the corpus callosum. That's the split brain. It turns out, if you

do that, it's relatively easy, for professionals, to train one hemisphere to do things one way and the other hemisphere to do them the other way. And that's the way it is with the split-brain cats.

Please get back to your reaction to the cats when you first saw Sperry's demonstration. What "boggled your mind?"

It's obvious when you look at the split-brain cat, that it has two minds. I arrived at that moment, in 1955, with a lot of prior convictions—by that time I was already almost 30 years old. One belief I had was that everybody's got another mind inside their head. And I believed that before I ever saw these cats. And another thing I believed was that anything that's psychological has to have a physiological basis. There it was, right there! There was the physiological basis for the duality of mind.

What happens when you split the brain of a cat? What's the most noticeable change in behaviour?

You can't tell it from a normal cat. I could, but you couldn't. Suppose we had 16 cats in a row, like a police line-up. And suppose 3 or 4 of them are split-brain cats. You could watch them walking around and you still wouldn't be able to tell.

What about a split-brain human being?

If you lined up people of comparable intelligence—police line-up thing again, you couldn't tell which one had a split brain. You'd go out to lunch with them and you couldn't tell which one's the split-brain. With the split-brain ones, 200 million nerve fibres have been cut and in a social situation they are ordinary, socially ordinary.

Then what is this all about?

One of the great questions in the study of mankind is how can somebody be *unified*, and not be conflicted. That's true for anything that's alive. Anything that you call an organism. That's what it means to *be* an organism. If you burn a giant sequoia near the bottom of the trunk, the tree dies down from the top an appropriate amount, to correspond with the loss of cambrium on one side. The whole thing is an entity. How does one end of the tree know what the other end is doing? The answer is hormones. Trees are full of hormones which carry messages around inside the tree. They don't carry messages as fast as the nervous system does, so trees react slowly. Whereas an animal has a nervous system. Both these things are unifying mechanisms to keep the thing organized into an organism. Well, the corpus callosum is one of the main unifying features in the nervous system. Not the only one, but a significant one.

But what's the effect of cutting the corpus callosum, disconnecting the two sides?
> Well, some simple little thing would be that the information coming in from one hand is not connected to the information from the other hand. If you can't see your hands, the hands don't work together very well—like underneath a table, or in the total dark, where you can't see what the hands are doing. Now, if you can look, then each hemisphere can see what's going on and the head can move from side to side, so whatever's going on with the hands is available to both hemispheres, even without a corpus callosum for transfer of information.

And what is the main point to be learned?
> There are two points. One is that the two hemispheres can operate separately, and they don't think in the same way. I think that this capacity for independent problem solving increases the likelihood of a creative solution to a novel problem. At the same time, there is an enormous increase in the likelihood of internal conflict. And so we have man, the most innovative of species and at the same time the most at odds with himself.
>
> And the second point is that there are two principal ways of knowing, hence of learning, and overemphasis on one to the exclusion of the other is a basic mistake.

IMPLICATIONS FOR EDUCATION

David Galin, Associate Professor of Psychiatry, University of California, San Francisco wrote:

> Joseph E. Bogen is one of the world's foremost scholars of hemispheric specialization. As one of the pioneers in split-brain surgery, we might expect that he would be expert in the neurosurgical and neurophysiological aspects; however, he is also one of the most penetrating thinkers concerning the philosophical, educational, and social implications of the scientific findings (Galin personal communication: 10/23/96).

What is the connection between this brain research and language teaching? In terms of general educational principles that could be derived from the split-brain research, a bit of history is useful. Classical Greek mental training used visual images as mnemonic aids for oratory and preparing for examinations. These images fixed a whole concept in the memory, to enhance the material being memorized. This ancient teaching approach continued throughout the Middle Ages, using elaborate artwork in educational and religious buildings for pedagogical purposes; that is one of the reasons medieval cathedrals were so rich in visual images (statues, gargoyles, stained glass windows, page illuminations, etc.). The use of imagery continued to be a principle of education until the advent of the printing press, at which point education turned in a radically different direction and began to rely almost entirely on linear presentation of the printed word (Wittrock 1985).

Robert Nebes, Professor of Psychiatry at Duke University, wrote:

> If there is any truth in the assertion that our culture stresses left-hemispheric skills, this is especially true of the school systems. Selection for higher education is based predominantly on the ability to comprehend and manipulate language—a fact which may help explain why it took so long for science to come to grips with right-hemisphere abilities .... Perhaps, when people talk about the inverse relationship between scholastic achievement and creativity, they are really talking about the effect of overtraining for verbal skills at the expense of nonverbal abilities (Nebes 1975:16).

Galin made the following comment about the importance of taking into account the strengths of both types of thinking:

> The verbal-analytic style is extremely efficient for dealing with the object world. Our modern technology, standard of living, and scientific achievements depend heavily on highly developed linear, analytic methods. The holistic mode of information processing is very good for bridging gaps; we can perceive a pattern even when some of the pieces are missing. In contrast, a logical, sequential mode cannot skip over gaps. In this imperfect world, since we are usually trying to operate with incomplete information, we very badly need to have a capacity to perceive general patterns and jump across gaps in present knowledge (Galin 1976:18).

This distinction is demonstrated with items from the Street "Gestalt Completion Test" (Figure 1, page 30). If you focus on the pieces, you will have difficulty seeing the whole. If you process the whole by ignoring or filling in what is missing, you will recognize a configuration (Rico 1987).

IMPLICATIONS FOR LANGUAGE TEACHING

In terms of listening comprehension, many researchers have studied the importance of the right hemisphere in perceiving the narrative-level signals necessary to understand stories and jokes. The following two discussions of the effect of right-brain injury describe the relevance of these narrative-level signals:

> A growing body of recent work documents the importance of an intact right hemisphere for narrative-level linguistic performance, e.g., understanding stories, jokes, and utterances in contexts (Brownell et al. 1990:375).

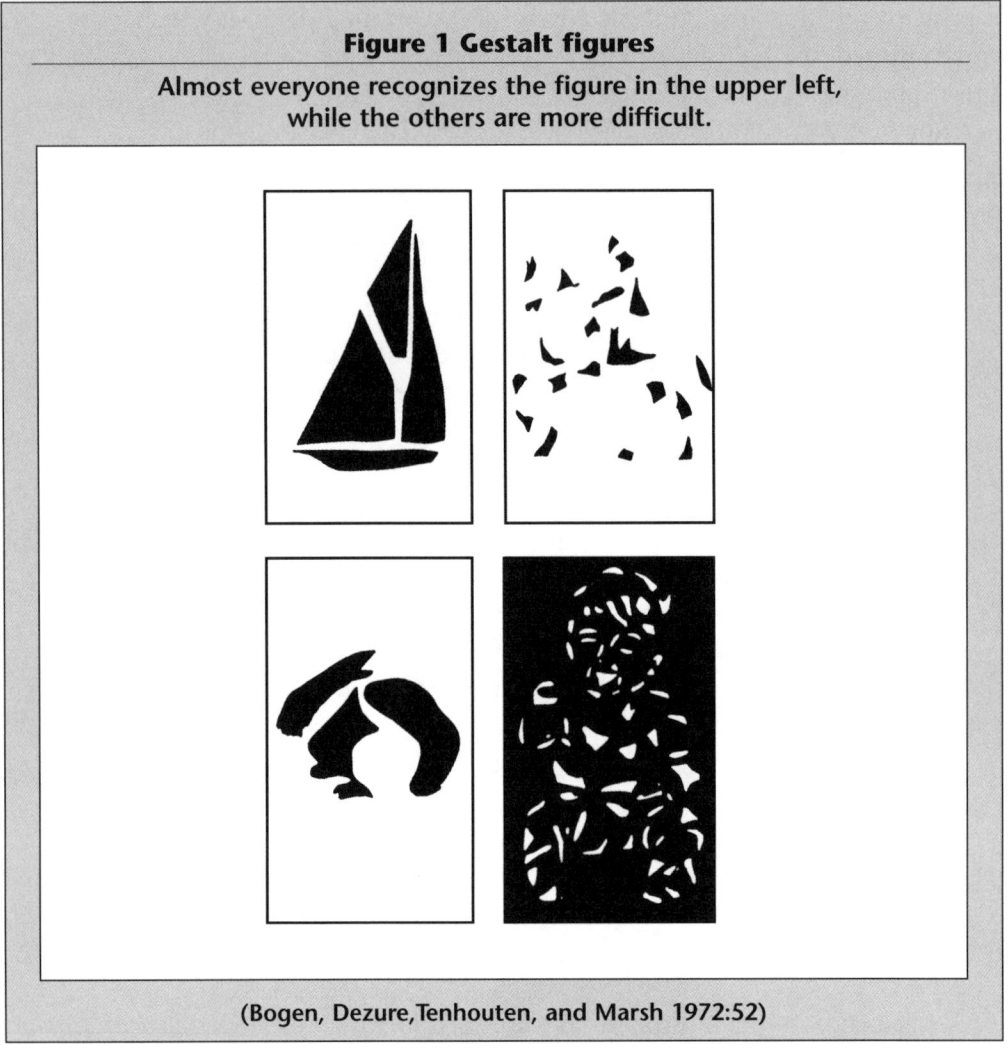

Figure 1 Gestalt figures

Almost everyone recognizes the figure in the upper left, while the others are more difficult.

(Bogen, Dezure, Tenhouten, and Marsh 1972:52)

> [Right brain-damaged patients] have seemingly normal syntax and phonology, and they often can carry on a reasonable conversation. However, closer inspection reveals that such patients often seem to lack a full understanding of the context of an utterance, the presuppositions entailed, the affective tone, or the point of a conversational exchange (Gardner et al. 1983:172).

In terms specific to language, neurolinguist Diana Van Lancker comments:

> Currently, perhaps the most richly mined cache of right hemisphere function is the use of language in communicative contexts—the field of pragmatics. Here we refer not to phonemes or grammar, but to the subtler, crucial interstitial knowledge used to connect sentences, infer meanings, follow conversation,

appreciate irony, recognize metaphor, comprehend discourse. [She then lists various research projects studying theme and topic maintenance, humour, context relevance, and inference.] (Van Lancker 1997:8).

These comments suggest that the right hemisphere is needed to integrate the various subtle cues into a single concept and to organize the whole situation in an appropriate way. Most of us have had the experience of "being of two minds" about something, and it is possible that this is because the two cognitive modes are in conflict. A suitable approach for observing details in a way that makes it possible to express them in words may be in conflict with, or inhibit, the ability to perceive the whole pattern. Gardner et al. discusses the importance of these discourse connections as going beyond individual clauses:

> [The right hemisphere specializes in] more complex linguistic entities, ones that involve redundant information, nonliteral information, and information that requires integration across the boundary of the clause (e.g., jokes, stories, adages) ... (Gardner et al. 1983:188).

"Getting the point" is related to the importance of integration across the boundary of the clause or sentence unit. This is a fundamental argument against the traditional reliance on lessons based on the grammar of individual sentences. Following is a description from *A Personal Matter*, by Nobel Prize winning novelist Kenzaburo Ōe, which illustrates the effect of teaching students to perceive the building blocks, but not the building. In this novel, Bird, the protagonist, is brooding about the students in his English cram school class, whose knowledge of rules of grammar far exceeds his own:

> The heads of Bird's students were so crammed with knowledge of details they were as complicated as hyper-evolved clams: the minute they tried to perceive a problem integrally, the mechanism tangled in itself and stalled. It was accordingly Bird's job to integrate and summarize the entire meaning of a passage. Yet he was in constant doubt close to an incombustible fixation about whether his classes were of any use when it came to college entrance examinations (Ōe 1969:61).

In terms of communicative language teaching, the concept of *hemispheric complementarity* suggests that: 1) we should balance traditional verbal explanations with visual and kinesthetic (physical) approaches/techniques, and 2) we should go beyond the kind of grammar exercise that depends on items only one sentence long. This traditional type of lesson seems designed to encourage slow, linear processing, conflicting with the need to "get the picture."

Two English Teachers

Following are accounts of how two teachers found relevance for education in Bogen's work with complementary hemispheric specialization.

A Composition Teacher

Dr Gabriele Rico, Professor of English at California State University, San Jose, had an unusual educational history. [Most of the information for this account came from an interview on 10/16/96 and from her books.] Born in East Germany during World War II, she was bombed out of her home three times, her mother being killed in the third raid. There was no opportunity to go to school until she was old enough to be placed in the 5th grade. Meanwhile, she had been educating herself with a copy of *Grimm's Fairy Tales*, and therefore came to school with opinions of her own about learning.

When she was 11 years old, she found herself in a new country, as a total beginner in English. This gave her an opportunity to think about language learning from a personal perspective. Then, when she graduated from college and began to teach high school German, the assigned textbook didn't strike her as an effective approach, so she invented her own activities. The school administration was nonplussed by her eclectic notions but, since her students seemed to achieve more than usual, she was allowed to continue her unconventional ways.

Later, as a graduate student of English at Stanford University, Rico crossed disciplinary lines into anthropology, linguistics, English literature, and biology. She felt that there must be a relationship between these diverse fields of study, but could not clearly articulate the connections. Then she attended a Bogen lecture for English teachers at UC Berkeley and felt she had found the unifying explanation for her life-long interdisciplinary searching. She asked Bogen if he would serve as the neurobiology representative on her cross-disciplinary dissertation committee. He agreed and thus began a fruitful educational relationship, combining Rico's instinct for seeking interrelationship between art and thought, and the technical findings of *hemispheric complementarity*. In her dissertation, *Metaphor and Knowing* (1976), she expanded the meaning of Bogen's term "appositional thinking" (that kind of holistic and unitary information processing used by the right hemisphere) by arguing that metaphor plays a powerful role as a tool of appositional thinking, just as logic is central to propositional thinking (analytic and fragmentary, used by the left brain.) Rico concluded:

> Lest I leave the reader with the impression that I am advocating a radical shift from propositional to appositional capacities in education, I would remind him/her that throughout this dissertation I have stressed complementarity, for the principle of knowing fully lies in the tension which connects the rule-abiding to the structure-seeking, literal truth with metaphorical truth ... (Rico 1976:296).

In 1976 Rico was the first guest speaker of the Bay Area Writing Project at UC Berkeley, which she later wrote "generated a kind of revolution in the teaching of writing and the springing up of Writing Projects all over the USA" (Rico personal communication: 11/29/96). She has written a number of books, one of which has been translated into several languages, but the book which illustrates the pendulum effect of reaction to "dichotomania" was a text she and a colleague wrote as a monograph for the Writing Project, *Balancing the Hemispheres: Brain Research and the Teaching of Writing* (1986). This was one of the most successful of all the publications of this group, but two years later, when the subject of a reprint arose, the editor of the series balked. He had read an article by C. Hardyck (1979) debunking the entire field of hemispheric specialization as "false science" and using *Balancing the Hemispheres* as an example. Based on this article, the Writing Project editor refused to allow the reprint. Rico then wrote to Bogen with a copy of the Hardyck article. She used his answering letter to help marshall an accumulation of research report summaries to date, which showed the scientific foundation for the principle of complementary hemispheric specialization (Milner 1980). The Bay Area Writing Project editor was then satisfied that this publication would be in a defensible position, and permitted the second printing. This kind of battle was typical of the struggles during the anti-hemispheric specialization pendulum period.

A Pronunciation Teacher

Like Rico, I attended two lectures Bogen gave for teachers. His conclusions and suggestions for educational implications so impressed me that I simply ignored the hoopla coming from less scientific sources and proceeded to base much of my subsequent teaching approach on the principles he put forth, developing visual and physical aids to enhance the verbal explanations I was using. Furthermore, I was convinced that intonational signals should have highest priority in order to help the student see "the whole," instead of concentrating mostly on the component parts (the building, rather than the building blocks).

Implications for Teaching Suprasegmentals (Stress, Rhythm, and Intonation)

Unlike many languages, English intonation serves as a discourse organizer, by making clear what goes with what and which words are most important (Brown 1990). The right hemisphere is specialized for these signals (Fromkin 1985), which are a crucial part of listening comprehension because "getting the point" means noticing the coherence between parts of discourse, i.e., "what goes with what." Therefore, when teachers begin to think about integrating the whole meaning of a passage, such aspects of pronunciation as stress, rhythm, and intonation must become central.

Efron (1990) claimed in *The Decline and Fall of Hemispheric Specialization* that sentences convey their meaning only by virtue of the sequential order of the words, and that this was true of both the spoken and written language. I asked Victoria

Fromkin, Professor of Linguistics at University of California, Los Angeles, how she reacted to this. She wrote me the following comment:

> I do think Efron has it wrong in more ways than just his ignoring the role of prosody [suprasegmentals]. The meaning of sentences may or may not be dependent on the word order. There are languages which have relatively free word order, whose thematic relations and grammatical relations depend on inflection rather than word order. Furthermore, even in a language like English, it is not word order which determines who did what to whom in a sentence like: 'It was the dog that the cat chased' (Fromkin personal communication: 9/24/96).

Intonational cues give us important information about what a remark is intended to mean because stress, rhythm, and intonation alert the listener to what the speaker thinks is most important, and to how the ideas relate from one thought to the next in a coherent, connected way. Notice how the focus of thought shifts in example 1 and how the focus on who is speaking shifts in example 2.

1. X: I want some <u>shoes</u>.
   Y: What <u>kind</u> of shoes?
   X: The <u>jazz</u>y kind.

2. John said, "The boss is an idiot!"
   "John," said the boss, "is an idiot!"

A learner who does not understand the use of intonation in English is apt to emphasize every word, in an effort to be understood. But English depends on *contrastive* emphasis and pausing. The great novelist, E.M. Forster, expressed it this way in *A Passage to India*:

> A pause in the wrong place, an intonation misunderstood, and a whole conversation went awry (Forster 1924:274).

However, it isn't enough for the teacher to be aware of the importance of rhythm and intonation; it is also necessary to have practical ways to teach these aspects of the spoken language. Following are a few ways to add images and physical activities to lessons on suprasegmentals.

Contrast
The fundamental mechanism for showing English emphasis is contrastive focus: words are highlighted for emphasis, and the surrounding words are "backgrounded." This principle of contrastive clarity/obscurity is more easily explained

when enhanced by a visual image. In Figure 2 below, the highlighted butterfly is easier to see. In the same way, intonationally emphasized words are easier to hear, as shown in the sentence below the butterfly pictures.

Rhythm

We all learn the rhythm of our language from infancy, and thereafter tend automatically to transfer the first language rhythm to any new language. Since many languages have a rhythmic principle in which all syllables are roughly the same length, transferring that rhythm to English produces a rhythm which is often described as "staccato" or "choppy." This is not simply a problem of sounding foreign; English speech *depends* on the lengthening of some syllables in order to convey meaning. So the transfer of the first language rhythm can seriously interfere with intelligibility in the new language and students need help with adjusting. Gillian Brown explained:

> ... rhythm in English is not just something extra, added to the basic sequence of consonants and vowels, it is the guide to the structure of information in the spoken message .... From the point of view of teaching production of stress, *length* is the variable that most students find easiest to control, and is a reliable marker of stress (Brown 1990:43-4).

The following aids are useful because rhythm is more of a physical than an intellectual matter, and students need to feel it, not just to think about it. See Figure 3 for visual images to encourage physical action: tapping for syllable count, lengthening for stress, and contracting auxiliaries.

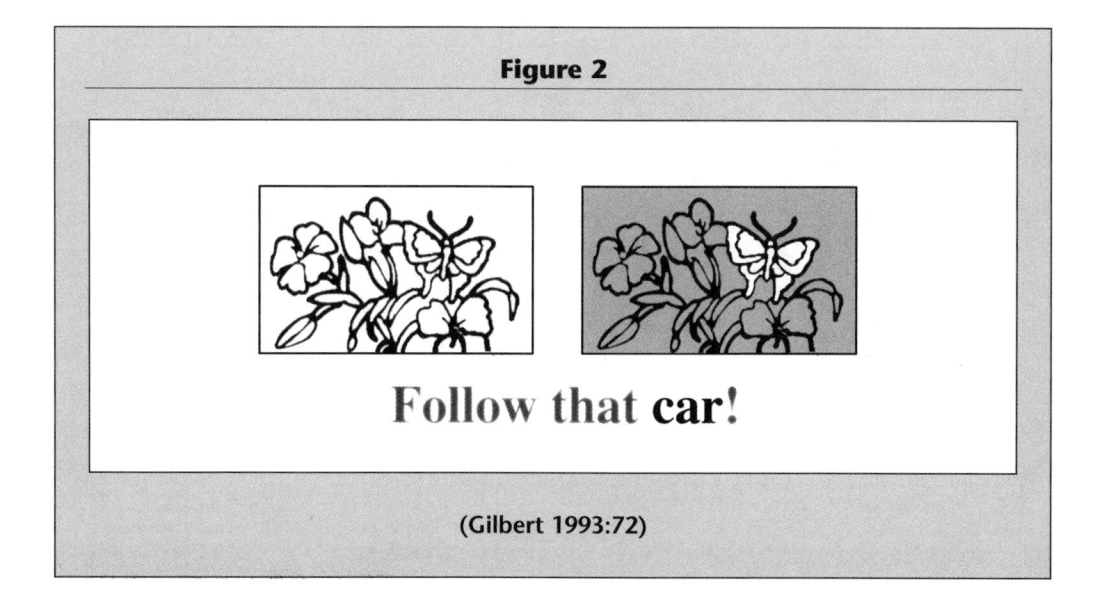

Figure 2

Follow that **car!**

(Gilbert 1993:72)

Aid 1 *Tapping.* L1 interference may cause syllables to be wrongly added or subtracted in the L2 (e.g., "eschool" or "sekalah" for "school"). Have students tap their hands or feet as they say pairs of words that are distinguished by the number of syllables (Figure 3).

EXAMPLES: prayed/parade can't/cannot walked/walk it
Wednesday ... chocolate ...

Aid 2 *Rubber bands.* They help show the difference between stressed and unstressed syllables. Have students pull heavy rubber bands (Figure 3) as they say the stressed syllable of a multisyllabic word, letting the rubber contract for the non-stressed syllables.

EXAMPLES: banana Canada atom/atomic general/generality/generalization

Emphasis
In every clause (thought group/tone group/pause group) there is one key word, and within that key word there is one crucial syllable. This crucial syllable is so important for English communication that it has several signals:
1. extra length, so that the listener will have time to notice it.
2. pitch change (usually up), followed by a drop of pitch.

The crucial syllable may also be louder, but these two cues are the most essential signals, and also the most specific to English. Other languages have other ways to

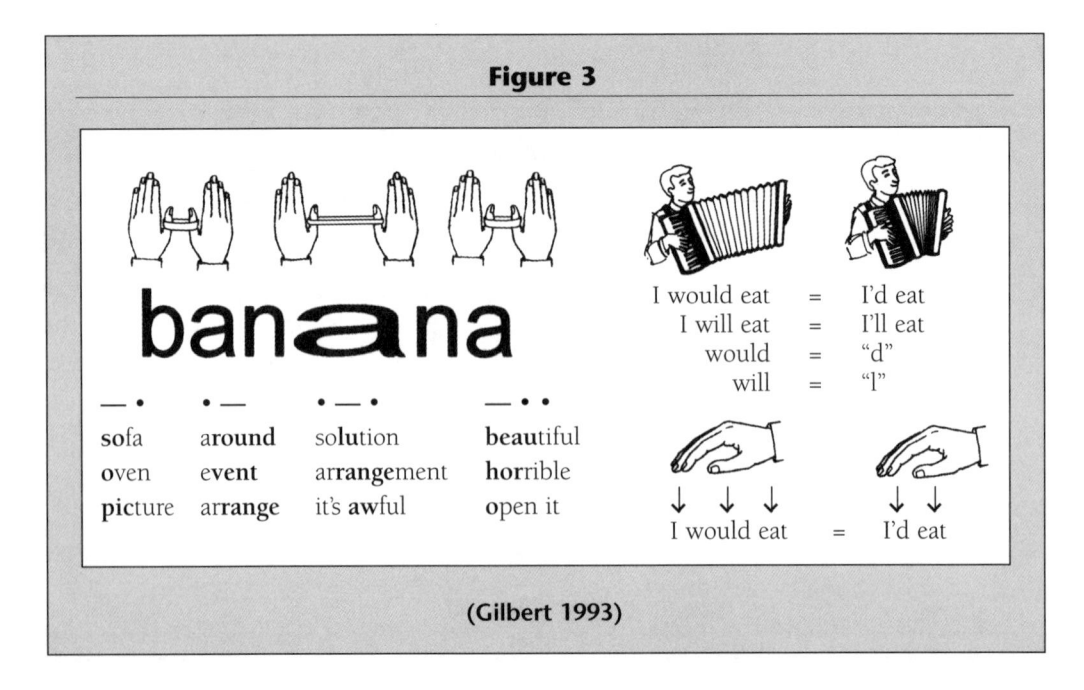

Figure 3

banana

sofa	around	solution	beautiful
oven	event	arrangement	horrible
picture	arrange	it's awful	open it

I would eat = I'd eat
I will eat = I'll eat
would = "d"
will = "l"

I would eat = I'd eat

(Gilbert 1993)

indicate emphasis. The signals of lengthening and pitch change can be heard in the stressed syllable of "wonderful" in the following spoken exchange:

> A: How good a singer is he?
> B: He's a wonderful singer.

Aid 1 *Whispering.* Have students recite dialogues or light poetry in a whisper so that they can pay attention to the extra lengthening of the crucial syllable.

Aid 2 *Highlighter pens.* Have students mark each crucial syllable (one to a clause or short sentence) with a highlighter pen, so that it will "jump off the page" while they are reading a script.

Aid 3 *Chair rising.* Have students recite polysyllabic words or short sentences, rising partly from their seats *only* on the crucial syllable. This wakes everybody up and requires concentration. A more modest version is the use of eyebrow raising, head lifting, etc.

Aid 4 *Kazoos.* It is difficult to listen for the pure melody pattern in normal speech, since there are so many distractions of sounds, vocabulary, and grammar. Kazoos are little plastic humming toys that can strip away the distractions and so direct learners' attention solely to the changing pitch at the crucial word. If you can't find kazoos (at a party goods store, for example), a possible substitute is a comb and tissue paper, or just "singing" a steady vowel like "*ahhhh.*"

EXAMPLES:
>   X: It's a big <u>dog</u>.   Y: No, it's a <u>wolf</u>.
>   X: It's a <u>big</u> dog.   Y: More <u>me</u>dium-sized.
>   A: You buy books at the library.   B: No, you <u>bor</u>row books at the library.

Once started on this pedagogical path, teachers can add visual and kinesthetic techniques of their own invention to many aspects of their teaching.

Conclusion

The innovative research of Joseph Bogen and his colleagues has presented us with a rationale for adding visual images, as well as other techniques similar to those described above, to enrich our teaching. His insight into the possibility of using the split-brain condition as a way to test the complementary attributes of the right brain has helped give a scientific basis for recovering the lost art of Greek and Medieval use of visual images to fix concepts in the mind. Furthermore, the importance of "whole concept" thinking implies the importance of stress and intonation to help convey cohesion—a sense of how the parts fit together.

In summary, although early hyperenthusiasm about the significance of the split-brain experiments caused some educational writers to make extravagant claims about curriculum and methodology, we can now come to some reasonable conclusions. There is a useful principle involved in the idea that there are different ways of "seeing" and it is advantageous to expand our teaching repertoire to take them into account. At the simplest level of pedagogical theory, variety of presentation of the same teaching point makes for a more interesting and productive class.

Finally, the three brief histories above (Bogen, Rico, and my own) suggest a general principle: Not only does it take time to clarify essential meaning, but expanding our vision may deepen our teaching.

REFERENCES CITED

* References especially useful for teachers

Benson, D. 1985. 'The Significance of Hemispheric Specialization for Clinical Medicine.' In *The Dual Brain,* edited by D. Benson and E. Zaidel. New York: Guilford Press.

Bogen, J. 1956. 'Some Student Concepts of Functional Disease.' *The Journal of Medical Education* 31 (11):740-45.

———. 1969. 'The Other Side of the Brain II: An Appositional Mind.' *The Bulletin of the Los Angeles Neurological Societies* 34 (3):135-62

*———. 1975. 'Educational Aspects of Hemispheric Specialization.' *The UCLA Educator* 17 (2): 24-32.

———. In press. 'My Developing Understanding of Roger Wolcott Sperry's Philosophy.' *Neuropsychologia.*

———. 1997. 'The Neurosurgeon's Interest in the Corpus Callosum.' In *A History of Neurosurgery,* edited by S. Greenblatt, 489-98. Park Ridge, Illinois: American Association of Neurological Surgeons.

Bogen, J., M. DeZure, W. TenHouten, and J. Marsh. 1972. 'The Other Side of the Brain IV. The A/P Ratio.' *Bulletin of the Los Angeles Neurological Societies* 37 (2): 49-61.

*Brown, G. 1990. *Listening to Spoken English*, 2nd ed. London: Longman.

Brownell, H., T. Simpson, A. Birhle, H. Potter, and H. Gardner. 1990. 'Appreciation of Metaphoric Alternative Word Meanings by Left and Right Brain-damaged Patients.' *Neuropsychologia* 28 (4): 375-83.

Efron, R. 1990. *The Decline and Fall of Hemispheric Specialization*. London: Lawrence Erlbaum Associates.

Forster, E.M. 1924, 1950. *A Passage to India*. New York: Harcourt Brace Jovanovich.

*Fromkin, V. 1985. 'Implications of Hemispheric Differences for Linguistics.' In *The Dual Brain*, edited by D. Benson and E. Zaidel, 319-27. New York: Guilford Press.

Galin, D. 1975. Quoted in *University of California San Francisco Magazine* (March 1979): 14-15.

———. 1976. 'Educating Both Halves of the Brain.' In *Childhood Education* 53 (1): 17-20.

Gardner, H., H. Brownell, W. Wapner, and D. Michelow. 1983. 'Missing the Point: The Role of the Right Hemisphere in the Processing of Complex Linguistic Materials.' In *Cognitive Processing in the Right Hemisphere*, edited by E. Perecman, 169-91. New York: Academic Press.

*Gilbert, J. 1993. *Clear Speech: Pronunciation and Listening Comprehension in North American English*, 2nd ed. New York: Cambridge University Press.

Hardyck, C. 1979. 'Educating Both Halves of the Brain: Educational Breakthrough or Neuromythology?' *Journal of School Psychology* 17: 219.

Harrington, A. 1987. *Medicine, Mind, and the Double Brain: A Study in Nineteenth-Century Thought*. Princeton: Princeton University Press.

Kipling, R. 1901, 1987. *Kim*. London: Penguin Books.

Levy, J. 1985. 'Right Brain, Left Brain: Fact and Fiction.' *Psychology Today* (May): 38-44.

Milner, B. 1971. 'Interhemispheric Differences in the Localization of Psychological Processes in Man.' *British Medical Bulletin* 27 (3): 272-77.

———. 1980. 'Complementary Functional Specializations of the Human Cerebral Hemispheres.' In *Nerve Cells, Transmitters and Behaviour*, edited by R. Levi-Montalcini, 601-28. Amsterdam: Eslevier/North-Holland Biomedical.

*Nebes, R. 1975. 'Man's So-called Minor Hemisphere.' *The UCLA Educator* 17 (2): 13-16.

Öe, Kenzaburo. 1969. *A Personal Matter*. New York: Grove Weidenfeld.

Ornstein, R. 1986. *The Psychology of Consciousness*, 2nd ed. New York: Penguin.

Rico, G. 1976. 'Metaphor and Knowing: Analysis, Synthesis, Rationale. (Unpublished doctoral dissertation).

———. 1983. *Writing the Natural Way*. Boston: Houghton Mifflin.

*Rico, G. and M. Claggett. 1986. *Balancing the Hemispheres: Brain Research and the Teaching of Writing*. Bay Area Writing Project, Curriculum Publication No. 14: University of California, Berkeley.

Sperry, R. 1974. 'Lateral Specialization in the Surgically Separated Hemispheres.' In *The Neurosciences: Third Study Program*, edited by F. Schmitt and F. Worden. Cambridge, MA: Massachusetts Institute of Technology Press.

Van Lancker, D. 1997. 'Rags to Riches: Our Increasing Appreciation of Cognitive and Communicative Abilities of the Human Right Cerebral Hemisphere.' *Brain and Language* 57: 1-11.

*Wittrock M.C. 1975. 'Introduction to Education and the Hemispheric Process of the Brain.' *The UCLA Educator* 17 (2): 1.

———. 1985. 'Education and Recent Neuropsychological and Cognitive Research.' In *The Dual Brain*, edited by D. Benson and E. Zaidel, 329-39. New York: Guilford Press.

Zaidel, E. 1985. 'Right-Hemisphere Language.' In *The Dual Brain*, edited by D. Benson and E. Zaidel, 205-26. New York: Guilford Press.

Zangwill, O. 1961. 'Asymmetry of Cerebral Hemisphere Function.' In *Scientific Aspects of Neurology*, edited by H. Garland. London: E. & S. Livingstone.

CHAPTER THREE

JANE JACOBS

※

EYES ON THE CITY

Robert Oprandy
Monterey Institute of International Studies

Introduction

Having recently moved to the Monterey Peninsula of California after living four blocks from New York City's Harlem, I have been acutely aware of how my physical surroundings affect me, my work, and my attitude toward life. I constantly contrast the profusion of bougainvillea in my present habitat with that of rundown tenements in my former locale, or the fragrances of a wide range of wild flowers and herbs with the smells emanating from garbage heaps and the staleness of worn-down, unfreshened apartment buildings. In Monterey there is the intricate texture of an old Mexican-style fishing town with its twisting, meandering narrow streets (that used to be cattle paths) making their way to the big open plaza at the foot of the wharf. On New York's Upper West Side, there was the predictable perpendicularity of consecutively numbered streets crossing Broadway and other avenues. These contrasts have brought me back to an earlier interest in city planning and to Jane Jacobs, a guru of many city planners since the 1960s, and to contemplating lessons language teachers can learn from the profound ideas of city planners.

In *The Death and Life of Great American Cities* (1961), Jane Jacobs' classic work (as well as in *Cities and the Wealth of Nations* 1984, for which she won *The Los Angeles Times Book Review Award* for non-fiction over 20 years later), Jacobs lays out guidelines that have clear implications not only for how we can create more vibrant cities. Upon closer inspection there are also lessons, by implication, for varying and enlivening school and classroom environments. By sampling her ideas, many connections to the language teaching/learning enterprise emerge. Some connections concern ideologies in both fields, others the practicalities of how to do city planning or schooling. There are also lessons for the (language) teaching profession in the meticulous way Jacobs does her research, and in her incessant advocacy for city dwellers.

From Grand Schemes to Person-Centred Approaches

For language educators, Skinner's behaviourist psychological tenets had profound implications for theorizing about language learning, the wake of which sent waves of audiolingual drills into classrooms. So, too, in city planning the Garden City concepts of British planner Ebenezer Howard (1902) at the turn of the 20th century reflected a vision of "not simply a new physical environment and social life, but a paternalistic political and economic society," according to Jacobs (1961: 18). Such a vision presumed that those behind the sketch pads and T-squares knew what was best for the diverse dwellers of the city projects they planned. Streets were seen as bad environments for people, so these planners chose to face houses away from the street toward sheltered green spaces. They considered frequent streets as wasteful and superblocks rather than streets as the basic unit of city design. They sought to segregate residential and green spaces from commercial areas and to attempt a suburban-like privacy and sense of isolation from the rest of city life.

As Chomsky, cognitive psychologists, and sociolinguists did to Skinner's behaviourism, Jacobs turned such grand designs upside down with her more grassroots view of cities. She uncovered several shortcomings of Howard's concept, characterizing what he considered good planning "as a series of static acts; in each case the plan must anticipate all that is needed and be protected, after it is built, against any but the most minor subsequent changes" (1961: 19). She exposed his disinterest "in the aspects of the city which could not be abstracted to serve his Utopia" and the fact that he did not really study or respect the needs of the cities' people. She calls, instead, for planning that would accept the basic nature of cities. "Think of a city and what comes to mind? Its streets. If a city's streets look interesting, the city looks interesting; if they look dull, the city looks dull" (1961: 29). Jacobs continues, "There must be eyes upon the street, eyes belonging to those we might call the natural proprietors of the street" (1961: 35) who keep "the public peace—the sidewalk and street peace" (1961: 31). That peace is not primarily kept by the police but "by an intricate, almost unconscious, network of voluntary controls and standards among the people themselves, and enforced by the people themselves" (1961: 32). To help keep the peace, she says each city district needs along its sidewalks a sprinkling of stores and other public places, including restaurants, bars, and shops that are open and used in the evening and at night.

The parallels to the focus on the learner since the 1970s in the field of language teaching are striking. The reaction against the Skinnerian-based audiolingual orthodoxy of Fries (1956) and Lado (1964) in language education reminds me of Jacobs' jousting at Howard and all his followers among 20th century city designers, including LeCorbusier (1924) and Mumford (1938). Calling them "sorter" planners, she decries their building of single-function land use projects which destroyed the diversity of effective city streets and neighbourhoods. The thinking of Howard and his followers also resulted in the monotony of suburbs, in which Jacobs denounces the "fake country lane" layout of streets and the sameness of housing developments constructed by a single developer. Galt describes this very clearly:

> What planners in the 50s and 60s were trying to accomplish was uniformity through urban renewal, a revolutionary rebuilding of Metropolis dominated by the replacement megaproject mentality. What Jacobs proposed was quite the opposite: a nurturing of the multiplicity of existing urban assets to allow for gradual, organic growth (Galt 1982: 11).

Jacobs' conceptualization, to me, is what caring, humanistic teachers do. They get to know the uniqueness each student brings to class. Then they draw out (education = *ex ducere* in Latin) the multiplicity of resources the students bring with them and the backgrounds they represent, so that the classroom environment allows for learning to unfold in an organic way.

Jacobs also advocates "zoning for diversity" (1961: 252), in which multiple land uses, a diversity of socio-economic classes, and a range of architectural forms would lend vitality to cities and their neighbourhoods. In the schools, many are arguing for a celebration of multiculturalism and for a "two-languages-for-everyone" philosophy, hoping to arrange for people to know each other better, lessening the stereotyping that separates people and makes them fearful of one another. People as resources for each other is central to such movements, both in school hallways and on city streets.

Audiolingualism was, as were Howard's utopian Garden City and LeCorbusier's Radiant City schemes, a BIG idea—one that imposed upon learners (and their teachers) carefully and seemingly logically sequenced structural patterns to be drilled in a mechanical way. That idea became orthodoxy after World War II, and vestiges of the audiolingual approach are still heard in classrooms around the world as we approach the turn of the millennium. The focus since the early 1970s on interlanguage and on the needs of individual learners in specific contexts with particular motivations eventually moved the language teaching field, if not all practitioners, to functional-notional syllabuses and to curricula with communicative competencies at their core.

Communicative language teaching has replaced audiolingualism as the preferred orthodoxy, even if it is not yet practised everywhere. The communicative approach requires a complexity in terms of planning and a tolerance for messiness and ambiguity as teachers analyze students' needs and design meaningful tasks to meet those needs. The pat solutions and deductive stances of audiolingual materials and pedagogy, like the grammar-translation texts and syllabi preceding them, are no longer seen as sensitive to students' needs and interests. Nor are they viewed as respectful of students' intelligence to figure things out inductively through engaging problem-solving and communicative tasks.

Curriculum designers, like the city planners Jacobs influenced, began to demand that careful needs analyses be done so that all stakeholders' perceptions of language learners' needs in particular learning contexts could be teased out and taken into consideration. Interviews, questionnaires, surveys, classroom and program observations, tapings, document and materials analyses, case studies, etc., would shed considerable light on a given context before making the inevitable interpretations leading to curriculum design. Such curriculum designers are like anthropologists. They size up a situation from multiple angles by communicating with and observing the gamut of people closest to the action; that is, those who will be most affected by their subsequent plans. They may even be participant observers, enmeshing themselves in the context they are studying. Jacobs has done the same by living in the urban neighbourhoods she has written about.

This complex manner of planning contrasts sharply with the way Jacobs describes Le Corbusier's Radiant City of skyscrapers within a park:

> His city was like a wonderful toy. Furthermore, his conception, as an architectural work, had a dazzling clarity, simplicity, and harmony. It was so easy to understand. It said everything in a flash, like a good advertisement ... Like a great, visible ego it tells of someone's achievement. But as to how the city works, it tells, like the Garden City, nothing but lies (1961: 23).

Le Corbusier's simple, clear conception is, in Jacobs' eyes, "irrelevant to the workings of cities. Unstudied, unrespected, cities have served as sacrificial victims" (1961: 25). Nevertheless, Le Corbusier's vision was hailed by architects and has had a great impact on the design of cities, similar to the widespread impact audiolingualism has had on language teaching.

Many of us who taught languages in the 1960s and 1970s were similarly taken by the simplicity of working students through clearly laid out imitation, substitution, and transformation drills and having them work on minimal pair drills to improve their pronunciation. Being sure never to present incorrect models or to let errors go uncorrected for fear our students would pick up bad habits, we stayed close to the structural patterns in a lock-step manner. We assumed once one grammatical pattern rolled automatically (for the most part chorally) off the tongues of our students in the fast paced stimulus-response drills, we could move on to the next pattern because the previous ones had presumably been mastered. This all seemed clear, simple, and easy to understand and accept, like the conceptions for cities that Jacobs castigates. Once a scheme for a section of a city could be put in place, the thinking goes, planners could move on to the next problem area and fix it, too, in the lock-step, controlled, and controlling approach.

For those of us who do schooling and who spend countless hours in language classrooms, there are many lessons in Jacobs' vision of people-centred cities. She talks of the primacy of security and the importance of trusting relationships, of people looking out for each other along a city's sidewalks. This is reminiscent of humanistic approaches to language teaching, including Charles Curran's Counseling-Learning precepts: "Feeling secure, we are then freed to approach the learning situation with an attitude of willing openness. Both the learner's and the knower's level of security determines the psychological tone of the entire learning experience" (Curran 1976: 6).

Likening the "complex order" of the city to a dance, Jacobs says it is not "a simple-minded precision dance with everyone kicking up at the same time, twirling in unison and bowing off en masse" (echoes of the choral drills of Fries and Lado). Instead, she describes the dance as "an intricate ballet in which the individual dancers and ensembles all have distinctive parts which miraculously reinforce each other and compose an orderly whole" (1961: 50). This metaphor can be used equally to express the learner-centred language pedagogy few would contest today, and the systems theory Bateson so well explains (see Chapter 9 in this volume). That individuals are part and parcel of an unfolding whole presupposes the importance of community and cooperation as important avenues through which we learn languages or anything else. According to Rardin and Tranel:

> The community and cooperative dimension to education ... enhances both the individual integrity of the person as well as the ability to participate and cooperate with others in the learning process. The unique individuality of each person—teacher and students—is important to the educational process and needs to be acknowledged and respected within the classroom, but in a way that furthers interpersonal communication and a genuine experience of community (Rardin and Tranel 1988: 6-7).

Jacobs would also have us strike a balance between "people's determination to have essential privacy" and a range of degrees of contact. This balance, she says, is largely made up of "small, sensitively managed details, practised and accepted so casually that they are normally taken for granted" (1961: 59). Similarly sensitive teachers afford students choices in terms of working independently or interactively, and find ways to allow for learners to move back and forth between the two modes. Such teachers also consider the needs of the entire class while celebrating the unique contributions of each student. In carrying out their carefully detailed lesson plans, they achieve a flexibility akin to the sense of balance Jacobs strives for in cities. Moment by moment in the hundredfold decision-making process that faces teachers daily, they notice a multitude of details and make necessary adjustments to their plans as they execute their lessons. They have a teaching presence of the sort Kessler describes:

> To be fully present is to be *open* to perceiving what is happening right now, to be *responsive* to the needs of this moment, to be *flexible* enough to shift gears, and to have the repertoire, *creativity*, and imagination to invent a new approach in the moment. Being present also requires the *humility* and *honesty* to simply pause and acknowledge that the new approach has not yet arrived (Kessler 1991: 13).

This teaching (as well as administrative) presence in schools contrasts with the practices of the city planners Jacobs chided for planning communities that had to be separated like self-contained islands, resistant to future modifications. In such project planning, "every significant detail must be controlled by the planners from the start and then stuck to" (1961: 20).

Jacobs also rails against planners who do not "seem to understand that spaces and equipment do not rear children," but that "only people rear children and assimilate them into civilized society" (1961: 82). The planners she attacks remind me of those who looked in the 1960s and 1970s to open classroom designs, language labs, and now to computers and distance learning as panaceas for the schools' ills. Only sensitive, caring language teachers (with or without the support of technology) who willingly enter into the worlds of their students can help them assimilate the kinds of linguistic, cultural, and interpersonal awarenesses they need to find a new "language self."

Issues of gender are also explored by Jacobs, who notes that most city architectural planners and designers are men. "Curiously they design and plan to exclude men as part of normal, daytime life wherever people live" (1961: 83). Men create a "matriarchy" in the residential areas of cities, where their own influence on chidren's lives is often absent throughout the day. I was privileged to grow up with a father who was a milkman and was home every afternoon and evening. After he and I completed our milk route, I remember going swimming at a nearby lake most summer afternoons. I felt very lucky when I noticed how many of my playmates were starved for my father's attention to their early attempts at floating, dog paddling, and other forms of swimming. Practically all the other fathers were at work; some did not show up at the lake until the early evening. The absence of men in children's lives in the New Jersey suburbs where I grew up and in the cities Jacobs observes is similarly evident in schools.

In training language teachers for the past 20 years, I have observed how many more teachers-in-training are women than men, particularly those intending to teach children. Observing numerous practice teachers in elementary, middle, and secondary schools, I have also noticed how many teachers working in those schools, and specifically language teachers, are women. This is especially true in elementary and middle schools. The schools in general, including language classrooms, are microcosms of what Jacobs discovered in the residential areas of cities. Why should one expect it to be any different? After all, schools are where children reside during the day; and few men cross their paths. Principals and other administrators, many of whom *are* men, are often tucked away in offices off the beaten paths of the hallways that school children travel. Their offices are often centrally located in terms of the entrances into school buildings, but are not, I have noticed, in closest proximity to the packed banks of classrooms where the central activity takes place. Men have important roles to play in children's lives in and out of schools, and Jacobs recognizes that in her vision of cities. Educators, including language teachers, should consider how to weave men more into both hiring and curricular decisions.

Jacobs also keenly observes that city park users "do not seek settings for buildings; they seek settings for themselves. To them parks are foreground, buildings background, rather than the reverse" (1961: 106). Similarly schools should not be settings for administrative showcasing, but for students, in interaction with teachers as well as others from the community. In the foreground we should see students, teachers, and others participating in problem-solving, play, and other arrangements for learning. This also reminds me of how persuasively Frank Smith argued against the teaching of writing and of other language skills in a formal way:

> All the busywork, the meaningless drills and exercises, the rote memorization, the irrelevant tests, and the distracting grades should go (to the extent that the teacher can get rid of them). And in their place teachers and children together should use writing (and reading, spoken language, art, and drama) to learn other things. Writing should be used to tell stories and to produce artifacts—books to be published, poems to be recited, songs to be sung, plays to be acted, letters to be delivered, programs to be consulted, newspapers to be distributed, advertisements to be displayed, complaints to be aired, ideas to be shared, worlds to be constructed and explored. Children should learn to write in the same manner that they learn to talk, without being aware that they are doing so, in the course of doing other things. Teaching writing should be an incidental matter also—teachers showing children what writing can do and helping them do it themselves (Smith 1994: 211).

All the stratagems for teaching writing in the traditional ways, while certainly well meant, have missed the important point of how writing is used in the real world. It is that sense of reality that Jacobs expounds when she exposes "the dishonest mask of pretended order, achieved by ignoring or suppressing the real order that is struggling to exist and to be served" (1961: 15). She cites a tenant of an East Harlem housing project who pronounced to a social worker why the tenants hated the rectangular lawn that was gratuitously made a centrepiece of the project design:

> Nobody cared what we wanted when they built this place. They threw our houses down and pushed us here and pushed our friends somewhere else. We don't have a place around here to get a cup of coffee or a newspaper even, or borrow 50 cents. Nobody cared what we need. But the big men come and look at that grass and say, "Isn't it wonderful. Now the poor have everything!" (Quoted in 1961: 15)

Language labs, curricula, thematic units, and lesson plans that do not meet the needs or interests of learners could be the foci of similar pronouncements. Meeting the varied needs of students demands varied arrangements through which they can access information, work with it, and apply it. Then it becomes vital to them and, if feasible, to other stakeholders in and outside of the school.

Creating Varied and Vital Spaces

Jacobs lists four elements she sees in the design of intensely-used parks: intricacy, centring, sun, and enclosure. How can these elements be applied to the design of schools and classrooms? I find intricacy to be of particular interest. Of parks characterized by intricacy, Jacobs says:

> Even the same person comes for different reasons at different times; sometimes to sit tiredly, sometimes to play or to watch a game, sometimes to read or work, sometimes to show off, sometimes to fall in love, sometimes to keep an appointment ... sometimes to get closer to a bit of nature ... (1961: 103).

She adds that intricacy at eye level is of most importance: "change in the rise of ground, groupings of trees, openings leading to various focal points—in short, subtle expressions of difference. The subtle differences in setting are then exaggerated by the differences in use that grow up among them" (1961: 104).

This intricacy strikes me every day in Monterey. The city's gently rising and also steep hills, the undulating lines of the bay shore punctuated by piers, the twisting narrow streets that used to be cattle paths, the mixture of residential and commercial buildings, mid-19th century adobes next to modern structures, small parks and wide open plazas, and the profusion of flowering and evergreen plants wherever you turn bring daily surprises and changes to the environment. Beach walkers, rollerbladers, joggers, ambling tourists, surfers, scuba divers, bicyclists, drivers, outdoor cafe patrons, workers and students of all descriptions and restaurant and shop frequenters all seem to blend together in almost all of the above-mentioned settings. At the same time, there is a centre that is readily identifiable, pervasive sunshine most of the year, and a sense of the town being enclosed between the surrounding hills and the bay.

These features bring to mind some of the most creative elementary school classrooms I have visited. In an elementary ESL classroom in New York City where I did a number of observations, the creative touches of the teacher were everywhere in evidence. She had a nature corner where beans and other plants were growing. There was also a prominently displayed chart and graph where the children could keep track of the growth and the amount of water the plants required each day. In another part of the room was a reading centre enclosed on two sides by short bookshelves, but open on the other two sides for easy access to other niches, as well as to the identifiable centre of the room. The classroom also included a little science centre, a place to play games, a cassette tape recorder and headset with lots of language tapes and songs available for free-time activities, a carpeted area with hanging pictures of the steps involved in doing sun salutations (a series of yogic stretches), small tables with three or four chairs around them, a big table with at least half a dozen chairs around it, and colourful yarn hung across the top of the room supporting the children's artwork. The little twists and niches of the room lent it the intricacy Jacobs seeks for city neighbourhoods. The children the teacher worked with on a "pull-out" basis seemed to enjoy coming to their space, often dropping by during lunch hour and after school.

I have seen similar evidence of intricacy in self- and group-access language learning centres for adults. When these have been carefully planned, especially after needs analyses of the students, they buzz with the energy of users engaged in self-chosen activities.

Jacobs offers several suggestions for how she would make cities and their neighbourhoods more vital. She decries the fact that there is too much area in cities "afflicted with the Great Blight of Dullness," reminding me of the teachers I have observed who merely go through motions to get from one chapter to the next in a charade of "covering the curriculum." Like many students counting the days to summer vacation, city dwellers would not travel willingly, Jacobs tells us, "from sameness to sameness and repetition to repetition, even if the effort required is trivial" (1961: 129).

Jacobs concludes that "differences, *not duplications*, make for cross-use and hence a person's identification with an area greater than his immediate street network." "Monotony," she adds, "is the enemy of cross-use " (1961: 130). Varying tasks, interactional configurations, and the modes of communication in classrooms would seem to be congruent with this notion. Emphasizing also the importance of good communication and morale, Jacobs lays out several conditions for generating "exuberant diversity" in city streets and districts. The first suggestion, "to think about processes," would certainly prick up the ears of today's educators, as would several other of her suggestions (e.g., working inductively). Both of these suggestions, thinking about processes and working inductively, will be re-examined in the discussion that follows of Jacobs' research methodology.

"ALL EYES:" ON OBSERVING AND DOING ETHNOGRAPHIC RESEARCH

Another important connection between Jacobs' approach to city planning and what we are learning about language teaching is her research methodology. "The way to get at what goes on in the seemingly mysterious and perverse behaviour of cities," she tells us, "is ... to look closely, and with as little previous expectation as possible, at the most ordinary scenes and events, and attempt to see what they mean and whether any threads of principle emerge among them" (1961: 13). In our field, the ethnographers of communication, the sociolinguists, the discourse analysts, and the researchers of classrooms who spend months or even years collecting data and observations from within and outside the walls of schools are serving us in the ways Jacobs has done for city planners. As one writer put it, "Jane Jacobs is all eyes. Her mission has been to see the city clearly, to penetrate the veil of rhetoric woven by planners, architects, and municipal politicians for most of the 20th century, and to discern the real dynamics of successful city life" (Galt 1982: 11). Consider, for example, her perceptive observations of something as seemingly trivial as how play on sidewalks is affected by their width:

> If sidewalks on a lively street are sufficiently wide, play flourishes mightily right along with other uses. If the sidewalks are skimped, rope jumping is the first play casualty. Roller skating, tricycle and bicycle riding are the next casualties (1961: 86).

She then goes on to contrast activities on 9 metre [30 ft.] wide sidewalks with 6 metre [20 ft.] wide ones. This is a minor but instructive example of how carefully she observes her surroundings. Her books are chock full of such observations of the particularities of city life and design.

Jacobs' careful, painstaking observations of particular streets and neighbourhoods, including those she has herself lived and worked in, allow her to put people's needs over institutional interests. Her penchant for seeing the accumulated effects of small details coincides nicely with her idea that "Big plans literally live off of little plans" (1981: 28). At an international conference on urban design in Boston, she talked about the market from which she gave her address, "Vital Little Plans," saying:

> This market ... would be nothing without all the little bookshops, restaurants, barrows, pillows, chocolate chip cookies, and the myriad of other things that came out of the little plans. One could write a six-volume study on the origins and ancestries of the little plans that made this market possible. Without them, the market would be an oven with no loaves (1981: 28) .

She went on to say that "big plans stifle the imagination" as well as alternatives. She then predicted that the market, too, would "become a stifler, a smotherer, and a routinizer as soon as enough big planners get hold of the idea"(1981: 29). If they see enough money in it, "they are going to imitate it in a big way. They will do it without love or imagination because imitators don't need those qualities and don't usually use them" (1981: 38). She predicted, "This market, which now seems to us so fresh and imaginative, will become a boring idea because of all its boring, trite repetitions."

This reminds me of the imitators of extremely innovative approaches such as Gattegno's Silent Way (1976) and Curran's Counseling-Learning (1976). I was fortunate enough to have had considerable training in these approaches, at both the theoretical and practical levels, from those closest to the formulation of the ideas behind them, that is, from Gattegno and Curran themselves and their proteges. Through the years I have cringed when teachers without such training take cuisenairre rods or tape recorders into their classrooms and tell me they are "doing Silent Way (or Counseling-Learning) today." They have no idea that the strategems or use of such materials does not really capture the essence, at the philosophical level, of these approaches. They claim to be imitating something they really know nothing about. As a result, in time, despite the incredible richness of these approaches, they fall into unfair disrepute.

Perhaps the same thing happened with the open classroom movement, and perhaps it is happening now with Collaborative Learning and the Whole Language approach. The imitations often pale in comparison with the creative and well-thought out original formulations by those who understand the essential nature of these innovations.

Jacobs' participant observer perspective on the neighbourhoods she has lived in reminds me of the calls for classroom-centred action research by teachers, those who truly know the particularities of the contexts in which they work. "Cities are an immense laboratory of trial and error, failure and success, in city building and city design," she tells us.

> This is the laboratory in which city planning should have been learning and forming and testing its theories. Instead the practitioners and teachers of this discipline (if such it can be called) have ignored the study of success and failure in real life, have been incurious about the reasons for unexpected success, and are guided instead by principles derived from the behaviour and appearance of towns, suburbs, tuberculosis sanatoria, fairs, and imaginary dream cities—from anything but cities themselves (1961: 6).

Her vision of cities as planning laboratories resonates loudly with those of us who promote teacher-driven research and development (Gebhard and Oprandy in press), and with the professional development school movement, which connects teacher training institutions with real schools (Darling-Hammond 1994).

In order to understand the organizations of people, like those of living protoplasm, Jacobs prods us to employ a detailed, microscopic view while keeping an eye on the whole. "Life is a web," she told me. This requires first-hand knowledge of the cities we plan for, just as effective school change is brought about by the collaboration of all those who participate in the lived reality of a school—the students, their families, teachers, administrators, staff, curriculum specialists, public officials, researchers, etc.

Jacobs proclaims that in order to truly understand cities, or the life sciences in general, we must think about processes. "Objects in cities—whether they are buildings, streets, parks, districts, landmarks, or anything else—can have radically differing effects, depending upon the circumstances and contexts in which they exist" (1961: 440). She says that such processes are not arcane and to be understood only by experts. Many ordinary people are capable of understanding the processes but do not have the experts' names for them or a full understanding of how they can be directed. To direct changes, she argues for inductive reasoning.

A deductive approach "ultimately drives us to absurdities," many of which she cites in her books. Instead, inductive reasoning, she claims, is terribly important "for identifying, understanding, and constructively using the forces and processes that actually are relevant to cities ... City processes in real life," she continues, "are too complex to be routine, too particularized for application as abstractions. They are always made up of interactions among unique combinations of particulars, and there is no substitute for knowing the particulars" (1961: 441). She goes on to say that ordinary citizens have an advantage over planners in this respect because the planners have been trained in deductive rather than inductive thinking. Instead of thinking of a neighbourhood in a generalized or abstract way, an ordinary person understands it through using it and experientially knowing its peculiarities.

An understanding of the particulars of city processes goes only so far in affecting change, however. It then requires the strength of character to advocate vociferously and often for one's beliefs. It is that passionate quality, along with her keen intellect and observation skills, that sets Jacobs apart from so many other intellectuals who hide behind their words. In her case, the actions accompanying her words help her speak more effectively for urbanites wherever she lives.

ADVOCATING FOR CITY DWELLERS AND STUDENTS

Jacobs demonstrates that inhabitants of successful neighbourhoods improve their schools by fighting for them. She credits the successes of city neighbourhoods to the concomitant successes in localized city governments, by which she means "both the informal and formal self-management of society" (1961: 114). Gathering together people with communities of interest, she says, is perhaps the greatest asset of cities. She led such gatherings, when, for example, she fought successfully against what might have become the Lower Manhattan Expressway, a boondoggle that would have destroyed most of what is now the New York City artist colony known as SoHo. She was even charged in 1968 with second degree rioting during demonstrations against the proposed expressway. Shortly afterwards, she moved from Greenwich Village to Toronto to protest US involvement in the Vietnam War and became a Canadian citizen in 1973. Not long after her arrival, she helped stop a wrecking crew from knocking down a beloved old house in her newly adopted home city, where she has lived ever since.

More recently, as an octogenarian, she battled but lost a fight to prevent Toronto from combining several separate municipalities into a megalopolis. The "No Mega City" sign that hung on the front door of her brick house on Albany Avenue is symbolic of the toughness she has shown against city officials. At an October, 1997 week-long symposium in Toronto on her and her work, she even suggested that the core city of Toronto secede from the megacity. Perhaps the sense of community she helps create and then fights for through her political action hearkens back to the strength of community she grew up with in Dunmore. Dunmore is a small town on the outskirts of the small city of Scranton in eastern Pennsylvania, and she remembers many of the townspeople there playing baseball together throughout the summer. (I told her of my Italian relatives who also lived in Dunmore and had great gatherings of their families at least once, if not twice a week for huge pasta dinners, followed, of course, by baseball.) Later, in Toronto and Manhattan, Jacobs has continually backed up her observations and writings, as well as her sense of community, through action and moving others to question the seemingly sensible and well-meaning grand schemes of city and suburban developers.

In our profession, we need more spokespeople with her tenacity and nerve—those willing to advocate for our students and the beliefs that emerge from our research. This is especially important when such beliefs and research run counter to popular, often more simplistic reactions to the issues that languages raise in our schools and society. The seductiveness of simple solutions to complex concerns seems dangerous in any realm of life. Jacobs exhibits the kind of spirit we admire in people with strongly-held convictions, especially when they have the vision, the facts, the articulateness, and the battle scars to go with them. Known widely for her toughness on matters urban, she is to her neighbours a very kind, accessible human being as well.

Entertainment columnist for *The Toronto Star* Sid Adilman, who is her neighbour, reports that "Everybody knows her. She talks to everybody" (DePalma 1997: B10). Her cheery voice, knowing smile, belief in people, and continued optimism in the face of all the problems that cities face is refreshing. The teacher in her came across when I spoke with her. Though she wanted to see this chapter, she made it clear that I could send it to her "not to mastermind it, though, because it's your chapter." Her encouragement in expressing my own unfettered voice about the connections between her work and education was very supportive. The idea of *Expanding Our Vision* excited her. She said, "There's not enough looking into different fields" to inform us of our own expertise. "It's one of the great diseases—to fragment everything," she added, just as in cities when urban planners "separate residents from work, cultural places, the traffic of the streets and sidewalks." Regarding language, she noted its connection "to biology and all the rules of self organization." She spoke passionately about the fact that "life is a web" and how important it is to see how connected everything is. While I had hoped to engage her in a much longer discussion, I could not. She had clearly set limits at the outset of our chat: "I can't get distracted right now from my writing." She had work to do on her next book, another one on economics, and she needed to get back to her 40-year-old Remington typewriter she borrowed from her daughter-in-law. Her clear statement of limits was more evidence of her persistence, whether in her writing or in the other ways she continually advocates for cities and their inhabitants.

The Death and Life of Great American Cities is "perhaps the most important book written about cities in the 20th century" (DePalma 1997: B10). One sees in that classic work, as well as in her other writings and in her political action, the power of painstakingly accomplished qualitative research, her person-centred approach to city planning, and the unflappable hold she has on her convictions. If you look beyond the half-smile and unassuming demeanour of "Jane," as her neighbours call her, her eyes pierce through to see what is going on, what more there is to learn. These are certainly qualities I aspire to as a language teacher and as a teacher educator and classroom researcher. She, like the mentors I have been most influenced by, has an integrity that rings through louder than the spoken or written meaning of her words. That integrity comes from observing carefully and from caring about the objects of her observations. It is a quality she also admired in her great aunt, whose memoirs Jacobs put together in *A Schoolteacher in Old Alaska: The Story of Hannah Breece* (1997). Of Breece, Jacobs wrote, "She was inexhaustibly interested in the ordinary—better yet, extraordinary—minutiae of daily life" (1997: viii). What was true of her pioneering great aunt in the remote reaches of Alaska in the first decade of the 20th century is also characteristic of the urban-oriented Jacobs in the waning years of the century. "Hannah was a truthteller," according to her grand niece, who has carried on the legacy (1997: xvii). That sense of integrity and scouring for the truth is what sets the great teachers or administrators apart from the others in schools who merely go through the motions, play acting the roles of educators and curriculum designers.

APPLICATIONS TO LANGUAGE TEACHING

Having lived on three continents and visited some 45 countries, I often view the world as divided not continentally or nationally but into urban and non-urban swatches. Jacobs talks about elephantine cities while we in the educating business struggle to deal with the particularities of "urban education." Her discerning perspective on, and deeply felt relationship with cities, and the impact she has had on generations of city planners, illuminates for language educators, once we see the parallels between her work and ours, a plethora of possibilities for enlivening schools and the classrooms that are their pulse.

Having already interwoven pedagogical lessons derived from Jacobs' vision of cities, I will now summarize some of the connections between her view of city planning and language education. Following the organization of this chapter, I will begin with broader, more theoretical considerations and then turn to the practicalities of curriculum design and the everyday realities of classroom teaching. Finally, I will revisit the spirit with which Jacobs observes cities and advocates for her fellow urbanites.

At the broader level, we need to be wary of the big, one-size-fits-all conceptions of education, particularly those being promulgated by professors of education who are removed from the everyday workings of a range of schools and classrooms. We need to consider Jacobs' observation that "Big plans live off little plans" (1981: 28), not the other way around. We also should heed her advice that inductive thinking about the particular processes observable in a unique context will lead us to understandings that deductive thinking about abstractions will not. This is important not only in planning at the school district and curriculum levels. It is also essential within a particular school and classroom setting and when teachers sit down at night to plan their next day's lessons.

At the planning stage, Jacobs reminds us, "Cities have the capability of providing something for everybody only because, and only when, they are created by everybody" (quoted in Galt 1982: 12). That is why curriculum planners also need to do full-blown needs analyses that take into consideration the perspectives of all the stakeholders involved in the education of those in their communities. Similarly, teachers need to know about the richest resources available to them, that is, the students who enter their classrooms. By celebrating the multiplicity of resources students bring with them—and the unique contributions each of them will make to the community of learners—teachers can more effectively allow learning to unfold in the organic way Jacobs tells us to observe and appreciate. The lock-step, fix-it mentality behind language teaching approaches of the past do not match this organic view of life, of cities, or of education.

It is incumbent upon us to see the language learning process from the perspective of our students, as Jacobs has done with city dwellers (herself included). It seems to me that the process approach that is now so popular in the teaching of writing should extend to the teaching of the other language skills, to vocabulary development, and to cultural and general language awareness. We also need to involve ourselves in the same processes so that we can more easily empathize with the struggles of our students. We can do so by learning another language, or other languages, and by increasing our knowledge of the workings of the language we teach, or at least of the processes we experience as we speak, listen to, read, and write languages. We need also to study more closely how, where, and for what purposes people actually use language and non-verbal strategies to accomplish communication and comprehension.

The gender issues raised by Jacobs 37 years ago should also make us take notice. That most city architects and planners have been men and that they have excluded themselves from the normal, daytime life of residential areas in cities are provocative observations. Have we done the same thing in elementary schools, and if so, how can we provide for more of a gender mix in our schools? Besides the implications for hiring faculty and staff, we can also consider inviting a mix of target language speakers to our classrooms for special sessions. To offer the kind of diversity Jacobs strives for, we can invite a range of working people from the neighbouring community into the classroom. Students can meet them and may later practise language with them outside of school. Why not make the hallways of our schools extensions of the sidewalks of our communities? Of course, we can also be more creative in taking students on short, nearby field trips that will help them know the people and the workings of their neighbourhoods.

When Jacobs claims that intricacy creates "subtle expressions of difference," as in all the changes one sees in a small Japanese garden, one thinks about the design of school buildings or the layout of classrooms. Creative teachers move desks and chairs around and use slide projectors, video monitors, transparencies, and butcher block paper, depending on the activities they have planned for a given lesson. If allowed the luxury, they can lay out their classrooms in ways that are artful, varied, and that provide novel twists, fresh perspectives, and eye surprises. Caring teachers also provide intricacy in the way they craft their unit and lesson plans, varying activities and interactional arrangements. Language teachers should be no less architecturally astute than city planners. After all, they are the architects each year of hundreds of hours of communicative and of multicultural possibilities.

Jacobs also argues for multiple and diverse uses of space, which, for me, translates into schools that allow for the range of reading, writing, spoken language, art, music, drama, and physical activity (including dance) that bring communication alive for our students. Only by doing the things for which these skills prove useful in the world outside of school will students truly appreciate their value and the joy they can bring. Jacobs' idea also makes me think about the meshing of school activities with those of the larger society. Consider, for example, the media teacher who had high schoolers in New York State do investigative reporting and scientific studies of a toxic waste dump on the outskirts of their town. Those adolescents felt compelled to present their findings at a city hall meeting, demanding, with the support of their parents, that politicians do something about cleaning up the dump. All the publicity that ensued resulted in action for which the students and their teacher had been the main catalyst. That is certainly the kind of action Jacobs would applaud.

There are also lessons in Jacobs' ethnographic research methodology and her belief in the ordinary citizen's knowledge of the processes in cities. Action research by teachers, perhaps done collaboratively with teacher educators (Gebhard and Oprandy in press), would seem to tap a knowledge base that is close to the processes governing schools and classroom interaction. Narrative accounts providing "thick descriptions" of the particularities of given schools and classes would seem to align well with Jacobs' penchant for observing the streets and telling stories about neighbourhoods that did and did not thrive.

Jacobs' model of how to advocate for city dwellers is inspirational for those of us concerned with the sociopolitical and economic realities that influence to a great extent what we can do in our educational institutions. She squarely puts the needs of people over the power of institutions. Her gentility combined with her unswerving tenacity and toughness make her a very likeable yet formidable advocate. Above all, though, I am in awe of her eyes, which see so much, and her gift for expressing all she observes. I like the way one writer described Jacobs, matching very well my own experience of her:

> The mobile, articulate voice swoops from an animated, bird-like face sending thoughts out in new test patterns: an intellect in flight. Sophisticated yet disarmingly direct, informed yet folksy, the author is still overflowing with

cogent opinions two decades after the book appeared that made her name (Galt 1982: 11).

That description was written, as you can see, 16 years ago. The crispness of her writing reflects her career in journalism, which she began right after high school in Scranton, Pennsylvania, and continued shortly thereafter in New York while raising her family in Greenwich Village. Sitting today at her typewriter in her 95-year-old brick house in Toronto, Jane Jacobs is still pounding out tales of cities she continues to fight for passionately and with every bit of her urban strength.

REFERENCES CITED

Curran, C.A. 1976. *Counseling-Learning in Second Languages*. E. Dubuque, IL: Counseling-Learning Publications.

Darling-Hammond, L., ed. 1994. *Professional Development Schools*. New York: Teachers College Press.

DePalma, A. 1997. 'Jane Jacobs, Fighting Toronto's Dragons.' *The New York Times* (6 November): B10.

Fries, C.C. 1956. *Teaching and Learning English as a Foreign Language*. Ann Arbor: University of Michigan Press.

Galt, G. 1982. 'The Seer of City Planning: Jane Jacobs and the Death and Life of Great Canadian Cities.' *Canadian Heritage* (May):11-12.

Gattegno, C. 1976. *The Common Sense of Teaching Foreign Languages*. New York: Educational Solutions.

Gebhard, J.G. and R. Oprandy. In press. *An Exploratory Approach to Language Teaching Awareness*. New York: Cambridge University Press.

Howard, E. 1902. *Garden Cities of To-morrow* (being the second edition of *To-morrow: A Peaceful Path to Real Reform*). London: S. Sonnenscheim.

Jacobs, J. 1961. *The Death and Life of Great American Cities*. New York: Random House.

———. 1969. *The Economy of Cities*. New York: Vintage Books.

———. 1981. 'Vital Little Plans.' *Urban Design International* 2 (2): 28-29, 38-39.

———. 1984. *Cities and the Wealth of Nations*. New York: Random House.

———. 1997. 'Foreword.' In *A Schoolteacher in Old Alaska: The Story of Hannah Breece*, edited by H. Breece, vii-xviii. New York: Vintage.

Kessler, S. 1991. 'The Teaching Presence.' *Holistic Education Review* (Winter 1991): 4-14.

Lado, R. 1964. *Language Teaching: A Scientific Approach*. New York: McGraw-Hill.

LeCorbusier, C.E. 1967. *The Radiant City*. New York: Grossman, Orion Press (English translation of *La Ville Radieuse* [1935]).

Mumford, L. 1938. *The Culture of Cities*. New York: Harcourt Brace.

Rardin, J. and D. Tranel with P. Tirone and B. Green. 1988. *Education in a New Dimension: The Counseling-Learning Approach to Community Language Learning*. E. Dubuque, IL: Counseling-Learning Publications.

Smith, F. 1994. *Writing and the Writer*. Mahwah, NJ: Lawrence Erlbaum Associates.

CHAPTER FOUR

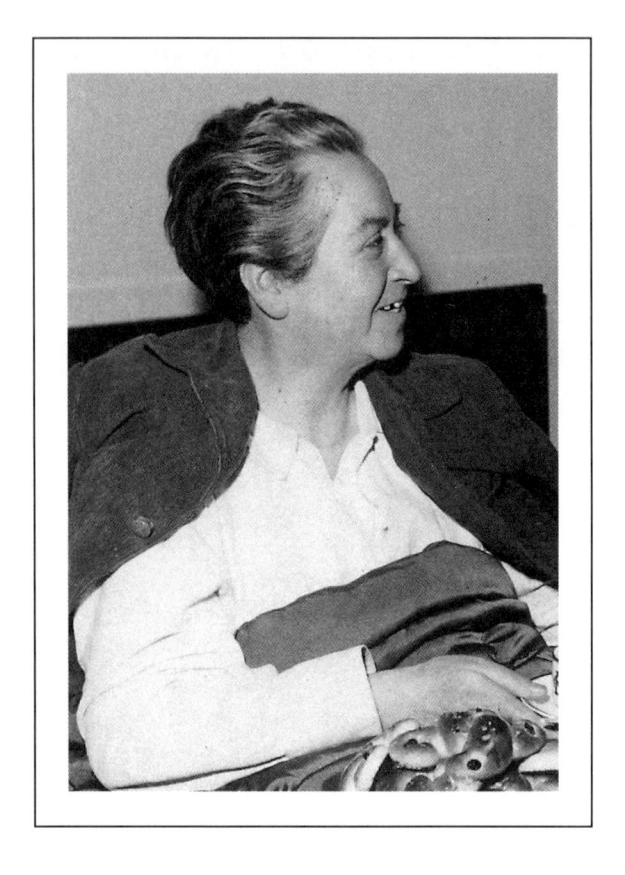

GABRIELA MISTRAL

❖

A LIFE OF SERVICE AND PASSION

Mary Ann Christison
University of Utah/Snow College

Aqui desde lejos
estoy con añoranza del tupido verdor
y el majestuoso andino de mi infancia.
Paso las horas de ilusión
que se pierden y se desvanecen lentamente
con los dias que corren veloces
al ocaso de mi existencia.

Here from afar
I long for the dense green
of the majestic Andes and my childhood.
Now, I pass my hours in illusion,
hours that are lost and slowly dissipate,
with days that pass too quickly,
days that are now the setting sun of my existence.

Jaime Cantarovici, *Desde Lejos* (*From Far Away*)
1975, written in the United States

INTRODUCTION

You may have never heard of Gabriela Mistral and may find it strange that I would choose her as the individual who has had the most influence on my professional life. Even though Mistral is perhaps the greatest Latin American lyric poet of the 20th century, and her work has been widely published in Latin America, France, and Spain, little is known about her in North America.

The works of Gabriela Mistral were first introduced to me in 1974 by Jaime Cantarovici (1942-1986), a professor of Spanish American Literature at Utah State University, a Chilean, and a poet in his own right (Cantarovici 1975). I was getting a Masters degree in Communication and had received permission from my department to pursue a creative foreign language thesis project using Readers' Theatre to present works from Spanish American literature. Dr. Cantarovici was one of my advisors on the project. He introduced me to a number of wonderful Spanish American poets—Juana de Ibarbourou, Alfonsina Storni, Pablo Neruda, Sor Juana Inés de la Cruz, Jorge Luis Borges, and Gabriela Mistral—whose works he thought might contribute to this creative endeavour. While I found the poetry of all of these writers interesting and thought-provoking, it was in the work and life of Gabriela Mistral that I found inspiration.

The Life of Mistral: Educator and Poet

Gabriela Mistral was born Lucila Gadoy Alcayaga on 7 April 1889, in the small rural village of Vicuña in northern Chile (Torres-Rioseco 1942: 120). She rose from these humble beginnings to become the most beloved and admired poet and educator in Latin America. Mistral's initial formal education was rural and minimal. The breadth of the knowledge she acquired and her facility with the Spanish language, however, indicate that she had acquired a great deal of self-taught knowledge, and that she was a voracious reader and an excellent, autonomous learner. As a teacher, I was encouraged by this fact about her life. Many second language learners in the public schools of North America face similar challenges. They have great talents and abilities, but may lack the opportunities to develop them. Mistral's life is a good reminder that much can be achieved by focusing on one's own natural talents and strengths.

After attending a teachers' college in Santiago, she became a school teacher at the age of 15. Her first job was in an elementary school in La Compañía, a village near Montegrande. I have thought many times of the difficulties that I encountered during my first year of teaching. I was 19 years old, inexperienced, and intimidated by some of the senior students who were close to my own age. I had difficulty finding time to prepare adequately for my classes, lacked patience with the students, and worried constantly over discipline problems. I was struck by Mistral's self-confidence and maturity at such a young age. During her first few years as a teacher, she was comfortable enough with herself that she began writing poetry and contributing selections to local newspapers—*Voz de Elqui* and *El Coquimbo* (Alcayaga 1906). She also published works in a Paris fashion magazine, *Elegancias*, which was edited by the Nicaraguan poet, Rubén Darío. It was in this magazine that she first used the pseudonym Gabriela Mistral. She chose the name, Gabriela, after her favourite poets—Gabriele D'Annunzio of Italy and Frédéric Mistral of France. "Mistral" comes from the fierce *mistral* wind that blows over the south of France.

In 1914, when she was just 25 years old, she submitted a trio of sonnets under this new pseudonym to a national poetry writing contest in Chile and won the grand prize. The sonnets were entitled "Los Sonetos de la Muerte." When the award was announced, literary critics were stunned to learn the identity of the new found Chilean poet. She was a 25-year-old teacher from a small, rural Chilean village. On the date of the prize's presentation, Mistral sent regrets that she would not be there to accept. The Chilean poet, Victor Domingo Silva, accepted the prize for her and read the laurelled verses. Later Mistral admitted that she had been in the audience the entire time but had been too shy to admit her presence, read the poetry, and accept the prize.

One of Chile's prominent literary critics at that time, Hernan Diaz Arrieta, said that Mistral's poems were " .... some of the most intense poems of love and sorrow in the Spanish language" (Dana 1971: xi). This is a powerful statement about any poet, but it is even more significant when one considers that Mistral was competing in a male-dominated literary circle against men who were highly influential and well-educated. She did not have the advantage of power, influence, or educational training and background. Her work had to speak for itself, and indeed it did. After her initial success in the Chilean national poetry writing contest, Mistral was not content to rest on these laurels. She continued writing at an incredible pace. In the years between 1914 and 1917, she published an additional 50 stories and poems and established herself as the most important national literary figure in Chile, all before the age of 30.

In spite of the fame that Mistral achieved as a poet and writer, she always thought of herself primarily as a teacher. She believed that teaching was her true vocation and that to sacrifice her calling would be worse than physical suicide. Mistral believed that if you do what you love, everything will fall into place. Her joy of teaching was contagious. In 1918, the Chilean Ministry of Education began to take notice of Mistral as both an educator and a writer. The Ministry advanced her teaching career by waiving the requirement for a pedagogic diploma and promoting her to the rank of a principal in a *liceo*. As a principal, Mistral was in a position to effect change in the educational system—change that she could not have carried out if she had remained solely a teacher. Mistral was passionate about her work as an educator and about educational reform. She cared deeply about Chilean rural children. As a principal, she was able to implement educational reform, create libraries, and work tirelessly on behalf of the education of rural children. Her attitude and her efforts on behalf of children serve as excellent reminders of the importance of commitment to one's goals and ideals. Mistral put her commitment to the education of Chilean children before her own needs and desires.

Many Chileans were inspired by Gabriela Mistral. Word of her achievements as a poet and educator spread throughout Latin America. In 1922, the Mexican Minister of Education, José Vasconcelos, officially invited Mistral to come to Mexico to collaborate with him in carrying out an ambitious program of educational reform (Bates 1971 in Dana 1971: xvi). The project was especially interesting to Mistral because it spoke to her passion. Being of Indigenous and Basque descent herself, she was well aware of the fact that the Indigenous population throughout Latin America had been denied educational opportunities. The program in Mexico included creating educational programs to teach Indigenous adults and children in the rural areas of Mexico. This population was not being served by the existing educational system. The project was successful. In fact, it was so successful that a school in Mexico City was named in Mistral's honour in 1922. Today every country throughout Latin America has a school named after Mistral.

The Works of Gabriela Mistral

The eventful project in Mexico in 1922 coincided with the publication of Mistral's first book of poetry, *Desolación* (*Desolation*) (Mistral 1923). *Desolación* reflects the remote and desolate landscapes of Patagonia where she was born. Poems on five themes—life, love, nature, sorrow, and children—are included. In this early work, she speaks to children with a compassionate, tender, maternal voice. The poems on children and teaching were inspired by her work in Mexico, as well as her work in Chile as a teacher and administrator. As is evident in these few excerpts from one of her poems in *Desolación* entitled, "La Oración de la Maestra" ("A Teacher's Prayer"), Mistral had a strong commitment to teaching and to making a difference in the lives of children. She put her own needs second to the needs of her students.

> *Dame el ser más madre que las madres, para poder amar y defender*
> *como ellas lo que no es carne de mis carnes. Dame que alcance*
> *a hacer de una de mis niñas mi verso perfecto y a dejarte en ella*
> *clavada mi más penetrante melodía, para cuando mis labios no canten más ....*
>
> *Dame el levantar los ojos de mi pecho con heridas, al entrar cada*
> *mañana a mi escuela. Que no lleve a mi mesa de trabajo mis pequeños afanes materiales, mis mezquinos dolores de cada hora.*

> Let me be more maternal than a mother; able to love and defend
> children who are not the flesh of my flesh.
> Grant that I may be successful in shaping one of my students into
> a perfect poem, and let me leave within her my deepest-felt melody
> that she may sing for you when my lips shall sing no more .....
>
> Each morning when I enter my school, let my vision rise above
> my own hurt. Let me never carry to my work desk my own small
> material cares or my personal sorrows.
>   (Mistral 1923)

Desolación was actually published in New York City by a group of Spanish teachers who expressed deep admiration and sincere affection for Mistral and her work. In 1921, a Spanish professor at Columbia University, Federico de Onís, read some poems by a Chilean school teacher to students of Spanish at the Hispanic Institute.

The poems were immediately recognized for the strength of their literary talent and for their great moral force. The students of Spanish who were present at the reading all wanted to know where they could get copies of the poems. Unfortunately, all that Professor Onís could give them was a handful of clippings from newspapers and magazines that Mistral had sent him. The students themselves worked to publish a collection of her poems because they were so powerful. Although Gabriela cooperated in the project with Onís and his students and ultimately gave her permission for all of the poetry to be published, she did have some difficulty with the project. In her genial modesty, she preferred to leave her work scattered (Dana 1971: xvi). Part of *Desolación* speaks to the pain that Mistral suffered as a result of losing a lover to suicide in her early life (Teitelboim 1996):

> *¡Y ser con él todas las primaveras*
> *y los inviernos, en un angustiado*
> *nudo, en torno a su cuello ensangrentado!*

> Just to be with him every spring
> and every winter, in naked anguish
> around his blood-stained neck.
>   (Mistral 1923)

Desolación was followed closely in 1924 (second edition 1945) by her second book, *Ternura* (*Tenderness*). The first edition was published in Madrid. *Ternura* was a collection of poems for mothers and children. Her deep sense of the maternal is evident, as is her devotion to her lifelong vocation of teaching. These elements are captured beautifully in the following four verses from her poem "Niño Mexicano" ("Mexican Child"):

> *Estoy en donde no estoy;*
> *en el Anáhuac plateado,*
> *y en su luz como no hay otro*
> *peino un niño de mis manos ...*

> *Yo juego con sus cabellos*
> *y los abro y los repaso,*
> *y en sus cabellos recobro*
> *a los mayas dispersados.*

> *Hace dos años dejé*
> *a mi niño mexicano;*
> *pero despierta o dormida*
> *yo lo peino de mis manos.*

¡Es una maternidad
que no me cansa el regazo,
y es un éxtasis que tengo
de la gran muerte librado!

I am where I am not,
on the silvery Anáhuac,
and by its light, like no other
I comb a little boy's hair with my hands ...

And I play with his hair,
part it, caress it,
and in his hair I find again
the dispersed Mayas.

Two years ago I left
my little Mexican boy,
but awake or asleep
I comb him with my hands.

It is a maternity
That never tires my lap.
It is an ecstasy I live
freed from great death.
        (Mistral 1945)

The poems were popular because of their humour. Her poems exalted children's innocence and sense of fair play and were an inspiration to all. An example may be found in the poem "Con Tal Que Duermas" ("If You'll Only Go to Sleep"), where she promises a little baby *"pez de luces"* (sequined goldfish) and more if only he'll go to sleep. The poems recall experiences that all mothers share. She found humour in these difficult and trying moments. Spanish-speaking children memorize many of the verses from *Ternura*, grown-ups read them for their own pleasure, and composers and choreographers put them to music and dance.

After the publication of *Desolación* and *Ternura*, Mistral's prose works also began to appear frequently in newspapers and periodicals throughout the Americas and Europe. Not only was she famous for her poetry, she also garnered an excellent reputation for articles on literature, education, and contemporary events (Pinilla 1945).

In 1938, 16 years after her first book of poems, she published her third book *Tala* (*Felling*) (1947). Mistral rushed this book to press because the Spanish Civil War had broken out, and she wanted to offer the book as a gift to the Basque children who were uprooted from their homes because of the war. The publication of

Tala produced great intellectual and emotional excitement among her colleagues. *Tala* was a departure in both theme and style from her previous works. The passion of love and the anguish of death that motivated much of her earlier work were missing. She wrote instead about recollections from her childhood as in her famous poem, "Todas Ibamos a Ser Reinas" ("We Were All to Be Queens"). This is a poem about Gabriela herself (Lucila in the poems) and three other little girls from her childhood. All three of the girls were Mistral's companions in the one-room schoolhouse she attended in Montegrande. In *Tala* she also wrote about her mother's death, hymns to the Andes Mountains, and *recados* (notes or messages) to friends in Chile, Argentina, Mexico, Spain, and the Antilles. The style of *Tala* was concise and terse. Her language revealed the colloquial speech of Latin America. The rhythmic pattern had also changed. It was no longer shaped by the classic modernists, as was her earliest work in *Desolación*. *Tala* had a rhythm all of its own with mythical simplicity and idiomatic innovations inspired by the rural speech of her native valley.

Her fourth book, *Lagar* (*Wine Press*) was published in 1954 in Santiago, Chile, 32 years after *Desolación*. This was her last and possibly greatest work and contained significant religious content. Mistral suffered great personal strife during the years in which she wrote *Lagar*. She encountered the Spanish Civil War and its terrible atrocities. Her sister, Emelina, and her close friend, Stefan Zweig, both died. Her adopted son, Juan Miguel (known affectionately as Yin Yin), died a tragic death. She had raised Yin Yin from childhood and lived with him as a son. In the poem "Liana," these expressions of personal grief are evident:

> ... *Por el tallo de la noche*
> *que tú amabas y que yo amo,*
> *ella sube despedazada*
> *y rehecha, insegure y cierta.*
>
> Up the stalk of night
> that you loved, that I love,
> creeps my torn prayer,
> rent and mended, uncertain and sure.
> (Mistral 1954)

The Bible had a profound influence on Mistral; it permeates her poetry in *Lagar*, such as in the poem "Marta y María" ("Martha and Mary") about the sisters of Lazarus. Mary is often identified as Mary Magdalene. *Lagar* also contains poems of intense social commentary. Mistral writes about the earth, its people, and their struggles and trials. She writes about the man who tills the soil, the miner who works in a cold tomb, the child who cries with hunger, and the mother who weeps because her child is hungry. For the people who had no voice, she became their voice. Mistral belongs to the group of humanists who see literature as a service. The poems in *Lagar* cry out against persecution, tyranny, racial hatred, war, and genocide. Through her poetry Mistral found a way to raise a collective social conscience and make a difference—particularly for women and children.

Of the four books of poetry Mistral published in her lifetime, the one that had the most popular acclaim was *Desolación*. This is the book that was written mostly before she was 17 years old. In it, she poured forth a virtual torrent of her emotional life. The poems in *Desolación* expressed the very depth of her being. Mistral was a poet who had a profound interior world and this interior world dictated to her rather spontaneously. The frankness that she expressed in all four of her books often scandalized the critics, but her vocabulary was so extraordinarily rich and original that her work was always embraced by her readers, and in the end, Mistral was forgiven by the critics. Mistral differs from other women poets of her time (e.g., Storni and Ibarbarou) because they are often painfully conscious of their femininity. Mistral seldom mentions herself in any of her books, unless to comment on her plainness.

On 16 November 1945 newspapers around the world announced the awarding of the Nobel Prize for literature to Mistral. She was the first Latin American ever to receive the award. The news surprised literary critics in North America. Although Mistral enjoyed great popularity in Spanish-speaking countries, as much for her deeds as for her words, few of her poems had been translated into English.

A Life of Service

Mistral travelled widely, fulfilling many educational and diplomatic postings. Her travels carried her to the United States, France, Spain, and Italy. She was a visiting professor at Barnard, Mills, Middlebury, and Vassar colleges and at the University of Puerto Rico. She was the Chilean Consul in a number of different countries, including Italy and the United States. In fact, she called the United States her home on two separate occasions and resided as the Consul of Chile in California and then in New York. Mistral was also a representative to the Institute of Intellectual Cooperation of the League of Nations in Paris and an official delegate from Chile to the United Nations. As a delegate to the United Nations, she was instrumental in the founding of UNICEF. During Mistral's later years, she came to New York to live with her longtime friend Doris Dana. It was in New York that she died in 1957, a resident of Roslyn Harbor, Long Island.

Inspirational Themes

Mistral lived an exemplary life—a life of service, passion, and creativity. Her life has been an inspiration to thousands of people, in particular, women and children. She has certainly influenced me in her roles both as teacher and writer. For many years I have carried her poetry and her life close to my heart, but I have not, until now, attempted to analyze the ways in which her influence has come to bear on my own professional development. In writing this chapter and talking to others about her life, I have been forced to think more clearly about not only the contributions she has made to my own professional development, but the possible applications for second language teachers and teacher educators. In order to clarify my thinking, I have focused on four themes from Mistral's life that I believe to have the potential to influence teacher development—recognizing one's roots, developing a commitment for learning, achieving balance in life, and developing humility and modesty.

Theme One: Recognizing One's Roots

Mistral felt connected to her place of birth. All of her life she carried within her a profound love for the small villages edged between the rugged Andes Mountains where she was born. Even though she lived in many places and countries throughout the world (Dana 1971: 123), her heart remained in Chile. Mistral was comfortable with her origins; they became a source of strength to her. She incorporated these early experiences into her writing; she was tied to the land; the mountains, the villages, and the people of her birthplace (Mistral 1923). Her ability to recognize and appreciate her heritage has held personal significance for me.

Because I was born in rural Utah, with my primary education taking place in a small school with six grades in three small rooms, I identified strongly with Mistral and have wondered if other teachers with similar backgrounds felt the same way. Her childhood and her early experiences were a source of strength to her, becoming the inspiration for much of her work. She integrated her life into her writing. In studying the life of Gabriela Mistral, it became clear to me that complete acceptance of self was important for success as a teacher and educator. Because Mistral accepted herself, she admitted to herself and to her readers both her strengths and her weaknesses. She was a successful teacher. Whether writing verse or interacting with friends, her words flowed naturally and spontaneously; her relationships with people were comfortable and easy. She was connected to all life's experiences and took the good with the bad.

Mistral's life and the complete acceptance of her roots, her humble beginnings, were a source of inspiration for me. In my own life, I, too, have felt connected to the land where I was born and felt that I would never be at my best if I left it completely. When I am travelling and far away from home, thinking about home becomes an oasis of comfort in my mind. Because of my background, I have worried about qualitative and quantitative issues relative to my own educational experiences. When I left primary school to attend a larger junior high school, it became immediately apparent that my primary education had been quite minimal. Some students at my grade level were already taking algebra and talking about literature that was foreign to me. Even though I had been one of the best students in my early grades, there were large gaps in my educational background. My response for many years was to feel that I had done something wrong, to keep those early experiences far away from me. Studying Mistral's life helped me to see how important it is for us to acknowledge every part of our lives. I am certain there are many gaps in my own educational background. I also know that there are benefits to the kind of education I had. I was never just a number, but always a name and connected to a family, a history with the land, and a community. This fact, alone, must have had a profound influence on my concept of self. Examining Mistral's life can help us understand the importance of valuing diversity in experience. Instead of believing that some experiences are better than others, we can begin to look at how our different experiences impact our lives and our students' lives and make us whole.

Theme Two: Commitment to Learning

Gabriela Mistral achieved national prominence and established herself as the leading lyric poet in Latin America all before the age of 30, but she was not content to stop there. She continued to write and expanded her talents into educational reform and politics. She travelled widely, serving her country as a diplomat and teaching at foreign universities. At any one point in Mistral's life, she could have stopped and been considered by most people's standards a complete success. Instead, she continued to grow, learn, and contribute throughout her entire life. The scope of Mistral's interests was immensely broad and profound. She was as enthusiastic about new events and opportunities in her later life as she was when she wrote *Desolación* in her teens. Her willingness to experiment and change is best captured in the varying styles of her poetry. *Lagar*, her final book, is a substantive departure in style from *Desolación*, her first book.

Early in my career as an educator, I thought it was important to define my professional parameters. In fact, on a couple of occasions, I turned down interesting work because I thought that it did not fit with the professional image that I had in mind. I wanted to be known as a specialist in some methodology or technique in language teaching. Mistral's life can inspire teachers to let go of limiting notions. Mistral believed that it was most important to be motivated to learn. If she was interested in the work and would learn from it, she did it. She didn't define herself in any particular way. As teachers, I believe we can benefit greatly from this inclusive approach to life. If we apply Mistral's principle to our own lives, they will become far richer. If an opportunity comes along, and we are interested in it, we should take it. If we can allow some of our decisions to be made from the heart, we might be happier in our work.

Theme Three: Achieving Balance

Gabriela Mistral possessed what some critiques call the "Basque equilibrium." She was steady and stalwart, never swaying in her commitment to her friends, her writing, her passions, or her life of service. This steadiness is a rare quality in people who have Mistral's bent for creativity, such passion for life, and such a flair for words. We often expect creative people to be flamboyant, eccentric, difficult, and frequently moody. Indeed, we are initially attracted to creative people because of these very qualities. The human characteristics of sensibility, loyalty, and commitment are often found to be flat and ordinary. We are only grateful for these qualities in other people when our own lives are difficult and uncertain.

Mistral, by many people's standards, was flat and ordinary. In her interactions with people, she was positive, practical, judicious, prudent, and sensible. What we can learn from studying Mistral's life is the importance of achieving balance. On the one hand, Mistral was the epitome of good, common sense; she was steady and constant. As a writer, however, she was intense and passionate; she was a balanced person, able to integrate the many parts of who she was—a simple woman from a small remote mountain village, a woman with a great capacity for love, an intellectual that made her a follower of the discipline of Buddha, and a devoted Christian. Mistral accepted fully all of these different parts of herself.

I think about my early days in the classroom; I worried that my students would either think that I was too boring or too strange. There were so many parts of myself that seemed not part of me. Coming to accept the fact that I was, at times, both boring and strange, and that these conditions were acceptable, was an enormous relief. Over the years, I have seen the value of this acceptance in the classroom. Students find value in the sensible, somewhat boring side of teachers when their lives, as students, are uncertain and difficult. They need to know what to expect from teachers, so they can be more open and relaxed and feel less pressure in completing assignments, taking tests, interacting in the classroom, and consulting with teachers about problems in their own lives or what they do not understand in the classroom.

Students can also benefit from the creative, somewhat flamboyant side of teachers' personalities, but they benefit in a slightly different way. When teachers use unfamiliar instructional techniques and promote controversial ideas, students are often resistant. When participation and discussion in classes move students beyond their current boundaries, their ways of thinking and knowing, the students themselves get a sense that they have learned and grown as a result of these experiences. They find value in this process.

Theme Four: Developing Humility and Modesty

Mistral's life was a model of humility and modesty. When I first read the story about Mistral being too shy and modest to personally accept the award for the national poetry contest she had won, I was stunned. I didn't, at the time, see how someone could not want to be recognized for what she had worked hard to achieve. What I came to understand from Mistral's life was that her motivation did not stem from wanting recognition for her work. There was something deeper within her that was the source of her motivation. She would do what she felt compelled to do, with scarcely a thought for an outcome that might bring her fame and recognition. She preferred to keep the attention on her work and not on herself. It was this same modesty that kept her work scattered for such a long period of time. She focused on the individual pieces of her work, giving little thought to achieving some sort of permanence to her voice. As support for this fact, it is interesting to note that the publication of her first book was not initiated by Mistral, but rather by her readers in the United States.

What teachers can learn from applying principles of modesty and humility is that it is much more meaningful and certainly easier to focus on one's work when the joy of the work itself is the motivator. It is always a bonus when someone else appreciates one's work or finds it useful. Doing work because one wants to be recognized by someone else is disappointing when the work is not recognized.

Conclusion

Mistral's life and works have been an inspiration to me for over 20 years. The strength of her character as much as her words continue to influence me today. Even in death, her legacy continues. To the children of her native village of Montegrande, she left her Latin American royalties. She hoped that the children of this poor, isolated mountain hamlet might never be forgotten by her country. To humanity, she left the influence of her good deeds and a life of service. To her faithful readers, she left her poetry.

>   *Mi último árbol no está en la tierra*
>   *no es de semilla ni de leño,*
>   *no se plantó, no tiene riegos.*
>   *Soy yo misma mi ciprés*
>   *mi sombreadura y mi ruedo,*
>   *mi sudario sin costuras,*
>   *y mi sueño que camina*
>   *árbol de humo y con ojos abiertos ....*
>
>   My final tree is not of the earth,
>   not of seed, not of wood,
>   not planted, not watered.
>   I myself am my own cypress,
>   my obscure shade, my circumference,
>   my seamless shroud that wipes the sweat from my brow,
>   and my dream that walks,
>   a tree of smoke with open eyes ....
>
>   "Luto" ("Mourning") from *Lagar* 1954

References Cited

Alcayaga, L.G. 1906. 'La Instrucción de la Mujer.' En *La Voz de Elqui* (8 March) Vicuña, Chile.

Bates, M. 1971. 'Introductions' In *Selected Poems of Gabriela Mistral*, edited by D. Dana, xv-xvii. Baltimore, Maryland: Johns Hopkins Press.

Cantarovici, J. 1975. *Desde Lejos*. Barcelona, Spain: Ediciones Rondas.

Dana, D., ed. 1971. *Selected Poems of Gabriela Mistral*. Baltimore, Maryland: Johns Hopkins Press.

Mistral, G. 1923. *Desolación*. Santiago de Chile: Ed. Nascimento.

———. 1945. *Ternura*. Buenos Aires: Collecíon Austral. (First edition published 1924).

———. 1947. *Tala*. Buenos Aires: Ed. Losada. (First edition published 1938)

———. 1954. *Lagar*. Santiago de Chile: Ed. del Pacifico.

Pinilla, N. 1945. *Biografía de Gabriela Mistral*. Santiago de Chile: Ed. Tegualda.

Teitelboim, V. 1996. *Gabriela Mistral*. Santiago de Chile: Editorial Sudamericana Chilena.

Torres-Rioseco, A. 1942. *The Epic of Latin American Literature*. Oxford: Oxford University Press.

Note: Translations of poetry selections in this article by Mary Ann Christison.

CHAPTER FIVE

Myra Scovel

✣

A Woman of Spirit

Thomas Scovel
San Francisco State University

INTRODUCTION

One of the most consequential changes that has taken place in the teaching of English as an additional language at the end of this millennium is the revolution from "methods" to "principles." In this post-methodological era, well-informed practitioners are no longer concerned with employing a single method or with comparing the efficacy of different methods; rather, they are now much more interested in considering the "principles" which have been established from decades of second language acquisition research and in translating these principles into practice through the selection of appropriate classroom activities (Brown 1994a). This quiet revolution has resulted in several benefits for our profession. For one thing, teachers are less likely to be misled by the overzealous claims of the proponents of a particular method. They are also more apt to examine the specific characteristics of their teaching situation rather than blithely to assume that a "one-size-fits-all" designer method, which might be appropriate for one classroom, will also be equally suitable for theirs (Brown 1994b: 58). By considering the abstract principles underlying their teaching, practitioners are also encouraged to be reflective: they are prompted to ponder on how these principles jive with their own assumptions about language learning and teaching (Richards and Lockhart 1994). Finally, the move toward "principled" rather than "methodological" instruction encourages teachers to be more disposed to making their classrooms student-centred. Rather than following the routines of a particular method and rotely adopting the techniques dictated by that method, irrespective of all the different variables that students bring to any language classroom, principled teaching encourages teachers to translate a common set of principles into tasks which fit their students' needs, aptitudes, and interests (Brown 1994b).

One could choose almost any method from the past and any principle from the present for the sake of illustration, but for a brief example, let's contrast Asher's (1977) "Total Physical Response" (TPR) method with the current post-methodological focus on principled, reflective teaching. When teachers commit to using TPR in their classrooms, the method appropriates, in many ways, their need to reflect on the pedagogical issues which surround their classes and their freedom to choose suitable activities which meet and match their students' communicative needs. For example, because this method is based on the notion that listening must precede speaking, and that at least initially, all linguistic input in the target language must be in the form of imperatives, teachers are not prompted to think about these assumptions critically. Nor are they allowed to choose linguistic forms and functions other than commands, at least during the early stages of TPR. This constraint, which is endemic to any method, was one of the primary reasons why practitioners and theorists alike have become much more attracted to a post-methodological, principled approach.

In contrast to following a method, consider the following principle as an example of the more contemporary perspective on language teaching. Comprehensible input is a necessary but insufficient condition for successful language acquisition (Krashen 1994). Of course, if one retreats to the immediate past, when methods reigned, a practitioner of TPR would immediately argue that this method (like many others) was validated by this principle because it provided plenty of "comprehensible input" in the form of spoken commands. But one crucial difference between the methodological and the principled approach to language teaching is that in the former, according to TPR, "comprehensible input" was defined and confined by the use of imperatives and by restricting students to only silent responses. Teachers did not think for themselves, nor did they make informed choices for their students. The method, not the teacher and not the student, was the centre of the classroom. Principled teaching prompts the teacher to reflect on the nature of "comprehensible input" in terms of students' needs and aptitudes. Should input be initially introduced through listening, or through reading, or through both? Why? What is the level of comprehensibility of my students considering their ages and their stages of acquisition? How do I know this? How can I introduce "comprehensible input" in the target language to my students in an interesting and relevant manner? How can I contextualize today's tasks and activities into the larger curriculum? What specific constraints do I face in teaching my class today? Notice that methods tend to provide answers; a principled approach tends to provoke questions.

It is not the intent of this chapter to promulgate principled teaching; that has been done eloquently and convincingly by others elsewhere, but I think the new consciousness about principled teaching underscores the timeliness of this volume of collected voices, for it raises a natural question. If the experiments of scores of applied linguists and the experiences of thousands of language teachers have demonstrated the value of *principles of teaching* for their professional lives as teachers, then are there not larger and more general *principles of professional living* that might have an impact on the personal lives of language teachers? Just as the experiments of sound research contribute to classroom teaching because they provide an objective, external viewpoint, so too do the experiences of extraordinary individuals from outside our ordinary pedagogical world bring us a refreshingly different perspective, and in doing so, they serve to expand our vision (Casanave and Schecter 1997). In both my professional and personal life, a person by the name of Myra Scovel has served to provide that outside perspective and has given me a fresh view of what it means to live a more wholesome life as a language teacher. Let me share her story.

COURAGE AND HUMOUR

Language classrooms do not normally evoke memories of railroads and even less do they elicit thoughts about refugee trains snaking through war-torn countrysides, but the juxtaposition of the classroom we teach in and a dangerous journey once taken many years ago may be an apt way to introduce the story of the remarkable woman I have in mind and to identify some principles from her life that might be relevant for ours.

During the late 1930s, the Japanese Imperial army, in its ambitious mission to co-opt its neighbours into Japan's "Greater East Asia Co-Prosperity Sphere," had swept across Korea and Manchuria and was spreading westward, battle by battle, across the Shandong peninsula of northern China. This war had completely disrupted the lives of millions of Chinese and would eventually result in hundreds of thousands of civilian deaths, the destruction of many of the towns and cities of coastal China, and a decade of colonial subjugation. The invasion also affected the lives of a handful of foreigners who happened to be living in Shandong at the time. Among these was an American missionary nurse who was temporarily trapped in the port city of Qingdao with her three children and mother-in-law, separated from her husband, a missionary doctor, and the Chinese town she called home many kilometres to the west by the ever shifting front of the war. It was late autumn, and she had fondly hoped that the fighting would diminish sufficiently enough for her to secure train transportation home so that she and her family could rejoin her husband by Christmas.

In late November, her husband telegrammed her that his small, inland hospital was filled with wounded Chinese soldiers and civilians, and they were in grave need of ether. Qingdao was the only city in the province where this precious surgical commodity was available, and his thought was that being an American and a "neutral" in the conflict, she might be able to get the ether to him through the battle lines. With pluck and prodding, she bought as many small tins of the volatile liquid as she could, placed them in a large suitcase, and with the throngs of refugees that are the invariable consequence of any combat, squeezed herself into one of the few trains that were still operating out of the city. Quite abruptly, she realized that the situation was much more desperate than she had realized from the shelter of her temporary residence in the colonial port enclave of Qingdao. Every few kilometres the train would squeal to a halt, precipitating a mass exodus of passengers into the fields on either side of the track. The first time she followed this lemming-like rush, she had not understood why the sudden panic, but after spotting a Japanese fighter ricochet by in a brief strafing attack, prompted by the expectation that the train was ferrying Chinese troops into the battle zone, she realized what was happening. Once the plane disappeared, there was another mad scramble to reboard the overcrowded train, and on again it would rumble, only to screech to a stop once more when the drill was frantically repeated. Because she was barely 152 cm [5 ft.] tall, and because she had to haul her valuable cargo of flammables with her every time there was a scrum for the door, she decided enough was enough. The next time there was an attack, more faithfully than fatefully, she simply stayed seated, and for the rest of the day she enjoyed the few minutes respite the empty carriage provided during each subsequent stop. Fortunately for all of them, there were more false alarms than actual attacks, and even the latter were brief and mercifully inaccurate.

The train arrived that evening at the provincial capital, where she disembarked, and hired a rickshaw to the other railroad station across town to see if there were any trains running south to her expectant husband. Providentially, one train was heading in that direction, but the station was ringed by a mass of refugees, frantic to escape the invading army. "I have ether to take to the mission hospital in Jining," she shouted in Mandarin to the few policemen trying to maintain an illusion of order. "If I don't get on the train, many will die." The impact of her terse plea moved the police and they half shoved, half carried her and her precious package into the sea of evacuees and through a window into a carriage packed with Chinese troops, escaping the front to regroup to fight another day against the relentless Japanese forces. They were so tightly stuffed together that as the train rocked slowly into the night, she soon had a head nodding off on each shoulder and one young soldier dozing on her suitcase at her feet. With all the armed men crowded around her, ironically, she must have felt both lonely and frightened. After all, she was a foreigner, perhaps the first one many of these young Shandong conscripts had ever seen, and she was a youngish woman, completely alone, spending the night in a room packed with military men.

Occasionally they would wake up and engage her in conversation. What was she doing in China? And what on earth was she doing on this train? But the only moment of her entire journey when she began to grow genuinely frightened was when a packet of cigarettes suddenly emerged, and the men surrounding her all started to light up. Smelling the fumes that seeped from the leaky tins in her suitcase by her feet, she pleaded with them to extinguish their smokes. "Younger brothers," she implored, "please do not smoke in here. My suitcase is filled with ether and can explode." "What difference does it make lady," one of them immediately replied, "if we get blown up here or in battle, a few days later?" "A very big difference, brother," she tartly rejoined, "I won't be with you on the battlefield!" The laughter that broke out in the carriage helped shorten the night, and by the next afternoon, she was able to deliver her much-needed cargo and enjoy a brief reunion with her husband before retracing the same perilous journey back to rejoin her children stranded in Qingdao.

Granted, there are no teachers or classrooms in this little episode, neither are there grammar patterns or lesson plans. And war, refugees, teeming trains, desperate journeys, and the smell of ether are, at least for the fortunate majority of us, faint recollections from past history. And were you to return to this part of China today, although the same cities and rail lines remain, about the only remnant that links this account to the present is the ubiquitous stench of cigarette smoke which still fouls the air of railway carriages. But life is much more holistic than it appears at first glimpse, and there is a reason I began with such an apparently remote and insignificant incident involving a woman whose life was seemingly unconnected to language teaching. When a few more details are shared, there begin to emerge several systemic connections between her life and the life we live as language teachers. So I believe that this brief history of her story can help expand our vision by providing us with some principles about how to teach more sensibly and yes, even about how to live more sensitively. Of course, I am not exactly an unbiased reporter. The American nurse was my mother.

The account just shared suggests at least two principles. Even though our contemporary lives are not nearly as harried nor as desperate as the train journey my mother was forced to endure, stress and uncertainty are frequently part and parcel of our daily life as language teachers, and we might do well to confront this pressure the way she did—with relentless courage and with spurts of spontaneous humour. Neither of these virtues diminished the dangers she experienced, but both allowed her to accomplish something which seemed almost impossible, and to accomplish it in a way that brought both her and her fellow passengers a brief moment of joy. Granted, courage and humour are largely gifts of our birth, but they can be nurtured too, and we would do well to kindle them if we can. They give us hope when things are desperate and they elicit smiles when life is grim. But this is not the only way in which my own vision was expanded by this remarkable woman.

APPRECIATION FOR THE SPOKEN AND WRITTEN WORD

I obviously have no direct memories of the first half of my mother's life, and the afflictions of Alzheimer's and her subsequent death a few years ago have deprived me of any recent opportunities for gleaning more about her past. But thanks to her prolific writing and my own storehouse of memories as a child growing up first in China and then in India, I have an impressive record of her life.

Myra Scovel is not the kind of person you would customarily include in a book about influential celebrities whose lives might impact ours as language teachers. She certainly was not famous in any conventional sense. Born just after the turn of the century in a small town along the Hudson River in upstate New York, the eldest daughter of a working class family, she never received a university education. From high school, she went directly to a nearby city hospital for her nursing training (the custom for that vocation at the time), and there she found both a profession and a husband—a young doctor who was interning at the same institution. After their marriage, the completion of her medical training, and the birth of her first child, it would seem that she was destined to enjoy a life of comfort and status close to her family in the familiar environs of her native Hudson river valley, but even during her engagement, she knew that this dream was not to be. The man she was about to marry had been given a book when he was only five years old by his father for "perfect church attendance." When my father read this account of David Livingstone, the famous 19th century missionary explorer to Africa (Mathews 1912), he was instantly inspired by this biography and by the fact that Livingstone's original aspirations had been to work in China. Even as a child, my father had always felt called to go to that then remote part of the world as a medical missionary. It was another testimony to my mother's courage (and her sense of whimsy as well, perhaps!) that in 1930, she agreed to be deputized with him as a missionary of the Presbyterian Church, packed their belongings for their first six-year assignment, said good-bye to friends and family, and with a baby son in her arms, accompanied my father on the train ride across the continent to Seattle where they caught a slow boat to China. She was 24 and had never been farther from home than Cleveland.

The voyage westward across the Pacific marked an important transition in her life; she was an emigrant from the safe but small and homogenized world of her childhood and had chosen to become an immigrant in a much wider, diverse, but also more dangerous realm of mission and adventure. From rather unpretentious beginnings, bound by her gender, socioeconomic class, geographical provincialism, and relatively limited education, she eventually grew to enjoy a life rich with education and service—a life which she initially shared only with her immediate family and friends, but in later years with a much broader audience through her writing. And despite the fact she was neither born nor educated into a literary life, she became an eloquent public speaker, an articulate poet, and a well-published and well-read author (see Bibliography). More significantly for the six of us who were her children, she was able to pass on this love of words to each of us. All of this attests to her nascent and ever-evolving fascination with language.

From the very first, during their year-long residence in Beijing to study Mandarin, barely a generation after the last emperor had been dethroned, she was thrust into a situation where language was obviously the *raison d'etre* and *sine qua non* of her daily life. Even before she was forced to confront the apparent vagaries of a new culture and language in China, she was already intrigued with the wonder of words, both spoken and written. Along with my father, who lacked her eloquence but not her linguistic curiosity, she nurtured in her children a lifelong interest in language, and it surprises me today (although in retrospect it shouldn't) that almost every one of them chose a career where the use of language was central. From her brood came two journalists, a preacher, a literacy teacher, and a linguist. A sixth followed her vocational example and chose a career in nursing.

A significant portion of our linguistic heritage stemmed from her direct teaching, an aspect of her life that I will share in a moment, but much of it seemed to seep through on a daily basis in the banter and arguments around the dinner table, in the bedtime stories, in the adventures she reported, embellished, and perhaps even created about what otherwise appeared to be rather pedestrian day-to-day encounters, but she also engendered this metalinguistic awareness within us through poetry and verbal humour. Each of us was encouraged to memorize poems, and to this day, I have been able to salt and pepper an otherwise bland ESL class on an obscure point in English grammar with a poem learned from my mother's side when I was probably only halfway through my first decade of life. The poems were short, simple, and traditional (verses from Stevenson, Tennyson, Dickinson, and Kipling), but their lessons linger on more than a half century later. They helped teach us the power of discourse, and the way words convey a memorable message only when they are couched in a comfortable context. My mother was quick to reward wit. I was about 10 when she gave me a typical linguistic puzzle. "A coin was found more than 2000 years ago with the initials 'B.C.' inscribed on it. How," I remember her testing me, "can you prove that it was not authentic?" My answer certainly did not demonstrate critical thinking, but it did verify the pervasive interest in language fostered in our household. "Easy," I replied "B.C. Bad Coin." The addition of this episode to her treasure trove of family lore was not the only positive reinforcement I received; many years later, she even enshrined this quip in one of her books (Scovel 1962: 169). Neither parent knew anything about reading research, but nowadays, there is a substantial body of evidence suggesting that reading readiness in young children is greatly enhanced by awareness of how words are composed of individual sounds (Crowder and Wagner 1992: chap. 10). Improving our reading scores was, I'm almost certain, not one of my mother's intentions while she was raising us in China. She loved puns and poetry, and she wanted to infect us with the same affection, but in that process, she afflicted us with a consciousness about language that invariably improved our verbal prowess.

There were other ways through which her natural love of language was shared. Present throughout our nurturing was the language of ritual, which as a youth I tended to remember only unappreciatively as large chunks of languid listening—monotonous "musak" for the most part. But as I aged, I realized that even these dull remembrances played a vital role in nourishing my linguistic awareness. We attended religious services religiously, and liturgy and sermons in those days, whether in Mandarin, or later in Punjabi, or English, tended to be longwinded. But the hours of quiet boredom sitting in malevolently designed pews in sanctuaries which, like cold-blooded creatures, seemed to absorb the heat or cold of the season, cultivated an appreciation for the spoken word and for the paralinguistic power of gesture, timing, cadence, and intonation.

Another shorter and more attractive form of ritualized language that formed a daily component of our comprehensible input was prayer. My mother loved to talk, and her proclivity for loquacity was not limited to her fellow humans. My parents began most of our meals with a blessing, mercifully short for the most part, and we always had bedside prayers before we retired for the night. Some of these petitions were rote routines, the shortest and most perfunctory of our table graces was intoned as if it were one polysyllabic word, "God for what we are about to receive make us truly thankful Amen!" But my mother or father created most of them spontaneously and as we grew older, we learned to do this too. Again, upon reflection, I realize that this was a valuable linguistic experience, not just because of the direct inculcation we received about religion, but also because of what the experience taught us about language. We learned different registers, for example (Joos 1964).

You don't talk to God the way you talk to your sibling, whether you're doing it in Chinese or in English. I also learned the power of oral language and the fact that there are speech acts. Only after a graduate course in linguistics where I had read John (not Jane!) Austin did I realize that prayers are often performatives (Austin 1962). By invoking God's help you were actually *doing* something, not just saying something.

Because we lived without electricity during the formative years of my childhood in China, and lacked radio, and certainly television, as a form of entertainment, reading out loud was a favourite method of passing the evening hours, especially during the darkness of winter. Although we can and should not replicate the historical past in the very modern world into which we have slipped so comfortably today, there was one of my mother's linguistic traditions that I as a parent was able to recapitulate when our own children were young. Every year, irrespective of our situation (and sometimes during my Chinese childhood this included incarceration, first by the Japanese army and later by the Communist government), my mother would read us the unabridged version of Charles Dickens' *A Christmas Carol* the week before Christmas (Dickens 1843). We would sit quietly for an hour or two each night, listening to her intone the voices of each character with dramatic flair and punctuate the prose with poetic prosody. I sense this annual ritual had several linguistic benefits. It nurtured within each of us an appreciation of the spoken word—an intuitive appreciation that if something is fun to hear, it is easy to hear, and if it is easy to hear, then it is easy to remember and thus easy to learn. We also increased our vocabulary by guessing from context, not a bad language learning strategy according to the recent research (Coady and Huckin 1997). Even if we didn't know what "covetous" meant, let alone how to spell it, we surmised it referred to something bad since it was used to describe Scrooge. Maybe it was a fancy way of saying "stingy."

We picked up other knowledge as well: that the ultimate act of literature is displacement, the ability to talk about other people in other places in other times—indeed, about people who never existed and never will. ("Once upon a time ..." was used to introduce a time that had never actually existed.) And we learned that language has emotions. Though my mother did all the reading, she relinquished her cherished stage on Christmas Eve, when she came to the part in the penultimate chapter of Dicken's timeworn story, where the Ghost of Christmas Past forces Scrooge to witness the death of Tiny Tim. Invariably, her voice would begin to choke, and she would hand the book over to my father, whose feelings were much more cloaked, to finish this portion of the chapter. It is then not so strange that many years later, my voice would catch as I began to read the same passage to our children on the night before Christmas. I don't think it ever crossed my mother's mind that those evenings of my growing up were anything more than a time for entertainment, and a chance, conceivably, for her to seize the family stage, and yet we young children could probably not have been given a more effective lesson in literacy.

BECOMING BILINGUAL

Certainly the most direct way the story of my mother's life would relate to any language teacher is the fact that she herself was challenged to learn not just one, but two languages which differed markedly from her own. Remember that she was living in a world much smaller and greatly more isolated than ours. Especially during the years she lived in a remote, interior town in China before and during World War II, the world was by no stretch of the imagination "a global village," to use the now popular and accurate metaphor. Back then and there, each village was a world to itself, and the geographical, pedagogical, and psychosocial barriers impeding linguistic and cross-cultural communication which my parents faced were formidable. It is all the more remarkable, therefore, that they were able to penetrate these barricades not once, but twice in their lives—first during their 20 some years living in China, and then, after they were forced to leave by the Communist government, for another six years when they moved in the early 1950s to a new mission station in northern India. We children learned much about language and culture from their commitment to live and serve in these two cultures which contrasted in so many ways with life in America. Ironically, because of my mother's conscious commitment to overseas mission, we children grew up with a mother culture which was not our mother's culture.

Clearly, my parents' decision to devote their adult lives to medical mission work in Asia had a profound effect on my life and that of my siblings. Four of the six of us were born in China, all of us were raised there, and the three youngest of us lived in India as well. Like tens of millions of other children all over the globe, we grew up bilingual and bicultural, not because we chose to, but because of our birthright, and this heritage has left an indelible mark on each of us. I cannot speak directly for my sisters and brothers, but I doubt if I would have chosen linguistics as a profession and language teaching as a career had I not been born and raised in China, and I know that I would not have opted to have spent so much of my adult life in Asia if I had grown up in the United States. This geographical heritage has been passed down to my own children, who were both born in Thailand, and even through our new granddaughter, who is named after the continent my mother chose to become her adult home. Although I know of no formal study of how foreign birthrights might determine future occupational choices, I would not be surprised if there is research by social psychologists confirming what I have found anecdotally in my frequent encounters with linguists, language teachers, missionaries, and diplomats. It seems like an inordinate number of them come from a background similar to mine. Still, in order to remain an honest participant-observer, I must also admit that there has been a downside to this heritage.

Being born and raised in a culture that is different from the home society you have chosen to live in as an adult offers many advantages, as some of the research in bilingual education has suggested; nevertheless, there are also limitations, especially when your ethnicity does not match your cultural heritage. On both sides of the Pacific, I have experienced the cognitive dissonance which is created by situations where I don't look like the kind of person I was raised to be. This feeling of anomie and discomfort was most pronounced when I graduated from high school in India and left to study at a small midwestern college in the United States. In the words of David Pollack (personal communication 6/28/96), who has talked about the phenomenon of "third culture kids," I was a "hidden immigrant." I looked and sounded like a "real" American, but inside I was an amalgamation of our family's life experiences as expatriates in China and India. Ironically, my parents did not have to experience this anomie because they were always correctly identified as adult immigrants from a foreign shore. Fortunately for me, this upbringing as a "third culture child" has been the most significant part of my education and has rewarded me with insights, experiences, and friendships which have far exceeded the limitations of growing up as a hidden immigrant. It has also given me a special empathy for the many foreign students and immigrants whom I have taught as ESL or graduate students for over two decades in the United States. But aside from the obvious point that my mother's life in Asia endowed each of her children with bilingual and bicultural experiences, what can we learn from her own situation about the process of becoming bilingual?

That first year in the capital city of Beijing was an exciting moment in my parents' lives. They were young, open-minded, and had consciously chosen this cross-cultural experience, not as a temporary educational opportunity, but as a lifelong vocational commitment. Having said this, however, from most of my mother's accounts, that year of Chinese language study was a frustrating experience. To characterize the teaching method as "traditional" would be charitable; a more accurate adjective might be atavistic! To begin with, the class was enormous: about 150 students from many different countries and with varying learning goals were crowded into a large room. Most of the time was spent with one teacher, nicknamed "Dearest" because of his smile, who instructed them entirely via the Direct Method, pointing, naming, and asking them to repeat in chorus (Kelly 1969). For the first few weeks, students never initiated conversation and emphasis was on accurate imitation. In due time, Chinese characters were introduced, and again the focus was on replicating the calligraphy as accurately as possible.

Fridays were proverb days, and my mother recalled trying to match the initial line of an aphorism with its appropriate pair. Once my parents learned the meaning of these sayings, my mother concentrated on adhering to the curriculum, and was consequently rewarded with good marks throughout the course. My father ran into disfavour with the teacher, however, because he would occasionally try to mismatch the paradigms as a declaration of creative independence. My mother recalls that his stock as a language student fell precipitously, at least in his teacher's eyes, when instead of automatically matching "husband and wife" with its appropriate pair, "the husband leads, the wife follows," he switched to the phrase that was supposed to be coupled with "the old and the new" and replied in his halting Mandarin, "if the old does not leave, how can the new enter?" Though my parents knew nothing about language teaching, not even about the work that people like Palmer and Richards were doing at that time in the early 1930s (Richards and Rodgers 1986), they were frustrated that this year of intensive inculcation provided them with virtually no communicative competence in colloquial Chinese. It was not until they arrived at the small mission hospital in Shandong province hundreds of kilometres from the capital a year later that they had a chance to acquire the language of daily experience and of health and healing in the common everyday *patois* of the local dialect. Many years later, when they were about 50, my parents repeated this experience when they were reassigned to India, and although my mother never learned Punjabi well, she acquired enough to run her household, purchase goods in the market, travel around the Punjab on her own, and participate in religious services. I think her natural love of words percolated through all the pedagogical barriers that would have impeded the typical foreign language student and allowed her to acquire relatively impressive competence in Chinese, an ability which abided quite faithfully with her the remainder of her life.

Soon after her arrival at their new home in Shandong, she discovered a unique way by which her study of Chinese resonated with her inherent fascination with language and created a new interest which soon grew to become her life's passion. Although their town was relatively small, remote, and historically insignificant, it did contain a small park with a pagoda which commemorated a visit over a thousand years earlier during the Tang dynasty by Li Po, one of China's greatest poets. His poetry, and that of other Chinese writers, captivated her. Their texts were short and clear and tended to evoke the beauty of nature. In a very real sense, they were verbal scrolls, painting in words the natural scenes for which Chinese art is so renowned. Soon she dared to start composing her own verbal portraits in English, and her lifelong passion for poetry began, ignited largely from her experience learning a strange but beautiful new language. Like many poets, she practised her craft privately at home, sharing her samples only with her husband and a small circle of friends, but later, when living in India, she began to publish a few in magazines here and there, and by the time my parents finally returned to the United States to live out the remainder of their lives, my mother had honed her craft so well that she was able to publish a well-received volume of her poems (Scovel 1970) and become active and acclaimed in several local and national poetry circles. Even her final and most mature poems tended to echo the succinct phrases, the natural images, and the enduring spirit of the Chinese poetry that served to inspire her in those early years in Shandong.

Crossing Cultures

My mother learned much more than new words and art forms during those 30 years in Asia. She also acquired an amazing ability to cross cultural barriers—not just the societal boundaries that separated her as an American missionary from the Chinese, and later the Indian medical personnel and townsfolk with whom she worked and lived, but she also gained the ability to penetrate the individual boundaries that tend to box us out from communicating with people from a very different racial, religious, professional, or socioeconomic upbringing. I guess it should have come as no surprise to me then when I learned that late in their life, my parents had entered into correspondence with a convicted felon and later, during his parole, had invited him into their home in an attempt to help him straighten out a troubled life. It still amazed me that an older, white, professional couple with extensive international experience would welcome into their home a young, African-American convict, whom they had never met. I think the social crucible of acculturating to completely new cultural environments as young adults forged in both my parents a tolerance of ambiguity and an aptitude to feel comfortable in the midst of strangers. Certainly, a great deal of their empathy and their affection for others stemmed from their Christian faith, but this faith was nurtured by those many cross-cultural opportunities my mother and father experienced as strangers in an alien land. They learned to look beyond what was alien, and they had an uncanny ability to accept strangers as friends.

    I think the most enduring legacy of her cultural and interpersonal empathy was displayed by my mother's lifelong attitude toward the Japanese. It is unmistakable from the anecdote with which I began this chapter that from her very first experiences in northern China, my mother was conditioned to consider the Japanese as enemies. After the Imperial army advanced across the Shandong peninsula to occupy the town where my parents laboured, they experienced direct and increasing evidence that Japanese soldiers were to be feared and even despised. One terrible consequence of the army's occupation of China was the soldiers' proclivity to rape Chinese women, and for a period of time, my parent's mission hospital was about the only sanctuary the women in the town could flee to to escape sexual attack. This constant terror culminated in an event that embroiled my parents in a very personal way with the Japanese army. In the process of trying to lead a drunken, off-duty Japanese soldier out of the hospital compound into which he had illegally wandered in search of Chinese women, my father was shot in the back and nearly had his head blown off. My mother, who had heard the shot while teaching us children during our morning studies in our house nearby, was hurriedly told that it was her husband who had been hit. Through the care that she and the hospital staff administered, my father miraculously survived, but just on the basis of that incident alone, any normal person could be forgiven for harbouring permanent feelings of resentment. But the situation worsened.

    On Pearl Harbor weekend, we were placed under house arrest by the Japanese and spent several years confined to the hospital compound. Eventually, my parents, brothers, and sisters and I were led away and incarcerated in a concentration camp which the Imperial army had erected to confine all Allied civilians residing in that part of China. Fortunately, for all of us, but especially for my mother who was pregnant with her last child, the International Red Cross was able to secure a prisoner exchange, and our entire family was successfully transported from the camp and around the war-torn world on a succession of ships. We eventually repatriated to the United States, where we lived for two years before returning to China at the end of the war.

Given these experiences, it would be understandable for my parents to dislike the Japanese people, based on the bitter incidents they had experienced directly, and on the historical record of the martial cruelty the occupying Japanese army had inflicted on the Chinese people, with whom my parents were so closely aligned. But their faith prompted them to be forgiving. I never once heard my mother speak deprecatingly of the Japanese people; indeed, she harboured a seemingly warm attachment to things Japanese. After their first furlough in America in the late 1930s, my parents had to spend several weeks in Japan en route back to China because of disruptions caused by the Japanese invasion of northern China. The few recollections of this summer that my mother shared are all positive. Quite recently, I was able to track down the old, rundown cottage where they stayed at the foot of Mount Fuji, where my mother enjoyed the time working on her poetry and my father began his lifetime avocation of drawing pastels. My father marvelled at the modern department store they visited in Kobe, and my mother delighted in amenities designed for people of her short stature. Japan, she loved to relate, was the only country she felt perpetually comfortable in, for she could always reach the straps when riding on the buses and subways. Somehow, my parents' faith, along with their many cross-cultural encounters, allowed them to see the difference between the evil wreaked by the Imperial Army during the war, and the Japanese people, as a society and as individuals. She loved her husband, her family, and the Chinese no less by not hating the Japanese. To me, this was perhaps the most enduring legacy to be gleaned from her life story because my mother taught us that love is not finite, nor is love diminished when we love those who are easy to hate.

THE GOOD TEACHER

Trying to provide an American education for a family growing up in the hinterlands of China 50 some years ago was no easy task, and this responsibility absorbed the majority of my mother's time and energy for much of her life as an overseas missionary. Despite the fact we were all eventually sent off to a boarding school for expatriate children for varying chunks of our secondary school education, my mother was responsible for almost all of our primary education. One room in our house was converted into a school, and depending on our age and the number of years separating us from the nearest siblings, this classroom would number between two to four pupils varying from kindergarten to seventh grade. Monday through Friday, except for holidays (happily for us, both American and Chinese), we would trudge upstairs after breakfast to our one-room schoolhouse and faithfully follow our lessons until early afternoon. Without a university education herself and with no training in education, my mother was fortunate to be able to follow a "teacher proof" curriculum prescribed, produced, and packaged by the Calvert School, a correspondence school in the United States which still operates to this day.

Once a year, a literal barrel-full of books, school supplies, and curricula would arrive via sea mail to stock our small classroom and supply my mother for another academic year. Like all home-schooled children, we did a lot of pair work teaching between ourselves, and this often extended into our free time. I remember subjecting my two younger sisters to many hours of "playing astronomy," where they were forced to memorize the names of all the planets, their number of moons, and the location of all the major constellations, and it is mute testimony to my fraternal dominance that I cannot recall a single instance where roles were reversed, and they were allowed to play teacher to me! My mother ran this classroom efficiently and with what seemed to be a happy balance between what Calvert had dictated (Monday, Week Seventeen, Period One: Read Chapter Seven of *The Child's History of Art*) and what she thought was good for us (here is a poem by Emily Dickinson I want you to memorize before lunch). She also was successful in wielding positive reinforcement. At the end of every school year, for example, "diplomas" appeared on our dinner plates at the evening meal, and there was much chatter about our successfully completing another grade. Based on her results and our subsequent boarding school education, she was an effective teacher. All six of us received a university education, and three of us completed graduate degrees; not bad considering the disruptions caused by war, imprisonment, geographical isolation, and lack of institutional support.

My mother's teaching was not confined to her children however, and especially during her early years in China, she devoted considerable time to a small school for nurses which she helped establish as part of my parents' endeavours as medical missionaries. Here, she was forced to rely solely on Chinese as the language of instruction, but the task of using a second language for special purposes was eased in part by the fact much of it involved hands-on training and direct patient care. Thirty years after my parents had left that Shandong mission station, my wife and I secured special permission from the provincial government to be the first foreigners ever allowed to return to Jining, and when we reported on that momentous visit to my aging parents when we flew back to America, I think one of the things that pleased them most was to learn that the small training centre for nurses had grown into a full-fledged school, preparing nurses for that entire provincial district.

Ironically, it is hardest for me, a teacher, to summarize my mother's contribution as a teacher for a readership made up primarily of educators, but, in sum, there are a few principles I value when I reflect on this aspect of her life. Through all of her teaching, she seemed to maintain a fair balance: she followed the Calvert course, but sprinkled each day's classes with her own interests and priorities; she did most of the teaching but gave us each significant freedom to help each other out; and though school work was serious stuff (she brought the materials to our bed when we were sick), she was able to respond to the moment (we could stop whatever we were studying and rush to the window to watch the dragon boats drum down the nearby canal). Another clear virtue was that even though she was never directly compensated for her tutoring, she was an extremely dedicated instructor. Very little ever superseded school: not illness, which was unfortunately quite common in our household, not the weather, which could be execrably hot and miserably cold at a time and place where there was neither air-conditioning nor central heating, and not even the Japanese or Communist occupations. Both the teacher and the school kept going. This dedication ensured a very predictable and consistent environment for us which, because of its constancy, created a haven of security in the midst of an outside world of change, and even chaos. With mom, somehow we always felt safe and secure.

We present-day teachers can, I feel, follow these same principles. For one thing, we need to be flexible enough to balance the dictates of our curriculum and our administrators with the demands of the day's events and the daily needs of our individual students. In addition, if we are truly professionals, we must profess a commitment to teaching, and this professional dedication must be intense enough so that despite the vagaries and insecurities that might surround our students in the larger world outside our classrooms, inside, with us, students can experience a consistent and continuous commitment to helping them learn. Good teachers are, in a very real way, good mothers.

INSPIRED BY SPIRIT

The final lesson that I feel is worth sharing about my mother's biography is the most important, for it seemed to infuse and energize all other aspects of her life. Both my parents were spiritual people and the depth and primacy of their religious faith sustained them and their marriage for almost six decades. Their Christian faith called them to devote their lives as medical missionaries from the very beginning; it was something that they openly shared throughout their lives in a sensitive and non-judgmental manner; it sustained them throughout all the calamities that befell them; and it nurtured them through their waning years to the very end. This faith touched all whom they encountered—fellow Christians, non-believers, and their many friends and acquaintances who shared differing religious convictions. But I think it pleased my parents most that their heritage of faith was successfully passed down to each of the six of us. Having said this, however, I think it is essential to emphasize that my mother's spiritual legacy was not confined to one particular religion. The most important lesson her life teaches us, I believe, is that the essence of living is spiritual, not material. To paraphrase a popular verse of Christian scripture, we are *in* the world but not *of* the world. This spiritual conviction transcends religious boundaries and, at the same time, leaves us with many implications about how we can try to teach and to live more successfully. It is no accident that all of these ideas are etymologically derived from the word "spirit."

Fair salaries and benefits are vital, of course, in our vocation as teachers, along with job security, social recognition, opportunities for professional growth, and all the other material rewards that are rightfully ours, but the life of the spirit argues that ultimately, good teaching and good living should be *inspired*. Inspiration and passion originate within us as individuals; they are not conditioned responses shaped by the positive or negative reinforcement of the outside world of matter. The life of the spirit also argues that our teaching should be *spirited*. We should be lively, active, and outgoing, in our classrooms, in our profession, and in the way we solve problems and accept new ideas. And finally, the life of the spirit suggests we should be *spiritual*— upholding our students' spirits and responding to their souls as much as to their minds.

Conclusion

I have felt somewhat uncomfortable sharing these few personal vignettes about my mother's life and in trying to spell out the impact I believe they have on our lives as teachers today. We have been trained to be impersonal and objective as academicians, and especially within the tradition of scholarly writing, it is difficult to write introspectively and honestly about a person who is so close. It is not unlike describing every detail of the face you confront in the mirror every morning. But irrespective of my discomfort and of how successful I may have been in portraying the way my mother's life might serve to expand our vision as language educators, I have found this experience beneficial. In sum, the principles her life depicts are ones which I believe are salubrious for us to follow—in our teaching and in our living.

To return to the metaphor with which I began this chapter, I would like to end with the image of a journey. As each of the Scovel children became young adults and had to leave our Asian home and our parents, sometimes for many years, and begin our university studies in America, my mother was forced to say good-bye many times. This concluding poem is one she wrote about these forced farewells, and these words have nurtured us for many years as we each of us have experienced our own separations. Although it is a poem written by a mother to her children, I do not think it is too condescending to consider it also as a poem written by a teacher to her students. And it captures, I believe, the gift of the spirit which was my mother's final and greatest legacy.

> Go where you will across the world,
> You cannot reach a point beyond our love.
> But do not fear,
> Love can never play the rope,
> To let you go, to draw you near;
> Let love be the wings on which you soar.
> (Scovel 1970: 71)

REFERENCES CITED

Asher, J. 1977. *Learning Another Language Through Actions: The Complete Teacher's Guidebook.* Los Gatos, CA: Sky Oaks Productions.

Austin, J. 1962. *How To Do Things With Words.* Oxford: Oxford University Press.

Brown, H.D. 1994a. *Principles of Language Learning and Teaching,* 3rd ed. Englewood Cliffs, NJ: Prentice-Hall Regents.

———. 1994b. *Teaching by Principles: An Interactive Approach to Language Pedagogy.* Englewood Cliffs, NJ: Prentice-Hall Regents.

Casanave, C.P. and S. Schecter, eds. 1997. *On Becoming a Language Educator.* Mahwah, NJ: Lawrence Erlbaum Associates.

Coady, J. and T. Huckin, eds. 1997. *Second Language Vocabulary Acquisition.* Cambridge: Cambridge University Press.

Crowder, R. and R. Wagner. 1992. *The Psychology of Reading.* Oxford: Oxford University Press.

Dickens, C. 1843. *A Christmas Carol.* London: Chapman & Hall.

Kelly, G. 1969. *Twenty-Five Centuries of Language Teaching.* Boston: Newbury House (Heinle & Heinle).

Joos, M. 1964. *The Five Clocks.* New York: Harcourt, Brace, World.

Krashen, S. 1994. 'Bilingual Education and Second Language Acquisition Theory.' In *Schooling and Minority Students: A Theoretical Framework,* edited by C. Leyba, 47-75. Sacramento, CA: California State Department of Education.

Mathews, B. 1912. *Livingstone the Pathfinder.* New York: Missionary Education Movement of the US and Canada.

Richards, J. and C. Lockhart. 1994. *Reflective Teaching in Classrooms.* Cambridge: Cambridge University Press.

Richards, J. and T. Rodgers. 1986. *Approaches and Methods in Language Teaching.* Cambridge: Cambridge University Press.

Scovel, M. 1962. *The Chinese Ginger Jars.* New York: Harper & Row.

———. 1970. *The Weight of a Leaf.* Philadelphia: The Westminster Press.

ADDITIONAL BIBLIOGRAPHY

Autobiographical

Scovel, M. 1962. *The Chinese Ginger Jars*. New York: Harper & Row.

———. 1964. *Richer by India*. New York: Harper & Row.

———. 1968. *To Lay a Hearth*. New York: Harper & Row.

———. 1971. *The Happiest Summer*. New York: Harper & Row.

———. 1980. *In Clover*. Philadelphia: The Westminster Press.

Children's Books

Scovel, M. 1963. *The Buffalo and the Bell*. New York: Friendship Press.

———. 1965. *George and the Chinese Lady*. New York: Friendship Press.

———. 1969. *How Many Sides to a Chinese Coin?* New York: Friendship Press.

Scovel, M. and P. Ragland. 1970. *Don't Just Sit There Reading: A Fun Book About the Americas*. New York: Friendship Press.

Miscellaneous

Scovel, M. 1959. *I Must Speak: The Biography of Augustine Ralla Ram*. Lucknow, India: Lucknow Publishing House.

———. 1966. *My Neighbor, the Wounded: The Widening Scope of the Medical Mission of the Church*. New York: Commission on Ecumenical Mission and Relations, The United Presbyterian Church, USA.

———. 1972. *The Gift of Christmas*. New York: Harper & Row.

Poetry

Scovel, M. 1970. *The Weight of a Leaf*. Philadelphia: Westminster Press.

CHAPTER SIX

REUVEN FEUERSTEIN

❋

RELEASING UNLIMITED LEARNING POTENTIAL

Marion Williams and Robert Burden
University of Exeter

INTRODUCTION

One of the tests of greatness in a thinker and writer must surely be that his or her ideas are transferable across disciplines, that they can give us new insights and visions, and that they can open up possible new pathways which we might explore. It was with this feeling of inspiration that we first began to investigate the ways in which the ideas of the Israeli psychologist and educator, Reuven Feuerstein, could be of value to the language teacher.

For many years the field of Teaching English as a Second/Foreign Language (TESL/TEFL) has drawn upon its parent disciplines of linguistics, or what language is; sociology, ethnography, and anthropology, or how language is used in a social context; and second language acquisition, or how languages are learned. In addition, the field of psychology has always influenced our language teaching methodologies. We have seen moves from audiolingualism, which is based on a behaviourist view of psychology, to cognitive approaches, through to communicative approaches which are based more on interactionist views of learning. More recently the works of Vygotsky have been *de rigueur* in the world of second and foreign language teaching (Lantolf and Appel 1994). However, the impact of the work of the great psychologist and educator, Reuven Feuerstein (b. 1921), on the profession has so far not been explored in any detail. The purpose of this chapter is firstly to introduce Feuerstein and outline his main theories, and secondly to consider the impact that these theories could have on the field of language teaching.

FEUERSTEIN AND HIS IDEAS

Reuven Feuerstein is one of the most charismatic characters in the parallel and sometimes overlapping worlds of psychology and education in the 1990s. Conveying, as he does, the image of an Old Testament prophet, Feuerstein proclaims his message to the world in a manner that brokes no argument. Interestingly, however, it is this manner in which Feuerstein presents his case that often causes greater controversy than the ideas themselves, and even seems to prevent some academics from giving those ideas the attention they deserve. Unlike many contemporary educational theorists, Feuerstein places great emphasis upon his religious faith and his cultural background. When he lectures, it quickly becomes very clear that values play an essential part in his work and form the underlying basis for all his theoretical writings. Until recently this has not been at all common in educational and, especially, psychological texts. For example, despite the brilliance of Piaget's (1966) writing, it is extremely difficult to uncover exactly what his values were. In psychology, for many years it was taboo to offer any ideas that could not be shown to be objective and open to scientific investigation. Values were definitely "out." Even Vygotsky was constrained by the dominant ideology of Soviet Stalinism to express some of his ideas more cautiously than others. Feuerstein, however, proclaims a value system at the heart of his theory, which shines with a religious fervour.

After growing up in a strictly orthodox Jewish family in Rumania under the influence of a father who believed that no more than three hours sleep per night were necessary, Reuven Feuerstein became a teacher committed to helping the disabled and disadvantaged children of Bucharest in the 1930s. This was roughly at the same time that Vygotsky was teaching and writing, though Feuerstein claims not to have come across Vygotsky's work until much later. The notion of service was a powerful driving force for him, as was the vision of individuals striving to better themselves in accordance with God's wishes. In this scheme of things, every person has a unique part to play in the world and should be constantly seeking to fulfil the potential with which he or she has been endowed. At the same time, it is the responsibility of the older generation to transmit wisdom and help young people take on the legacy of their culture and civilization so that it will not die out. This is done by imparting valued knowledge, but also by preparing the young to think for themselves in ways that will enable them to solve new problems as and when they arise. Thus the two central tenets of Feuerstein's view of education, which arose directly from his Jewish religious convictions, are (a) the transmission of culture from one generation to the next, and (b) the preparation of young people to think and solve problems for themselves.

World War II and, in particular, the persecution of the Jewish people throughout Europe brought an end to the first phase of Feuerstein's teaching career. As a survivor of the Holocaust and as a member of the organization known as Youth Aliyah, Feuerstein played an early active role in the education of young immigrants to the fledgling state of Israel from all corners of the world. It was here that he first began to puzzle over the differences between those from different cultural backgrounds in their response to formal education. Unprepared to accept the standard explanations later to become so fashionable in many Western societies that some individuals and even some races were simply more intelligent than others, Feuerstein set out on a lifelong quest for alternative explanations. He studied the works of Carl Jung and joined Piaget's team of researchers in Geneva where he was greatly influenced by André Rey's alternative approach to psychological assessment.

THE IMPORTANCE OF CULTURE IN LEARNING

As part of his doctoral thesis Feuerstein made an intensive study of Moroccan immigrant Jews, which provides the foundations for one important aspect of his developing theory of human learning. This was the growing conviction that we are all products of our culture and that we need to understand our own culture before we can fully understand how people from different cultures learn best. The distinction is made here between *cultural difference* and *cultural deprivation*, but Feuerstein's definition of the latter state is radically different from that first proposed by Basil

Bernstein (1961) and his supporters amongst English sociologists in the 1960s and 1970s.

In this instance the term "culture" can be defined in terms of characteristics of any society or civilization which are deemed to be worthwhile by the members of that society and which can be taken as representational in distinguishing it from any other society. It is the traditional customs, habits, and general ways of behaving of the people within that society which they may not be able to explain but which they hold dear alongside more tangible and physically representational aspects of that society. It is also the language and its usage within that society, what is *not* said or done as much as what is. It is mirrored in people's hopes and expectations for themselves and their fellows, which in turn are rooted in their society's history. It is a process as well as a product, something which is constantly changing while at the same time remaining constant in many respects. Without having a sense of our own culture and that of others, it is extremely difficult, sometimes impossible, to make sense of what is going on in a particular place at any specified time. Culture provides a context for our actions and helps us to make sense of otherwise incomprehensible behaviour.

The first point that Feuerstein makes is that no culture is better than any other; they are just different. However, a civilization which loses touch with its culture or destroys all that is worth preserving is a civilization in decline. This is one of the most important messages of history. Societies which do not preserve their cultural traditions, while at the same time creating new ones, are destined to die out.

For the Jews in Israel after World War II, this was an issue of massive importance. Thousands of people flocked in from all over the world with only one thing in common: their religion. It was even sometimes difficult to identify any commonality in this as, like most religions, Judaism has a variety of manifestations. The key question for Jewish educators thus became one of how to prepare their young people to shape a new society whilst enabling them to take pride in and preserve important aspects of the different cultures of their forebears. His work with Moroccan, Ethiopian, and other immigrant groups left Feuerstein in no doubt that despite their difficulties in adjusting to life in "the promised land," all of these groups possessed a rich cultural heritage of their own, much of which needed to be preserved.

However, most of these people were also "culturally deprived" in Feuerstein's terms, in that they did not possess the skills and strategies that would enable them to gain access to the new culture into which they were entering or to share in the shaping of that new culture. Thus, for Feuerstein, cultural deprivation refers to a lack of access to one's own or any other culture mainly because one has never developed the tools that are necessary to gain access to that culture. What is needed for this are tools such as language, and also an ability to think and to solve problems in a way that is necessary to function appropriately in the particular culture. It is interesting to note here the striking similarity to Vygotsky's ideas (Vygotsky 1978, Moll 1990).

Low Intelligence as a Form of Cultural Deprivation

As he turned his attention more and more towards working with disabled children and adults, especially those who had been designated "mentally retarded" (a term commonly in use at that time), Feuerstein became convinced that they too were suffering from a form of cultural deprivation. He realized that such people were failing in school and the workplace not because they possessed a lesser amount of so-called "intelligence," but because they had never been taught the necessary strategies, skills, concepts, language, and vocabulary that would enable them to know how to learn and solve problems effectively within their particular culture.

The idea that such people were "mentally retarded" was the result of the commonly accepted notion of intelligence. Traditionally, intelligence has been seen by psychologists as simply what is measured by IQ tests. Such a view leads to the assumption that anyone scoring poorly on an IQ test must be lacking in intelligence, and therefore incapable of learning as well as others. Feuerstein's argument, however, is that such people are merely deprived of the skills that would enable them to think and act appropriately, and that such skills can be taught. This became one of the cornerstones of Feuerstein's belief that most of the failures in our educational system are a result of a lack of knowledge of how to learn. It is the responsibility of all educators to foster such knowledge.

The means of learning how to learn may differ from culture to culture (see Fry 1984 for a helpful set of readings on the contextual nature of intelligent behaviour). However, in our Western post-industrialized societies, the application of logical thinking and hypothetico-deductive problem-solving techniques, using language in what is commonly agreed to be an appropriate manner, is most likely to lead to success in school and at work. Unfortunately, many children who enter school without having been prepared to think and act in a considered and logical manner may never be taught to do so.

The Foundations of a Theory

This brings us to the next aspect of Feuerstein's theory which emanates from his work with children and adults with severe learning difficulties. As his work with survivors of the Holocaust and with Jewish immigrants from all over the world began to show remarkable results, so, too, many who had been diagnosed as "mentally retarded" often revealed far greater learning potential than had been predicted on the basis of conventional IQ test results. This led to two further developments in his thinking with regard to the importance of our underlying assumptions about human potential and to the way in which such potential is measured.

Firstly, one of the major tenets of Feuerstein's theory is a fundamental belief that anyone of any age, however disabled can become a fully effective learner. It does not matter that we have not yet found ways of accomplishing this, but if we do not begin with such a belief about the plasticity of the human mind and its capabilities for life-long change and development, we shall always find ourselves setting limits to our expectations of others.

For language teachers such a belief is liberating. It frees us from the confines of seeing individuals' potential for learning a language as being limited. What it tells us is that anyone can become an effective language learner; what we should concern ourselves with is not whether people have sufficient aptitude, but how we go about developing any individual's potential to become proficient in language.

Dynamic Assessment and the Learning Potential Assessment Device

The second development is concerned with assessment. As far as the measurement of this limitless potential is concerned, Feuerstein became convinced very early on that an alternative approach to "static" assessment by means of conventional tests needed to be found. He and his co-workers therefore set out to construct an alternative methodology which became known as "dynamic" assessment. This particular methodology, which is akin in many ways to the Vygotskian notion of investigating a learner's "zone of proximal development"(Vygotsky 1978), gave rise to the construction of the Learning Potential Assessment Device (LPAD) that is celebrated in the Israeli group's first important book *The Dynamic Assessment of Retarded Performers* (Feuerstein et al 1979). More recently, alternative but complementary forms of dynamic assessment have been well summarized in an excellent compendium edited by Carol Lidz (1987).

There are several important ways in which dynamic assessment differs from the more conventional "static" assessment. Firstly, the assessor is much less interested in whether the person being assessed can obtain a correct answer than in the process by which that person attempts to find a solution. Help may be given in the form of rules or clues to see if the person being assessed can apply them to similar problems. The assessee is encouraged to talk out loud and to ask questions if it is felt that this would be helpful. Here the assessor is particularly interested in identifying the strengths and weaknesses of the processes the assessee is using, and where he or she might need help in carrying out the tasks given. Is he or she too impulsive in reaching for answers? Does he or she have a sound grasp of such concepts as similarity and difference? Is there a well developed sense of space and time? Are words and concepts used in a precise and unambiguous way? These and other related questions are constantly in the assessor's mind when assessing dynamically. In fact, this form of assessment would be better described as a series of "mini-learning experiments" than a type of psychometric measurement.

Despite Feuerstein's claims to the contrary, many of the items in the LPAD are very similar to conventional IQ test items. Raven's Progressive Matrices, a long-standing and widely used intelligence test, is a key element of the LPAD. However, it is the way in which these materials are used that constitutes the main difference between the two forms of assessment. In fact, almost any material which involves problem-solving can be used to form the basis of a dynamic assessment. The other major difference is Feuerstein's insistence that when we assess someone we need to remember that we are only assessing his or her performance on a particular day under a specific set of conditions. It is a huge and often unjustified step to relate this performance to other tasks under other conditions, but this is the basis for many test predictions.

Although the LPAD is very much concerned with the assessment of intelligence or thinking ability, there are parallels which can be drawn with language testing. The notion of evaluating the process by which learners arrive at a solution with the aim of helping them to go through similar processes more effectively is not one we have taken on board to any great extent. So, for example, a tester might be interested in such questions as: Is the learner using the available contextual cues to work out the meaning of a word? Is he or she making use of the discourse clues to understand the meaning and illocutionary force of the text? What processes is the learner going through to select a word to complete a blank?

This might be illustrated by giving a child a reading comprehension passage—a standard and very popular language test. A conventional question would be to ask the testee to write down the meanings of particular words. A dynamic assessment would involve saying to the child: "There are several words you don't know in this passage. I want you to tell me which words you don't know. Then I want you to tell me what you think they mean and why you think this." What is important in carrying out such a procedure is the nature of the interaction between the assessor and the assessee, in particular the nature of the questions asked by the assessor.

It is also important to note that true dynamic assessment should involve the further stage of teaching more appropriate learning strategies and observing how effectively the learner is able to transfer these to other aspects of language learning. So, in the example above, the assessor might go on to teach the child how to look at the context of the whole passage, to think about what sorts of words they might expect to find, to guess at some possible meanings, and to try these out. Thus dynamic assessment can be seen as an ongoing, reflective, and reflexive process requiring a committed interaction between assessor and assessed. The traditional power differential in assessment is thereby transformed into one which resembles far more one of a shared partnership leading to autonomy on the part of the assessee. The success or failure of any dynamic assessment must be judged in these terms, which differ markedly from traditional notions of test reliability and validity. Thus the notion of assessment becomes broader to encompass also effective teaching or mediation.

INSTRUMENTAL ENRICHMENT

One further problem about applying the results of IQ testing to educational issues is the "so what?" phenomenon. Of what practical value to the teacher is the information that this child has an IQ of 79 or that child has an IQ of 103? What can the teacher do with such knowledge apart from passively accepting that the second child might conceivably learn more quickly than the first?

Feuerstein and his co-workers recognized from the beginning both the essential flaw in this kind of approach, (i.e., it does not tell us anything meaningful about how and why people learn different things in different ways at different speeds), as well as its inherently pessimistic message. They recognized firstly that the hypothetical construct of intelligence as some kind of brain power with which people were endowed in different measures at birth and which was incapable of modification after about the age of five was in need of redefinition. What was needed was reconceptualization of the notion of intelligence in terms of *the ability to learn how to learn*. By redefining intelligence in this way, it becomes axiomatic that anyone can be helped to improve in this respect and thereby become more intelligent.

The next important question therefore becomes: "How can we teach people to learn how to learn?" Dynamic assessment can often be helpful here in identifying the strengths and weaknesses in people's cognitive functions and suggesting ways in which these can be developed. At a more general level, however, there needs to be a radical rethinking about the nature of the school curriculum and the process of education. Firstly, the curriculum itself needs to be much more process-orientated, with a greater emphasis upon teaching thinking skills and problem-solving strategies. Secondly, there needs to be a reconceptualization of teaching away from the notion of instruction and information-transmission towards the facilitation of independent thinking and problem-solving. This ties directly with the call by numerous second/foreign language experts today for more strategy instruction and even a "strategy-based methodology" for the language classroom, with the ultimate goal being learner autonomy. Feuerstein's response to the curriculum issue was the production of a complex thinking skills program known as Instrumental Enrichment (IE) (Feuerstein et al 1980). He saw the nature of appropriate teaching as being facilitated by the provision of *mediated learning experiences*.

Instrumental Enrichment (IE) is, as its name implies, a series of "instruments" designed to enrich cognitive processes or thinking skills. As such, it serves an "instrumental" purpose in helping people to learn how to learn. There are 14 different instruments, each of which consists of about 20 sets of paper-and-pencil tasks. Each set of tasks should form the basis of about a one-hour lesson, which will include a considerable amount of discussion and the "bridging" of newly-learned vocabulary, skills, and concepts into other curriculum areas. It is generally assumed that two IE lessons per week, taught for a continuous period of two to three years by a specially trained teacher, is necessary to bring about significant cognitive change. However, claims for improvement in the cognitive functioning of quite severely "retarded" and disabled groups and individuals have been made on the basis of considerably less than this. (See Burden 1990 for a full discussion of the issues involved in attempting to evaluate IE and other similar programs together with a summary of many of the key findings.)

The Instrumental Enrichment program was gradually produced over a number of years by a highly trained team of Israeli experts. The instruments are based on Feuerstein's notion of a *cognitive map*, which is a representation of what is involved in any mental act or act of thinking. The program itself consists of 14 different areas of cognitive functioning. These range from simple organization of our thoughts, through orientation in time and space and following precise instructions, through to higher order inductive and deductive reasoning. Each instrument, such as "Orientation in Space," contains a series of graded tasks which progress from simple to highly complex. By varying the different elements of the cognitive map such as the nature of the content, the modality, the level of abstraction, or the kinds of cognitive operations required to carry out the tasks, learners can be helped to move into more complex modes of thinking. A helpful summary of the instruments is provided by Sharron (1994).

FOREIGN LANGUAGE TEACHING: MEANING AND PURPOSE

Most current approaches to teaching a foreign language tend to be communicative in nature. Such approaches are based on the premise that the most effective way to learn a language is through using it in interacting with other people. Learning tasks therefore typically are activities where learners need to communicate with each other and exchange information to effectively complete the task. Alternatively, learners interact with a text or spoken language in order to obtain meaning. The main point about such activities is that the language used is *meaningful*; that is, it conveys information that the listener does not already know and needs to know. However, we would argue that any learning activity also needs to contain some *value* or *purpose* for the learner. This may be an educational value such as learning about the world, or it may be an intrinsic sense of purpose such as interest or enjoyment. In the next section, we suggest that it is possible to create purposeful tasks for language learning based on Feuerstein's Instrumental Enrichment activities, which develop thinking skills but do it in the foreign language, thus creating a context for development of the target language. These suggestions are further developed in Williams (1998) and Williams and Burden (1997).

INSTRUMENTAL ENRICHMENT AND LANGUAGE TEACHING

The tasks presented in this section as an example are adapted from Feuerstein's "Orientation in Space" instrument. Our understanding of spatial relationships is crucial for the organization of objects and events in our lives. When carrying out these tasks the learners will engage in different cognitive processes concerned with spatial orientation, which become increasingly complex as the learners are removed from the concrete objects and need to describe them in a more abstract way. At the same time, the learners need to do this in a foreign language, thus developing the language needed to describe position precisely in the foreign language. In doing so, they must also learn to take account of the needs and viewpoint of the listener.

In the first task (see Figure 1), the learners need to perceive the directional relationship between the drawing of a boy and four different objects. They need to understand that position is a concept that changes according to the relative positions

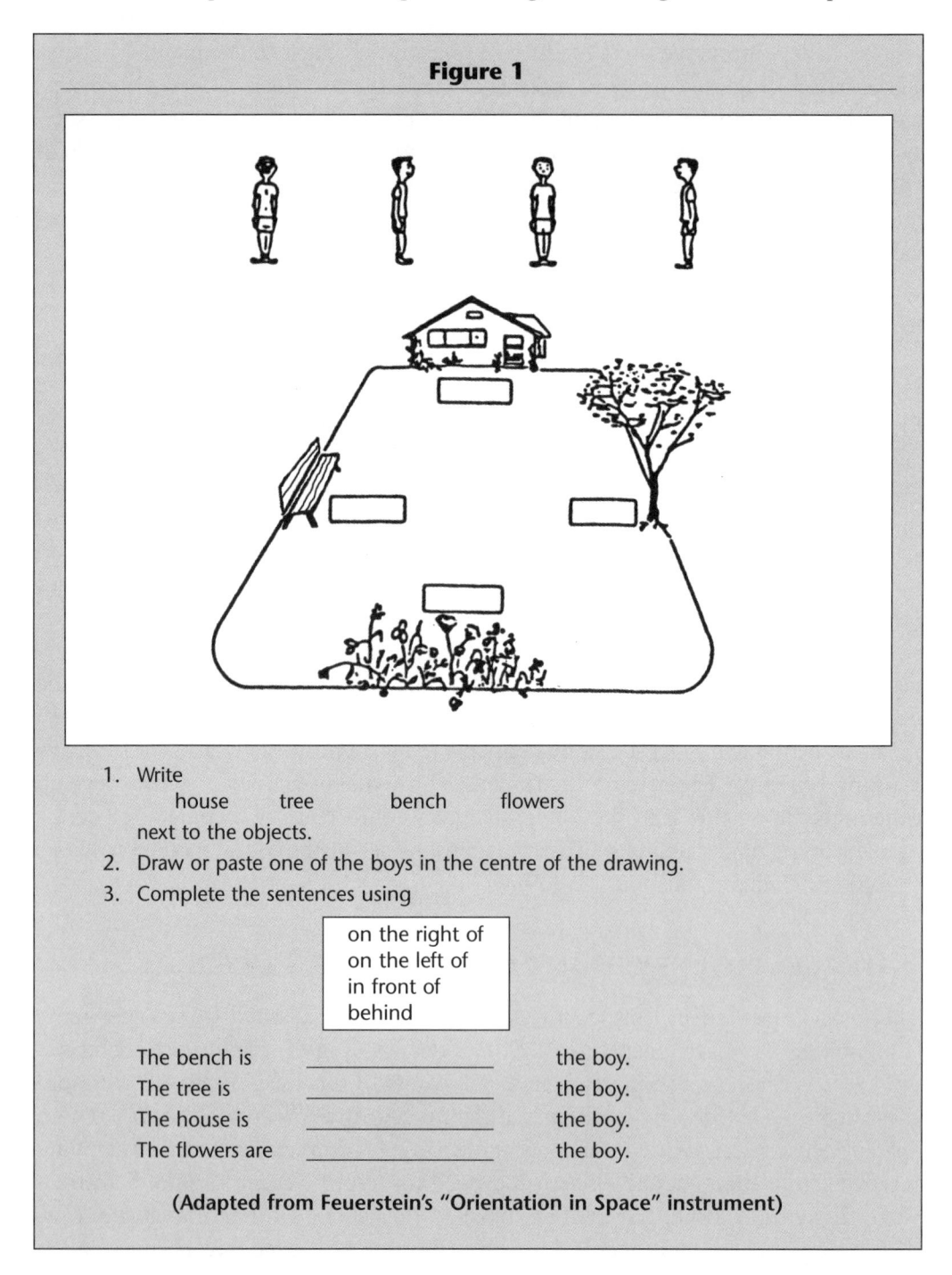

Figure 1

1. Write
   house   tree   bench   flowers
   next to the objects.
2. Draw or paste one of the boys in the centre of the drawing.
3. Complete the sentences using

   | on the right of |
   | on the left of |
   | in front of |
   | behind |

   The bench is _____ the boy.
   The tree is _____ the boy.
   The house is _____ the boy.
   The flowers are _____ the boy.

(Adapted from Feuerstein's "Orientation in Space" instrument)

of different objects. They must also perceive that direction is not merely egocentric. There is often a need when thinking to put oneself in the shoes of another. Taking another person's perspective is a valuable life skill.

In the second task (see Figure 2), the learners need to be able to understand that a number (1, 2, 3, or 4) is representative of a position, and to make mental transformations accordingly. They also need to be able to hold more than one piece of information in their heads at a time. These concepts again extend beyond orientation in space to other aspects of life where we often need to understand representations and frequently need to act on several pieces of information.

In the third task (see Figure 3), the learners have to manipulate the change of direction in their heads, thus seeing that relative position changes if one of the objects moves. The way in which a language expresses these concepts is different

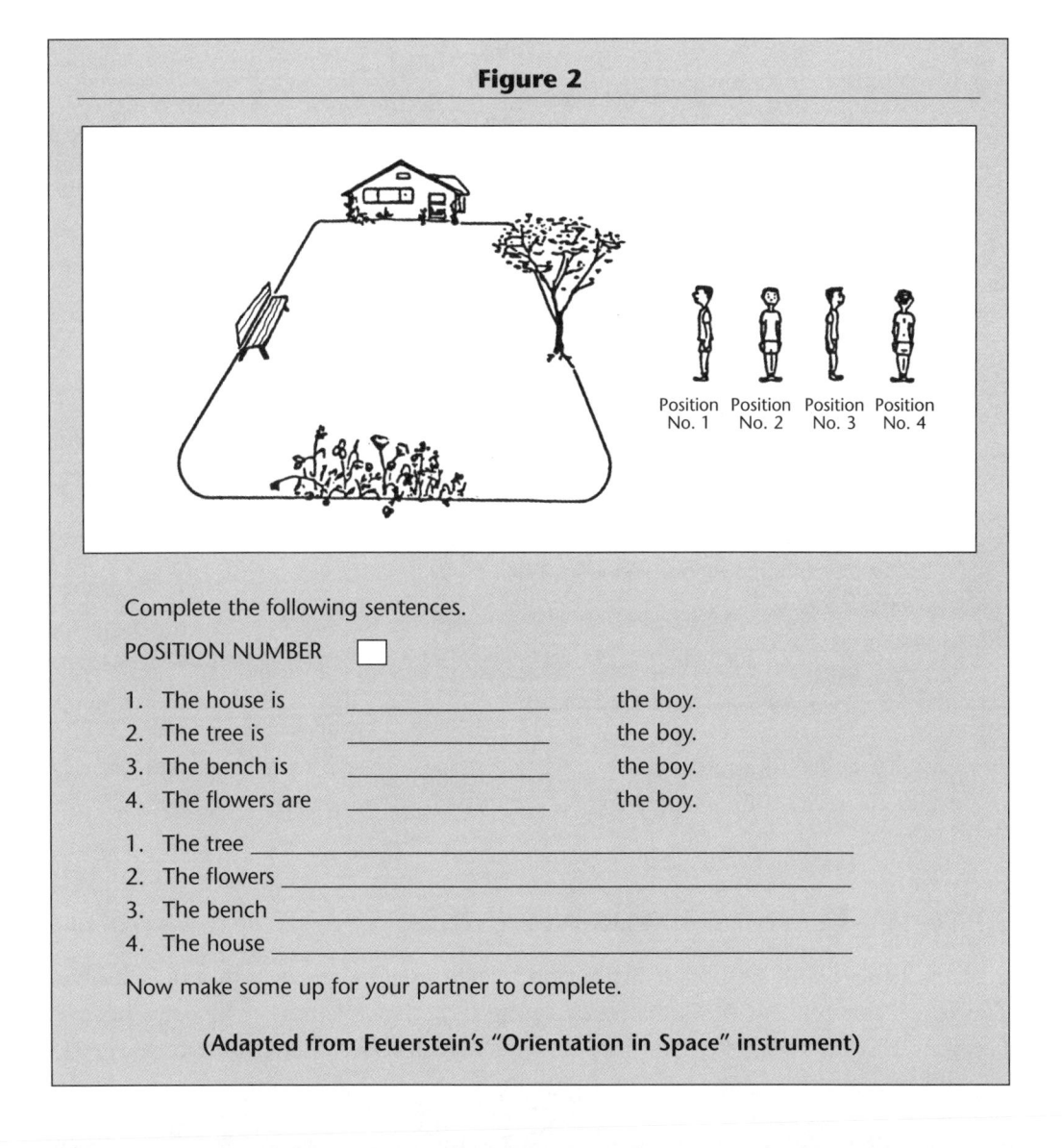

Figure 2

Position No. 1   Position No. 2   Position No. 3   Position No. 4

Complete the following sentences.

POSITION NUMBER ☐

1. The house is _____ the boy.
2. The tree is _____ the boy.
3. The bench is _____ the boy.
4. The flowers are _____ the boy.

1. The tree _____
2. The flowers _____
3. The bench _____
4. The house _____

Now make some up for your partner to complete.

(Adapted from Feuerstein's "Orientation in Space" instrument)

Figure 3

Choose one of the boys to put in the centre of the drawing.

Write the number of the position here. ☐

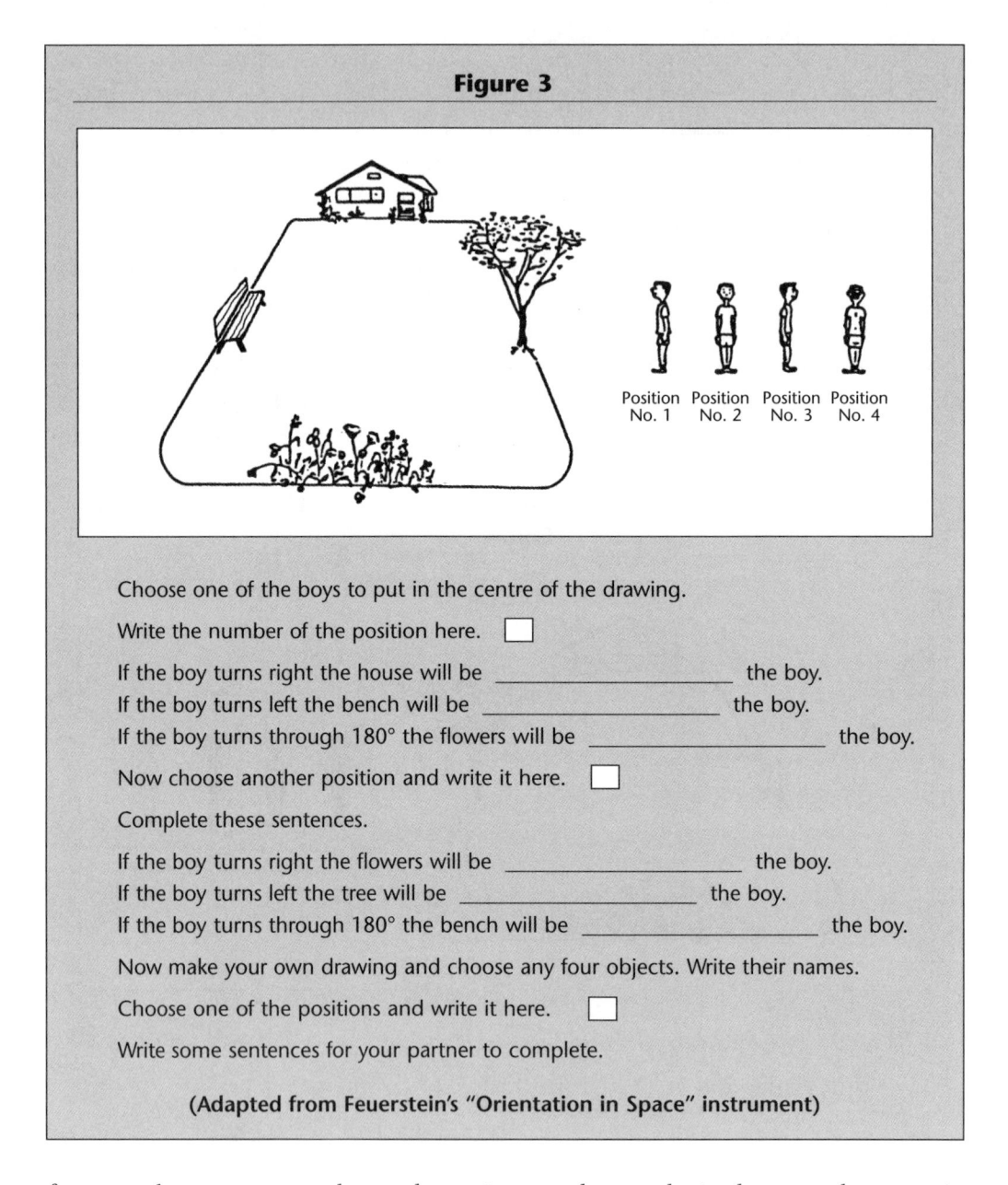

If the boy turns right the house will be _____ the boy.
If the boy turns left the bench will be _____ the boy.
If the boy turns through 180° the flowers will be _____ the boy.

Now choose another position and write it here. ☐

Complete these sentences.

If the boy turns right the flowers will be _____ the boy.
If the boy turns left the tree will be _____ the boy.
If the boy turns through 180° the bench will be _____ the boy.

Now make your own drawing and choose any four objects. Write their names.

Choose one of the positions and write it here. ☐

Write some sentences for your partner to complete.

(Adapted from Feuerstein's "Orientation in Space" instrument)

from one language to another and carrying out these tasks in the target language is important to develop in learners the way in which these concepts are expressed in that language.

Mediated Learning Experience (MLE)

Perhaps Feuerstein's greatest contribution to pedagogy is the way in which he has developed the concept of Mediated Learning Experience (MLE), which we believe contains his strongest message for the language teacher (Feuerstein et al 1991,

Sharron 1994). Essentially this notion seeks to provide an answer to the question faced by all those concerned with the teaching/learning process, namely "How can I help my learners to learn most effectively?" In this way, Feuerstein allies himself with other social constructivists such as Vygotsky and Bruner, in contrast with radical constructivists such as Piaget (Bruner 1960, Piaget 1966). While Piaget sees the development of cognition as arising from individual exploration by the child who gradually comes to make sense of the world, Feuerstein, like Vygotsky and Bruner, believes that a child is born into a social world in which two-way interaction takes place. Right from birth, a child's learning is shaped by interaction with other significant people. Feuerstein refers to these important figures as "mediators," and the experiences that they provide "mediated learning experiences." These people shape and organize the stimuli presented to children in ways they consider most suitable to promote learning. Thus the way in which significant adults, whether parents or teachers, interact with children plays a central role in their cognitive development.

Before presenting Feuerstein's theory of the different ways in which teachers can mediate, some important points must be made about mediation. First, it is concerned with empowering, with helping learners to acquire the skills they will need to learn, to tackle problems, and to function effectively and independently in society. It therefore involves helping learners to become autonomous. Second, the learner is an active participant in the interaction with the mediator. Third, there is an important emphasis on *reciprocation*, that is, the learner reciprocating the intentions of the mediator. Feuerstein calls this the principle of "reciprocity." This means that learners are ready and willing to carry out the tasks presented to them, and that there is an agreement as to what should be done and why. This may involve a process of negotiation. Fourth, learner autonomy involves more than the provision of self-access materials; the mediator needs to help the learners to interact with the materials to help them to become self-directed.

Key Features of Mediation

Feuerstein identifies 12 ways in which the teacher or other adult can mediate. The first three are considered by him to be essential for all learning tasks. The other 9 do not necessarily apply to all tasks or all situations. They are not presented here in the order in which Feuerstein normally presents them in his writings, but one that we feel will make them clear to the reader.

Significance. The teacher needs to make learners aware of the significance of the learning task so that they can see the value of it to them personally, and in a broader cultural context.

Purpose beyond the here and now. Learners must be aware of the way in which the learning experience will have wider relevance to them beyond the immediate time and place.

Shared intention. In presenting a task, the teacher must have a clear intention, which is understood and reciprocated by the learners.

As well as these three essential factors, teachers can enhance the significance and strength of learning experiences if they encourage and develop the following in their learners:

A sense of competence—the feeling that they are capable of coping successfully with any particular task with which they are faced;

Control of own behaviour—the ability to control and regulate their own learning, thinking, and actions;

Goal-setting—the ability to set realistic goals and to plan ways of achieving them;

Challenge—an internal need to respond to challenges, and to search for new challenges in life;

Awareness of change—an understanding that human beings are constantly changing, and the ability to recognize and assess changes in themselves;

A belief in positive outcomes—a belief that even when faced with an apparently intractable problem, there is always the possibility of finding a solution;

Sharing—co-operation among learners, together with the recognition that some problems are better solved co-operatively;

Individuality—a recognition of their own individuality and uniqueness;

A sense of belonging—a feeling of belonging to a community and a culture.

In our work with language teachers we have identified a variety of practical ways in which teachers can mediate in teaching a second/foreign language. Many of these are discussed in Williams and Burden (1997). The following list shows some of the main features of the techniques we have developed. However, the scope for the language teacher in further developing these ideas is limitless.

- Make clear to learners the reason for doing a particular activity.
- Help learners to perceive the value to them personally, both for the here-and-now and beyond.
- Make the instructions absolutely clear and check they are clearly understood.
- Build up learners' confidence in their ability to learn the language.
- Help develop skills and strategies that enable learners to learn a language.
- Help learners set their own long-term and short-term goals.
- Make sure activities are challenging.
- Provide ways of helping learners to assess their own progress.

- Encourage sharing and working co-operatively.
- Recognize people as individuals.
- Develop a feeling of belonging to a learning community.

Conclusion

In this chapter, we have attempted to bring to life the revolutionary ideas underpinning the work of the great Israeli psychologist and educator, Reuven Feuerstein. For the best part of 40 years he spoke and wrote as if he were a lone person in the wilderness, taking issue with the received wisdom of the times about such notions as intelligence, cognitive development, cultural deprivation, and "mental retardation." In his own way Feuerstein placed as great an emphasis as did Vygotsky on the relationship between language and thought.

Although each of the different aspects of his work provides a rich source of material for research and theory development, we believe that the true contribution of Feuerstein can only be understood if this work is taken as an integrated set of interlocking pieces which contribute to a coherent whole. Much of the criticism of Feuerstein lacks this overall perspective.

The main purpose of the chapter, therefore, has been to provide a comprehensive overview of Feuerstein's work and ideas by relating these directly to the specific area of language teaching. In doing so, we hope to have conveyed some of the excitement we have felt in drawing upon these ideas in our work with language teachers from many different countries and cultures. The application of these ideas to language teaching have been explored in detail by Williams and Burden (1997).

Readers who wish to further their knowledge of Feuerstein will find the most accessible introduction to Feuerstein and his work is almost certainly Howard Sharron's *Changing Children's Minds* (1994). Both the BBC (*The Transformers*) (1989) and the Open University in UK (1990) have produced informative films which are available to the general public. Feuerstein himself has provided chapters alone or with colleagues to books by Ben-Hur (1994) and Lidz (1987), as well as the two central volumes of his work, *The Dynamic Assessment of Retarded Performers* (1979) and *Instrumental Enrichment* (1980). In-depth appraisals of Feuerstein's ideas and the status of supporting research are provided by Bradley (1983), Savell et al (1986), Burden (1987), and Blagg (1991).

References Cited

BBC publications. 1989. *The Transformers*.

Ben-Hur, M. 1994. *On Feuerstein's Instrumental Enrichment: A Collection*. Palatine, IL: IRI/Shylight.

Bernstein, B. 1961. 'Social Class and Linguistic Development: A Theory of Social Learning.' In *Education, Economy and Society*, edited by A.H. Halsey, J. Floud, and C. Anderson. New York: Free Press.

Blagg, N. 1991. *Can We Teach Intelligence?* New York: Erlbaum.

Bradley, T.B. 1983. 'Remediation of Cognitive Deficits: A Critical Appraisal of Feuerstein's Model.' *Journal of Mental Deficiency Research* 27 (2): 79-92.

Bruner, J.S. 1960. *The Process of Education*. Cambridge, MA: Harvard University Press.

Burden, R.L. 1987. 'Feuerstein's Instrumental Enrichment Programme: Important Issues in Research and Evaluation.' *European Journal of Psychology of Education* 2 (1): 3-16.

———. 1990. 'Whither Research on Instrumental Enrichment? Some Suggestions for Future Action.' *Cognitive Education and Mediated Learning* 1(1): 83-86.

Feuerstein, R., Y. Rand, and M. Hoffman. 1979. *The Dynamic Assessment of Retarded Performers*. Baltimore: University Park Press.

Feuerstein, R., Y. Rand, M. Hoffman, and R. Miller. 1980. *Instrumental Enrichment*. Baltimore: University Park Press.

Feuerstein, R., P.S. Klein, and A.J. Tannenbaum. 1991. *Mediated Learning Experience: Theoretical, Psychological and Learning Implications*. London: Freund.

Fry, P., ed. 1984. *Changing Conceptions of Intelligence and Intellectual Functioning*. Amsterdam: Elsevier.

Lantolf, J. and G. Appel, eds. 1994. *Vygotskian Approaches to Second Language Research*. New Jersey: Ablex.

Lidz, C. 1987. *Dynamic Assessment*. London: Guildford Press.

Moll, L.C. 1990. *Vygotsky and Education*. Cambridge: Cambridge University Press.

Open University. 1990. 'Making Up Our Minds.' Part of Course E271 *Curriculum and Learning*. Milton Keynes: Oxford University Press.

Piaget, J. 1966. *The Origins of Intelligence in Children*. New York: International Universities Press.

Savell, J.M., P.T. Twoling, and D.L. Rachford. 1986. 'Empirical Status of Feuerstein's Instrumental Enrichment Techniques as a Method of Teaching Thinking Skills.' *Review of Educational Research* 56 (4): 381-409.

Sharron, H. 1994. *Changing Children's Minds*. Birmingham: The Sharron Press.

Vygotsky, L.S. 1978. *Mind in Society*. Cambridge, MA: MIT Press.

Williams, M. 1998. 'Teaching Thinking Through a Foreign Language.' In *Thinking Through the Curriculum*, R.L. Burden and M. Williams, 84-95. London: Routledge.

Williams, M. and R.L. Burden. 1997. *Psychology for Language Teachers*. Cambridge: Cambridge University Press.

CHAPTER SEVEN

LOUISE ROSENBLATT

❖

A VOICE THAT WOULD NOT BE SILENCED

Carol Hosenfeld
State University of New York at Buffalo

INTRODUCTION

Reading theory and the teaching of reading have a long history both in native and second language education. At any point in this history, different theorists have proposed different paradigms describing reading processes performed by children and adults in their first and second languages; the same theorists and their followers have described implications of these theories for teachers who wish to help students to become effective readers, and readers who read for pleasure. In some cases, such as with Whole Language, teachers themselves have spawned the teaching approaches and underlying philosophy that guide their interactions with students' attempts to become more literate, casting theoreticians in the role of debating the merits of an approach already in place in multiple forms in many classrooms. (For an example of this ongoing debate, see the *Reading Research Quarterly* 29 (4):1994).

In addition to this "hand in glove" aspect of reading; that is, that a theory (or theories) underlie(s) the practices teachers use with their students, another aspect of reading is that practices once deemed important for students may disappear from curricula and then later reappear with new vigour, new underlying assumptions, and new reasons for their inclusion into current teaching curricula. An example is a growing trend for both first and second language teachers to include literary texts into subject matter that recently included only expository texts. It is becoming more common to see teachers integrate literature into science instruction (Morrow, Pressley, Smith, and Smith 1997), history instruction (Smith, Monson, and Dobson 1992), and second language instruction (Silva personal communication 1998; Hosenfeld, Russell, Silva and Campbell 1998).

The purpose of this chapter is: (1) to provide ESL teachers with a rationale for including literary texts into reading syllabi that currently include only or chiefly expository texts, and to provide a rationale for helping students respond aesthetically to them; (2) to describe why I think Rosenblatt is a great educator who expands our vision of reading; (3) to present her efferent and aesthetic reading continuum; (4) to describe her suggestions for teaching literature by providing seven of her teaching principles that ESL teachers can use to guide them in embedding literary texts into their ESL classes and in fostering aesthetic responses to them; and (5) to provide examples that illustrate these principles— either as they were demonstrated in a reading and speaking class for international students in an English Language Institute in western New York, in three teacher-education classes in reading and writing with native and non-native speakers of English, or modified or created by the author. (See Note 1.)

A RATIONALE TO INCLUDE LITERARY TEXTS

What is a rationale for suggesting that ESL teachers include literary texts in their reading classes and foster aesthetic responses to them? Why suggest that ESL teachers include narratives in an advanced reading and speaking class and foster aesthetic responses to them in an English Language Institute where students' academic goals include improving their reading and speaking skills either to go on to higher education, to achieve a higher score on the TOEFL exam, or to return to their own country more proficient in English?

Current literature provides many reasons for teachers to include short stories and poems (and longer tracts for advanced students) in many types of ESL reading classes, e.g., EAP, ESP. Some of these reasons are expressed by Bakhtin (in Holquist 1981; Liapunov and Holquist 1993; Emerson and Holquist 1996), a philosopher of communication, who has broadened our notion of text by erasing the boundaries we once held between types of text; and by Scardamalia and Bereiter who urge teachers to encourage students to become experts in reading and writing which would require their dealing with a breadth of text types (Scardamalia and Bereiter 1991, Bereiter and Scardamalia 1993). For teachers, the most compelling reasons are expressed by Rosenblatt (1940, 1972, 1982, 1994, 1995 5th ed.) who argues that we need to view students as whole people with age-related needs, concerns, and goals that often exist in addition to their academic goals. Several of these needs and concerns stated by the students we observed and interviewed in the English Language Institute reading and speaking class were: "Who will I marry?" "What kind of person should I be looking for?" "What profession will I pursue?" "What job do I want to have?" "How can I prepare for it?" "What do I want to do with my life?" "Am I improving my English in this class?" The latter concern was an important one but for many students in this class it was a sub-goal of their larger life goals.

Does this mean that teachers of English as a Second Language who would embed literature in their classes (whether they be EAP, ESP, etc.) and foster students' aesthetic responses to them would forsake or diminish their teaching of reading expository texts, idioms, vocabulary, grammar, and skills their students need to increase their proficiency in English? Not at all. They would be adding another dimension to their course in an attempt to satisfy a broader range of student needs and goals, some of which they believe could be met by aesthetic responses to literary texts. They would also hope that enhanced interest in readings would motivate students to learn the component skills necessary to comprehend them.

Who is Louise Rosenblatt?

Louise Rosenblatt is both a pioneer and a contemporary in the fields of reading theory, literary criticism, reading education, and teaching literature in English as a native language. For six decades she has made significant contributions to all of these areas. She continues today, at the age of 95, from her home in Princeton, New Jersey, to participate in the ongoing debates in these fields. Through her publications and communications to colleagues, she continues politely to correct theorists who misinterpret her work, to disentangle her ideas from those who misperceive similarities between her work and theirs, to critique aspects of their positions, and to express her disappointment at high illiteracy rates.

Rosenblatt's message for reading teachers is the same today as it was 60 years ago. That message is best told in her book *Literature as Exploration*, first published in 1938, in which she presents her "transactional theory of reading" and its implications for teaching. In brief, her theory views reading any text, expository and literary, as a "transaction" among the reader, the text, and the meaning—all of which she views as three aspects of a single structure. To Rosenblatt (1969, 1994, 1995 5th ed.), meaning does not reside in a text, but results when a specific reader, at a specific time, and in a specific place "transacts" with a text and in so doing gives birth to its meaning for that reader, at that time, and in that place.

A characteristic of a great educator is perseverance against more powerful prevailing antithetical forces. Rosenblatt persisted for two generations in presenting her views and having them implemented by teachers in schools. In the late 1930s, her views differed from the prevailing view of the New Critics, who, while neglecting both author and reader, believed that meaning resided in the text, that texts including literary texts had one correct meaning, and that reading for students should consist of discovering that meaning. In the mid- and late 1960s and mid-1970s, when the second (1965), third (1968), and fourth (1976) editions of *Literature as Exploration* were published, her view differed from that of the prevailing view of reader response theorists whom Rosenblatt saw as swinging too far away from the New Critics and too far from centre by focusing too much upon the reader. They proposed that any "read" was as good as any other.

During the 1970s and 1980s, theories of reading were chiefly based upon "information-processing" in the fields of first and second language reading. To Rosenblatt (1978, 1980, 1982, 1985), the implications of interactional theories of reading led teachers to implement "efferent" reads of both expository and literary texts. In her transactional theory there is a place for both kinds of reading by students, but she alerts teachers to the differences between reading efferently and aesthetically, and explains in detail how her transactional view of reading differs from the interactional view of many of her colleagues.

Now, in the 1990s, her message appears to be taken more seriously by some leading theorists in first language reading. Several publications that serve as barometers of what is going on in that field are the *Reading Research Quarterly*, the *Journal of Reading*, the *Handbook of Reading Research* (Pearson 1991), and *Theoretical Models and Processes of Reading* (Ruddell, Ruddell, and Singer 1984, 1994). While the third edition (1985) of the last publication contains no chapter by Rosenblatt and only one reference to her work (Goodman 1985), the fourth edition (1994) contains a chapter authored by her, over 50 references to her work, and appreciation for that work by Goodman (1994) and Tierney (1994). The fifth edition of *Literature as Exploration* appeared in 1995. Its entry in *Books in Print* (1997) is framed and formatted in much larger and bolder letters than the surrounding entries, setting it apart as though it were a special book in some way—perhaps because it has remained in print for 60 years and now is in its fifth edition. Her work is now beginning to receive the attention it deserves by educators of reading in English as a first language (Cunningham and Fitzgerald 1996, Almasi and Miller 1996, Farrell and Squire 1990, Clifford 1991). Hopefully, her influence will continue to grow in first language reading and begin to be felt in second language theories of reading, in ESL reading materials, and ESL language teaching in its multiple forms (EAP, ESP, etc.). (See Note 2.)

ROSENBLATT'S EFFERENT/AESTHETIC CONTINUUM OF READING

Rosenblatt's transactional theory of reading encompasses the entire range of reading which includes non-literary and literary texts. She posits that at any moment all of a person's inner resources—cognitions (thoughts, intuitions, critical evaluations, etc.) and affects (emotions, feelings, attitudes, etc.) are available for selective attention. Cues surface either from the text or from the reader and attending to them can mark the beginning of an evolution of a stance toward a text. The stance suppresses some inner resources and allows others to rise to the surface. These processes are then attended to by a reader to create a specific read at a specific time in a specific place. Rosenblatt uses the term "efferent" to refer to a read of a non-literary text and "aesthetic" to refer to that of a literary text. As described above, a reader's inner resources are continuously available during the different reads; and, at times, an aesthetic read may interrupt a generally efferent read and vice versa. Also, a reader can read a literary text efferently and a non-literary text aesthetically. In a basically efferent read, readers evoke a different kind of "experience;" they respond to the ideas, arguments, conclusions, etc. Some responses may consist of agreeing with some thoughts and disagreeing with others, but the underlying purpose is to "take away" information from the text. In an aesthetic read, the reader evokes and experiences the events in the story world of the characters, at times feeling, simultaneously with the character, that character's sorrow, disappointment, relief, etc.; later, the reader can reflect upon the entire reading experience, abstract from it the essence of the meaning of the work to the reader, critically evaluate the lived experience, compare it to other experiences, and attempt to analyze why it had so much or so little impact on the reader.

Concrete examples of adopting the two stances with the same literary text and the processes involved in the two stances are the following. I could read *The Great Gatsby* by F. Scott Fitzgerald (1995) in order to identify and describe the metaphors and similes that refer to class, money, and power. For each of these, I could describe how they operate in their specific context; for example, what they reveal about the character who is using them, and what they reveal about the political, cultural, and economic climate of the early 1900s in America. In so doing, I would suppress much of the story world of the text and much of my experiential matrix. On the other hand, I could experience the text in such a way that I would have a lived experience with it; that is, evoke the story world and the characters who inhabit it, identify with the characters, and live through the events with them. I could reflect upon my experience and raise to consciousness the personal interpretation that for me, Jay Gatsby, although idiosyncratic in many ways, was a better person than the woman he wanted and many of the people with whom he surrounded himself. Rosenblatt would call the first reading "taking an efferent stance toward the text;" that is, reading it for the purpose of taking away specific information. She would call the second reading "taking an aesthetic stance toward the text," which involves bringing my personal culture, gender, political views, feelings about class and power—my lived experiences—to the "black marks on the pages" and through them evoking a world. I would be living through that world; that is, experiencing "a lived event" with the work often from the perspective of the different characters who inhabit it, and add another lived experience to the store of experiences that I bring to my daily living and to my transactions with other texts.

Concrete examples of adopting the two stances with the same text, but this time with a non-literary one, and the processes involved in the two stances could be the following. I could read *Ludwig Wittgenstein: The Duty of Genius* by Ray Monk (1990) with an efferent stance; that is, with the purpose of taking from the text the information I needed to present it to a class I might be teaching. I could diagram the major episodes of Wittgenstein's life on a timeline; on another horizontal line drawn below the first, I could describe the places he was in during those episodes; and on a third line I could place the personal relationships he had at those different times in his life. In contrast, I could decide to select this book as pleasure reading for the summer. With no intention of using it in my teaching or in my writing, I might simply become immersed in Wittgenstein's life experiences, his troubled relationships, and his continual striving to produce his philosophical works. Seeing the world through his eyes in his diary entries, I could wrestle with his decisions as he made them, feel with him how mundane life often can be, and sense how life often takes its own turns and makes some choices for us while we must wrestle with other decisions, make them on our own, and live with their consequences. To this read, I bring my own standards and beliefs about when actions are ethical or unethical, and when they are wise or naive. I judge Wittgenstein's decisions and actions, and I wrestle with creating other plausible interpretations of them.

PRINCIPLES AND EXAMPLES IN FACILITATING AESTHETIC RESPONSES

1. Selecting Appropriate Materials

To Rosenblatt (1995 5th ed.), there are two aspects in the selection of literary texts and both are important: some texts need to be selected by the teacher and some by the students.

Teacher Selection

According to Rosenblatt, in choosing material, teachers should be guided by students' "needs and conflicts and a recognition of any circumstances in their personal and social backgrounds that would make certain ... [material] of the past or present particularly interesting and illuminating" (1995 5th ed.: 69). She states that if teachers are aware of the conflicts and anxieties that recur most frequently in their students' lives, they will be able to make available work that has relevance to them. She affirms that what is important is not the "great works" themselves, but "the quality of the actual reading experiences" (1995 5th ed.:269).

In her reading-speaking class at the English Language Institute, the teacher added short stories and poems to two up-to-date, high-quality textbooks. One text, entitled *Timely Topics* by Aquilina (1993), contained appropriate expository readings for students. The other text, *All Clear! Advanced Idioms and Pronunciation in Context* by Fragiadakis (1997), contained current idiomatic expressions and dialogues to help students improve their speaking skills. About a month into the semester when students were reading "Chapter 2: Issues in Education" in *Timely Topics* and "Chapter 3: In Class—Bored to Death or on the Edge of Your Seat?" in *Advanced Idioms*, she assigned the short story "Housepainting" by Chang (1994) from *American Eyes: New Asian-American Stories for Young Adults* and played a videotape of the story entitled "Double Happiness" by Shum (1990). Both stories deal with generational conflicts that can arise when first-generation Asian American women begin dating and planning to marry either American or first-generation Asian men. The two narratives show contrasts among different responses by parents, relatives, children, siblings, and suitors at this critical moment in their lives.

The two stories deal with issues that the young men and women in the class were dealing with in their own lives. As reported earlier in this chapter, several of the main concerns voiced by 15 of the 17 students were: who they were going to marry, what kind of person they should be looking for, what kind of profession or job they should prepare for and seek. For these students, these two concerns (marriage and profession) cut across all national boundaries—Korean, Japanese, Taiwanese, Icelandic, and Mexican. They wanted to know how their peers were dealing with these issues, which they discussed consistently both in and outside of class. Because the two narratives resonated with students' immediate concerns, the students had a great deal to say about the two main fictional characters, Frances and Jade, and the different decisions made by the two women in the stories. (See Note 3.)

Student Selection

Rosenblatt (1995 5th ed.), in talking about a teacher's role, says that it probably would be much better if a teacher could select a wide range of books and place them on the shelves of a library, then turn students loose to work out a personal approach to literature. But, she realizes this is not always possible and that a teacher does have an important role to play in keeping an eye on the transactions between students and the texts they read.

Rosenblatt (1995 5th ed.) still feels that teachers should provide a broad selection of material for students and help them develop sufficient independence to seek out works for themselves. In class, they should learn to develop habits of selecting their own books. On the topic of developing these habits, in a footnote on page 70 of the 1995 edition of *Literature as Exploration,* she provides several sources ESL teachers can read and adapt to their own teaching situations.

While personal selection was not an aspect of the English Language Institute reading-speaking course, the reading coordinator, who is a member of the research team on the ethnographic study, said that this dimension could be worked into a class like that one at a later date (Campbell personal communication 1997). For example, a few weeks of the course could be set up as a workshop on how to select reading material and where to find it in the library. Copies of a wide variety of short stories and poems appropriate for students could be made available to them and in groups in class, they could share their interpretations. (See Note 4.)

2. Fostering a "Lived Experience" with the Text

Rosenblatt writes that "students' reactions will be in terms of their own temperaments and backgrounds" and that even if their responses "do injustice to the text .... the students' primary experience of the work will have had meaning for [them] in ... personal terms and no others. No matter how imperfect or mistaken, this will constitute the present meaning of the work for [the students] rather than anything they docilely repeat about it" (1995 5th ed.: 50). In other words, Rosenblatt tells teachers that they need to elicit a spontaneous, personal response from students to literary texts and help them to discover what the texts mean to them. Teachers also need to give students time to grapple with their own reactions. Whatever the teacher's approach, a teacher can help students develop their understandings in the context of their own thoughts, emotions, cultures, and their own curiosity about life and literature. "To attempt to ignore these student reactions would destroy the very basis upon which any greater literary sensitivity could be built" (1995 5th ed.: 225).

3. Allowing the Format of Responses to be Dictated by the "Lived Experiences"

Rosenblatt (1995 5th ed.) advises teachers to expand their repertoire of forms in which students can frame their responses. Students should be encouraged to express themselves freely and to let their comments take the form dictated by what they lived through in reading the work. Rosenblatt cautions teachers against framing students' responses for them by requiring that they appear in a preconceived form; e.g., the compare and contrast essay (as it is now used in many ESL reading classes). In developing questions for the two stories, "Housepainting" and "Double Happiness," it is customary for ESL teachers to present something like the following: "How does

Frances'/Jade's (the main character's) behaviour reflect her Chinese identity? Give specific examples." Or, "How does Frances'/Jade's behaviour reflect her Western identity? Give specific examples." In developing questions that ask students to *combine* the two readings, teachers often develop questions like: "Among the characters in 'Housepainting' and 'Double Happiness' that you compared, which pair (meaning the dating pair: Frances and Wei and Jade and Mark) did you find most interesting? Why? What similarities and/or differences did you note between the characters?"

Questions designed in this way will promote class discussions, but they encourage the student to format what we hoped was "a lived event" with the narratives; that is, an aesthetic reading into an efferent format. And if we use only efferent questions like these, they may very likely encourage students to take an efferent stance when they read assigned and selected literary texts.

What questions could we ask students to foster framing their responses more closely to what they actually lived through? What prompts might help them to capture "their lived events" with the text in preparation for sharing these with others? Several examples are the following: "What do you think is worth talking about when we talk about this story?" "How did you interpret the story? What in this story is meaningful to you? Why?" "What questions do you have about this story for which there are no answers?" (Donelson 1990: 17).

Some ESL teachers who may wish to use a more structured approach with their students might consider the following lesson plan that would be appropriate for both "Housepainting" and "Double Happiness."

Purpose: Individual and Collaborative Interpretation of "Housepainting"

Activity: 1. Read the short story silently to understand it.
2. Briefly write down your interpretation of the story in five to six paragraphs.
3. Share with the whole group your interpretation of the story. During the discussion, listen carefully to the interpretations of members in the group and respond to their interpretations. Ask questions of the speaker to gather information or clarify the speaker's interpretation, or to help you understand the speaker's reasons for interpretations that differ from yours. For example: "What did you mean by such and such? Did you think that such and such happened? Why? Where in the story did you understand that such and such ... ?" (Time depends upon number in the class.)
4. In three or four paragraphs, write down whether and how your interpretation was affected by the group discussion (15 minutes).

5. With a partner or two, discuss what occurred in the full group discussion; that is, what interpretation you heard from other members and what you learned from the questions asked. Share your initial interpretations and whether and how you decided to change or keep all or part of your initial interpretation and your reasons for doing so (15 minutes). Write down what you observed and felt happened in your small group discussion and describe whether and why you did or did not change any section of your interpretation of the story (15 minutes).
6. With the whole group, share what happened in your small group discussion (10 minutes).

A teacher might then wish to follow up the last whole group discussion by saying: "I hear that four of you interpreted the story in this way, six of you in this way, and eight of you in this way. Do you hear any agreements or contradictions among these three interpretations? What are they?" Targetting specific interpretations either because they need clarification or provide good examples, the teacher might ask: "Could you expand upon your interpretation and share with us how you arrived at it using information in and outside the text?"

At times, a teacher may wish to use a structured approach with a poem. In each of the teaching environments described in Note 1, the poem "My Papa's Waltz" was assigned in class (Roethke 1996). (See Appendix I for the poem and Appendix II for the lesson plan.)

In the four classes referred to in this chapter, the responses to this poem were different. For example, in the literary class, I was paired with a student from China who interpreted the event in the poem as a happy one—after all, it was a "waltz." She felt the father had come home after a long day's work, relaxed by having a few drinks, became light-hearted, and waltzed around in a happy mood with his son. She told me that in her experience in China, men would often have a few drinks after work, but this did not lead to their becoming alcoholics or abusive. I, on the other hand, interpreted the word "waltz" as ironic and viewed the event as negative. I saw a father being abusive to his son as his wife looked on disapprovingly.

4. Facilitating Comparisons of Students' Responses

Rosenblatt (1995 5th ed.) writes that another of a teacher's major tasks involves helping students become aware of possible alternative interpretations and responses. They can then be led to compare and examine further their own reactions with those of other students and of the teacher, and with information in the text itself. She cautions teachers against using set routines and urges them to let the discussions grow out of the ideas, perplexities, and questions formulated by the students themselves. She asserts that this approach does not imply "sheer improvisation" by the students and teacher. To elicit and scaffold students' responses, the teacher must have "a firm grasp of the work and concepts relevant to it." Only then will the teacher be able to engage in "an inductive process" in which students are motivated to ask questions to clarify their own interpretations and to listen to alternative meanings. After this listening, they can decide for themselves what meaning the text has for them.

First used by Almasi and Miller (1996) in their Literacy class, a different version of the lesson plan for "Papa's Waltz" (Appendix I) was assigned in the four classes referred to in this chapter. In the Literacy class at numbers 1.4, 1.5, 2, and 3 of the lesson plan (Appendix II), I learned that the reader to my left, who was from China, interpreted the poem in a similar way as had the student to my right with whom I was paired for the small group activity; that is, she heard a positive tone to the poem and experienced a happy event in reading it.

In contrast, many American readers responded as I had to the poem. They heard a negative tone. They saw an alcoholic father "roughing up" his son who was fearful of him. To them the "waltz" had an ironic meaning. Although waltzes are usually happy events, this was not a happy occasion for either the mother or her son. To these readers, of the three characters in the poem, only the father, in a hypnotic, alcoholic trance, seemed to them to enjoy the dance. In this class, did culture and/or language level play a role in determining the "tone" the reader heard in the poem, which played an important role in the interpretation of the events? For many, but not all of the Americans, that tone was negative; while for many Asians, it was positive. In my two teacher-education classes, the interpretations did not differ so strikingly along cultural or language proficiency lines (Hosenfeld 1997b). In those classes, several American as well as Asian students experienced the occasion as a happy one. In the ELI study class, in which students were from five different countries, many students expressed that they heard a positive tone and had a positive experience from reading the poem. (An analysis currently being carried out may provide more information about students' different arguments supporting their assessment of the waltz as a happy event.)

During or after these discussions, students can also deepen their "understanding of concepts such as voice, persona, point of view, and genre" (Rosenblatt 1995 5th ed.: 214). (For shifts in point of view in narratives see Hosenfeld, Duchan, and Higginbotham 1995; Costello, Bruder, Hosenfeld, and Duchan 1995; Segal 1995; Segal, Miller, Hosenfeld, Mendelsohn, Russell, Julian, Greene, and Delphonse 1997; and Talmy 1995).

Rosenblatt writes:

> If the literary works [have] had little emotional impact, any discussion would [be] empty verbiage. The discussions ... [are] fundamentally attempts by the students to work out some rational understanding of their reactions. They [are] involved in the task of managing their emotions—something very different

from ignoring or repressing them. In this way, they [are] encouraged to bring thought to bear on emotional responses—the starting point for intelligent behaviour (1995 5th ed.: 226).

This quotation leads into the next phase of transacting with a text which involves managing one's own thoughts and emotions as they emerge during the personal read and in discussions with others; that is, "going meta" on the lived event.

5. "Going Meta" On Lived Experiences

According to Rosenblatt (1995 5th ed.), evoking a personal response and clarifying that response by comparing it with the responses of others are necessary but insufficient conditions in responding to literary texts. A third task for the teacher consists of seeing that students reflect on their "lived experience;" that is, that they "go meta" on that experience (Bruner 1995, 1996; Hosenfeld 1997a). Rosenblatt says: "[Students] can begin to achieve a sound approach to literature only when [they] reflect on [their] response to it, when [they] attempt to understand what in the work and in [themselves] produced that reaction, and when [they] thoughtfully go on to modify, reject, or accept it" (1995 5th ed.: 72).

The following questions given by Rosenblatt could help students to reflect upon their lived event with short stories and poems. They could be added as number 7 in the author-constructed lesson plan for "Housepainting" and as number 5 in the plan for "Papa's Waltz."

> Why was [my] reaction different from those of the other students? Why did [I] choose one particular slant rather than another? Why did certain [events]/phrases of the [short story] or poem strike [me] more forcibly than others? Why did I misinterpret or ignore certain elements? ... What was there in my state of mind that led me to a distorted or partial view of the work? What in my temperament and past experience helped me understand it more adequately? What questions and obscurities remain? (1995 5th ed.: 75).

6. Moving Toward Warranted Reads

A sixth principle focuses upon the importance of students' arriving at valid interpretations of texts. Rosenblatt writes:

> Fundamentally, the process of understanding a work implies a recreation of it, an attempt to grasp completely all of the sensations and concepts through which the author seeks to convey the quality of his sense of life. Each of us must make a new synthesis of these elements with [our] own nature, but it is essential that [we] assimilate those elements of experience which the author has actually presented (Rosenblatt 1976: 113).

Rosenblatt (1995 5th ed.) posits that a portion or even an entire text can be misinterpreted as it is experienced by a student; that is, the student's "lived experience" can be warranted or unwarranted relative to a given text. She asserts that while she doubts that we can arrive at a consensus of a best warranted interpretation for any text (because one does not exist), we can come to a consensus on many unwarranted interpretations of texts. (For a description of the processes involved in an ESL student providing an unwarranted read of a text, see Hosenfeld 1995).

In helping students move from unwarranted to warranted reads of a passage, we can begin with their initial responses and as described above, in small groups have them listen to interpretations of the same passage by others. Either with individual groups or with the whole class, a teacher may hear certain students interpreting a section one way and other students another way. Paraphrasing or repeating the two interpretations, a teacher might say: "Do you hear these interpretations as similar or different? In what way(s)? What in the text justifies these interpretations? What background knowledge about the topic do you have that would seem to support or contradict either of the responses? What are the bases of your interpretation of the text?"

Some may think Rosenblatt is encouraging teachers to have one "best" interpretation in mind and be in the process of guiding students toward that one interpretation. Not at all. The teacher is assuming that there is no one best interpretation, but still some interpretations are better than others. (For a discussion of this same issue by Bruner, see Note 5.)

7. Creating a Relationship with Literary and/or Non-Literary Texts
Rosenblatt writes:

> Unless teacher[s] [themselves] value literary [and/or non-literary experiences with text], revision of [their] aims or methods will be futile. By implication, [a] definition of ... a relationship between the student and the literary [and/or non-literary] work applies also to the teacher. As long as an artificial and pedantic notion of literary culture persists, students will continue in their indifference to the great works of the past and present (Rosenblatt 1995: 63). (See Note 6.)

Rosenblatt adds that a teacher's personal love of literature or non-literary texts is not always proof against their using teaching methods that inhibit students' own personal responses to texts. She cautions us that a person who has aesthetically read and experienced a great deal of literature can also be ill-equipped to help students experience their own "lived events" with literary texts. A teacher needs to have both a personal relationship with texts and the abilities and methods needed to foster students' developing their own experiences with them.

Conclusion

Through her lifelong work, Rosenblatt offers all reading teachers, including ESL teachers, a theoretical foundation and explicit classroom practices that will foster students' having an aesthetic experience with literary texts and an efferent experience with expository ones. Based upon her work, teachers can help students to read efferently when that response is appropriate—often with expository texts or when their purposes for reading are efferent. Teachers can also help students to read aesthetically when that response is appropriate—often with literary texts or when their purposes are aesthetic. Students will be able to manage the different stances and know when and how to engage in one or the other.

While Rosenblatt's primary audience is theoreticians and teachers of reading in English as a native language, her work can expand the vision of teachers of non-native readers of English. By grasping Rosenblatt's essential insight into reading, I believe ESL teachers will be motivated to reexamine the methods and materials they use and see that, presently, many of our questions and prompts encourage chiefly efferent stances and efferent responses to both expository and narrative texts.

Furthermore, the characteristics Rosenblatt exemplifies in her life and work make her a model for teachers. These include her tenacity in sticking to what she believed in the face of fierce opposition, her courage (from the French word *coeur* which means "great heartedness") expressed in her unwavering view that great literature belongs to everyone, and her continuance in giving her gifts every day to the world. She continues to publish with her knowledge that the work is always beginning and never done.

Notes

1. Several examples in this article are intended to clarify some of the concepts in Rosenblatt's transactional theory of reading. Two reads of *The Great Gatsby* and of *Ludwig Wittgenstein* are intended to help the reader understand the differences between "efferent" and "aesthetic" reads of texts. Other examples are intended to show ESL teachers how Rosenblatt's vision is applied to concrete examples they can modify and adapt for their ESL students. These latter examples come from three sources: (1) An ethnographic study of an advanced reading-speaking class in an English Language Institute in western New York conducted by Hosenfeld, Russell, Silva, and Campbell. The data consist of field notes and videotapes of 100 hours of class sessions and individual interviews taken during the Fall semester of 1997; (2) Two teacher-education courses in writing and reading in a second language for native and non-native teachers taught by the author during the Spring and Fall semesters of 1997; and (3) A teacher training course in Literacy for native and non-native speakers of English taught by Almasi and Miller during the Spring semester of 1996.

2. For a cogent argument that much of instruction today is based upon a view that text is autonomous; that is, that meaning resides in the text, see Cheryl Geisler's book *Academic Literacy and the Nature of Expertise* published by Lawrence Erlbaum Associates in 1994.

3. Two of the women students enrolled in the course were already married. One had chosen a profession and her personal focus in and outside the course seemed more exclusively on improving her English in order to pursue a Master's degree in her chosen field. She reported that she enjoyed listening to her peers, all of whom were from different countries than her own, discussing their views about marriage, work, and other issues and listening to their different perspectives on them. The other woman student who was married was not looking for a profession and was more interested in the social aspect of being a student in the English Language Institute. While a student at the ELI, she and her husband travelled to five major cities in the United States and belonged to a social conversation group led by a native speaker who was retired and enjoyed inviting international students to his home.

4. My primary focus in this chapter is on the aesthetic part of Rosenblatt's continuum because, to me, fostering aesthetic responses seems absent from many ESL reading classes and reading materials in both EAP and ESP. I think in many reading classes, teachers should use materials that elicit processes along the entire range of Rosenblatt's continuum. In self-selection, as described in principle number 7, a teacher should support a student's selection of non-literary texts, e.g., biography, history, if these are the student's choices. Of course, experiencing reading a breadth of text types would seem the most prudent long-term goal for teachers to hold for their students.

5. In his book *The Culture of Education*, Jerome Bruner (1996) discusses these same issues under the notion of "hermeneutic composition." He writes: "What does it mean to say that the comprehension of a narrative is hermeneutic?" For one thing, it implies that no story has a single, unique construal. Its putative meanings are in principle multiple. There is neither a rational procedure to determine whether any particular "reading" is necessary as logical truths are necessary, nor any empirical method for verifying any particular reading. The object of hermeneutic analysis is to provide a convincing and non-contradictory account of what a story means, a reading in keeping with the particulars that constitute it. (See Bruner, page 137 for further discussion of this matter and references to other works on this issue.)

6. I have broadened this quote from Rosenblatt to include expository text such as biography, history, science, etc. I feel certain that she would agree with broadening this section for the purposes of this paper and breadth really exists in her own theory of reading, though it was not her primary focus in this specific section of her major book.

REFERENCES CITED

Almasi, J. and Miller, L. 1996. Literacy Course. Spring semester: State University of New York at Buffalo.

Aquilina, P. 1993. *Timely Topics: An Advanced Reading, Grammar, and Vocabulary Book*. Boston: Heinle & Heinle.

Bereiter, C. and Scardamalia, M. 1993. *Surpassing Ourselves: An Inquiry Into the Nature and Implications of Expertise*. Peru, IL: Open Court Publishing Company.

Books in Print 1996-1997, vol. 3. New Providence, NJ: R.R. Bowker.

Bruner, J. 1995. Speech at the Cognitive Science Center, State University of New York at Buffalo.

———. 1996. *The Culture of Education*. Boston, MA: Harvard University Press.

Chang, L. S. 1994. 'Housepainting.' In *American Eyes: New Asian-American Stories for Young Adults*, edited by L. Carlson. New York: Holt, Rinehart, and Winston.

Clifford, J., ed. 1991. *The Experience of Reading: Louise Rosenblatt and Reader-Response Theory*. Portsmouth, NH: Heinemann.

Costello, A., G. Bruder, C. Hosenfeld, and J. Duchan. 1995. 'Epilogue: A Structural Analysis of a Fictional Narrative: 'A Free Night.' In *Deixis in Narrative: A Cognitive Science Perspective*, edited by J. Duchan, G. Bruder and L. Hewitt, 461-85. Hillsdale, NJ: Lawrence Erlbaum Associates.

Cunningham, J. and J. Fitzgerald. 1996. 'Epistemology and Reading.' *Reading Research Quarterly* 31 (1): 36-60.

Donelson, K. 1990. 'Fifty Years of Literature for Young Adults.' In *Transactions With Literature: A Fifty-Year Perspective*, edited by E. Farrell and J. Squire. Urbana, IL: National Council of Teachers of English.

Emerson, C. and M. Holquist, eds. 1996. *M.M. Bakhtin: Speech Genres and Other Late Essays*. Translated by V.W. McGee. Austin, TE: University of Texas Press.

Farrell, E., and J. Squire, eds. 1990. *Transactions With Literature: A Fifty-Year Perspective*. Urbana IL: National Council of Teachers of English.

Fitzgerald, F.S. 1995. *The Great Gatsby*. New York: Simon and Schuster.

Fragiadakis, H. 1997. *All Clear! Advanced Idioms and Pronunciation in Context*. New York: Heinle & Heinle.

Geisler, C. 1994. *Academic Literacy and the Nature of Expertise*. Hillsdale, NJ: Lawrence Erlbaum Associates.

Goodman, K. 1985. 'Transactional Psycholinguistic Model: Unity in Reading.' In *Theoretical Models and Processes of Reading*, 3rd ed., edited by H. Singer and R. Ruddell, 813-40. Newark, DE: International Reading Association.

Goodman, K. 1994. 'Reading, Writing, and Written Tests: A Transactional Sociopsycholinguistic View.' In *Theoretical Models and Processes of Reading*, 4th ed., edited by R. Ruddell, M. Ruddell, and H. Singer, 1093-1130. Newark, DE: International Reading Association.

Holquist, M., ed. 1981. *The Dialogic Imagination: Four Essays by M.M. Bakhtin*. Translated by C. Emerson and M. Holquist. Austin, TE: University of Texas Press.

Hosenfeld, C. 1995. 'Reading in a Second Language: Theory, Research, and Practice.' *College ESL* 5 (2): 21-34.

———. (1997a). 'Theories of Mind: Metacognition.' Paper presented at the Fifth Annual Conference of the American Association of Applied Linguistics. Orlando FL: 11 March 1997.

———. (1997b). 'Teaching Writing in a Second Language,' Spring semester course; 'Teaching Reading in a Second Language,' Fall semester course at the State University of New York at Buffalo.

Hosenfeld, C., J. Duchan, and J. Higginbotham. 1995. 'Deixis in Persuasive Texts Written by Bilinguals of Differing Degrees of Expertise.' In *Deixis in Narrative: A Cognitive Science Perspective*, edited by J. Duchan, G. Bruder, and L. Hewitt. Hillsdale, NJ: Lawrence Erlbaum Associates.

Hosenfeld, C., W. Russell, J. Silva, and B. Campbell. 1998. 'An Ethnographic Study of an Advanced Reading and Speaking Class in an English Language Institute.' Study in progress, State University of New York at Buffalo.

Liapunov, V. and M. Holquist, eds. 1993. *Toward a Philosophy of the Act*. Translated by Vadim Liapunov. Austin, TE: University of Texas Press.

Monk, R. 1990. *Ludwig Wittgenstein: The Duty of Genius*. New York: Penguin Books.

Morrow, L., M. Pressley, J. Smith, and M. Smith. 1997. 'The Effect of a Literature-based Program Integrated into Literacy and Science Instruction with Children from Diverse Backgrounds.' *Reading Research Quarterly* 32 (1): 54-76.

Pearson, D. 1991. *Handbook of Reading Research*. New York: Longman.

Roethke, T. 1966. 'Papa's Waltz.' In *The Collected Poems of Theodore Roethke*, 45. Garden City, NY: Doubleday.

Rosenblatt, L. 1938 1st ed.; 1965 2nd ed.; 1968 3rd ed.; 1976 4th ed.; 1995 5th ed. *Literature as Exploration*. New York: The Modern Language Association.

———. 1940. 'Development of Reading Interests and Critical Appreciation in Secondary Schools and Colleges.' In *Reading and Pupil Development*, edited by W.S. Gray, 223-29. Chicago: The University of Chicago.

———. 1969. 'Towards a Transactional Theory of Reading.' *Journal of Reading Behavior* (Winter): 31-49.

———. 1972. 'The Enriching Values of Reading.' In *Reading in an Age of Mass Communication*, 2nd ed., edited by W.S. Gray, 19-38. Hallandale, FL: New World Book Manufacturing Co.

———. 1978 1st ed., 1994 2nd ed. *The Reader, the Text, the Poem: The Transactional Theory of the Literary Work*. Carbondale: Southern Illinois University Press.

———. 1980. 'What Facts Does this Poem Teach You?' *Language Arts* 57 (4): 386-94.

———. 1982. 'The Literary Transaction: Evocation and Response.' *Theory into Practice* 21(4): 268-77.

———. 1985. 'Viewpoints: Transaction versus Interaction—A Terminological Rescue Operation.' *Research in the Teaching of English* 19 (1): 96-106.

———. 1994. 'The Transactional Theory of Reading and Writing.' In *Theoretical Models and Processes of Reading*, 4th ed., edited by R. Ruddell, M. Ruddell, and H. Singer, 1057-1092. Newark, DE: International Reading Association.

Ruddell, R., M. Ruddell and H. Singer. 1984 3rd ed; 1994 4th ed. *Theoretical Models and Processes of Reading*. Newark, DE: International Reading Association.

Scardamalia, M. and C. Bereiter. 1991. 'Literate Expertise.' In *Toward a General Theory of Expertise: Prospects and Limits*, edited by K.A. Ericsson and J. Smith, 172-94. Cambridge: Cambridge University Press.

Segal, E. 1995. 'Narrative Comprehension and the Role of Deictic Shift Theory.' In *Deixis in Narrative: A Cognitive Science Perspective*, edited by J. Duchan, G. Bruder, and L. Hewitt, 3-17. Hillsdale, NJ: Lawrence Erlbaum Associates.

Segal, E., G. Miller, C. Hosenfeld, A. Mendelsohn, W. Russell, J. Julian, A. Greene, and J. Delphonse. 1997. 'Tense and Person in Narrative Interpretation.' *Discourse Processes* 24 (2): 271-307.

Shum, M. 1990. "Double Happiness" videocassette 246 m. Bedford, MA: BASF Corporation Information Systems.

Smith, J., J. Monson, and D. Dobson. 1992. 'A Case Study on Integrating History and Reading Instruction Through Literature.' *Social Science Education* 56: 370-75.

Talmy, L. 1995. 'Narrative Structure in a Cognitive Framework.' In *Deixis in Narrative: A Cognitive Science Perspective*, edited by J. Duchan, G. Bruder, and L. Hewitt, 421-60. Hillsdale, NJ: Lawrence Erlbaum Associates.

Tierney, R. 1994. 'Dissensions, Tensions, and the Models of Literacy.' In *Theoretical Models and Processes of Reading*, 4th ed., edited by R. Ruddell, M. Ruddell, and H. Singer, 1162-1182. Newark, DE: International Reading Association.

ADDITIONAL BIBLIOGRAPHY

Dewey, J. 1931. *Philosophy and Civilization*. New York: W.W. Norton.

Dewey, J. and A. Bentley. 1949. *Knowing and the Known*. Boston: The Beacon Press.

Peirce, C.S. 1932; 1933. *Collected Papers*, vols. 2,3. Edited by P. Weiss and C. Hart. Cambridge, MA: Harvard University Press.

Rosenblatt, L. 1968. 'A Way of Happening.' *Educational Record* 49: 339-46.

———. 1969. 'Pattern and Process—A Polemic.' *English Journal* 58 (7): 1005-1012.

———. 1977. 'What We Have Learned: Reminiscences of the NCTE.' *English Journal* 66 (8): 88-90.

———. 1989. 'Writing and Reading: The Transactional Theory.' In *Reading and Writing Connections*, edited by J. M. Mason, 153-76. Boston: Allyn and Bacon.

———. 1991. 'Literature—SOS!' *Language Arts* 68: 444-48.

———. 1993. 'The Transactional Theory: Against Dualisms.' *College English* 55 (4): 377-86.

———. 1995. 'Continuing the Conversation: A Clarification.' *Research in the Teaching of English* 29 (3): 349-54.

Rosenblatt, L., H.M. Jones, and O.J. Campbell. 1938. 'Statement of the Committee of Twenty-four.' In *Publications of the Modern Language Association of America*, vol. 53: 1367-1371. Menasha WI: George Banti Publishing Company.

APPENDIX I

My Papa's Waltz
by Theodore Roethke

The whiskey on your breath
Could make a small boy dizzy;
But I held on like death
Such waltzing was not easy.

We romped until the pans
Slid from the kitchen shelf
My mother's countenance
Could not unfrown itself.

The hand that held my wrist
Was battered on one knuckle;
At every step you missed
My right ear scraped a buckle.

You beat time on my head
With a palm caked hard by dirt;
Then waltzed me off to bed
Still clinging to your shirt.

APPENDIX II

Lesson Plan for "My Papa's Waltz"

Purpose: Individual and Collaborative Interpretation of a Poem

Activity:
1. Discussion of "My Papa's Waltz" (30 minutes).
    1.1 Two students volunteer to read the poem aloud.
    1.2 Pick a word, phrase, or sentence that seems to you to be significant in the poem and write it down.
    1.3 Briefly write your interpretation of the poem in two or three paragraphs.
    1.4 Share with the group the word(s) you selected and tell why you selected it/them.
    1.5 Share with the group your interpretation of the poem. During the discussion, listen carefully to the responses of members in the group and respond to their interpretation with comments; e.g., "I heard you interpret the poem in this way and you interpreted it another way. Could you both expand upon your interpretations and share with us how you arrived at them using information in and outside the text?"
2. Write down how your interpretation was affected by the group discussion in two or three paragraphs (5 minutes).
3. With a partner or two, discuss what occurred in the group discussion (10 minutes). Write down what you observed and felt happened in the discussion, as well as if and why you did or did not change any sections of your initial interpretation of the poem (5 minutes).
4. In a whole group discussion, share what happened in your small group discussions.

CHAPTER EIGHT

SIDNEY SIMON

✻

PRIZING OUR PERSONAL AND CULTURAL VALUES

Sharron Bassano
University of California, Berkeley

Introduction

> Every day, every one of us meets life situations which call for thought, opinion-making, decision-making, and action. Some of our experiences are familiar, some novel; some are casual, some of extreme importance. Everything we do, every decision we make and course of action we take is based on our consciously or unconsciously held beliefs, attitudes, and values. Students face problems and decisions every day of their lives. Students, too, ponder over what and how to think, believe, behave. So often what goes on in the classroom is irrelevant and remote from the real things that are going on in students' lives—their daily encounters with friends, with strangers, with peers, with authority figures; the social and academic tasks that assault or assuage their egos. This is a confusing world to live in. At every turn we are forced to make choices about how to live our lives.
>
> (Simon et al. 1972)

So begins the classic text, *Values Clarification: A Handbook of Practical Strategies for Teachers and Students*, first published in 1972. Though Sidney Simon and his colleagues, Howard Kirschenbaum and Leland Howe, address learners in general in this early work, they also perfectly describe the specific challenges faced by immigrants—those learners experiencing the arduous task of language acquisition within a new and strange cultural milieu. This is so much so, that Simon's philosophy of education and the basic strategies of Values Clarification have been the most significant guiding force—the touchstone, if you will—in both my ESL/EFL classrooms and in my teacher education courses over the past 22 years. His work has, in fact, influenced the teaching practice of most of my fellow English instructors—though they may not know his name nor be aware that the prototypes of so many language teaching strategies they commonly use were created by someone completely outside of the language teaching discipline.

Sidney Simon, professor emeritus at the University of Massachusetts at Amherst, was a founder of the Values Clarification movement in the early 1970s in the United States. An internationally-known pioneer in Psychological Education, he helped develop a theory and a set of principles that have influenced and altered counselling practice, education, parenting styles, medical care, and social work both in the United States where he worked and developed his theories, and abroad.

Beginning his professional career in 1950 as a high school English teacher, Simon subsequently served as Associate Professor in Education at both Queens College and Temple University, and later became Professor of Psychological Education at the University of Massachusetts, where he taught for 20 years.

Among numerous affiliations, Simon was a long-term member of the Association for Supervision and Curriculum Development, he served on the board of directors of the John Dewey Society, and he was an editor for the *Journal of Humanistic Education*. Author and co-author of more than 100 professional articles and 16 books, including *Helping Your Child Find Values to Live By* (1978), *Forgiveness* (1990), and *In Search of Values* (1993), Simon continues to conduct training workshops worldwide.

How, exactly, does the Values Clarification process relate to or fit in with teaching English as a Second or Foreign Language? And how has this model continued to remain current and valid in our profession after more than 25 years, and in the face of so many new and fleeting paradigms?

ESL: Immigrant and Foreign Student Instruction

In addition to instruction in listening, speaking, reading, writing, grammar, vocabulary, social functions, basic lifeskills, academic skills, learning strategies, and the specific subject matter that make up our diverse curricula, ESL instructors also have facilitating acculturation as a curricular goal. We are often the primary source of assistance for immigrant and visiting academic English learners who must quickly learn to understand, cope with, and adapt to the new cultural setting. We build awareness of the learner's adopted culture, we highlight cross-cultural similarities and differences, we role-play misunderstandings. We encourage our learners to teach others about their own cultural folkways, customs, and academic cultures while concurrently asking them to learn about, tolerate, and even appreciate the different ways and behaviours of others. We may be the only informant they have initially to help them make sense of the fundamentally incomprehensible and often incongruous world in which they find themselves. It is in these essential areas that Values Clarification principles and practices come into play in our classrooms at all proficiency levels.

All of us, young or old, may become confused about our values—about the things we believe in and hope for. But for our immigrant and visiting academic students, the internal conflicts—both personal and cultural—may be much more acute. They may be confronted by many more choices, and, paradoxically, by many more limitations than they have ever before experienced in their lives. Surrounded by a vast, bewildering array of alternatives and an unknown quantity of possible consequences for their actions, it is not surprising that they often experience intense disorientation and anomie.

Regarding immigrants, specifically, confronting such a major life upheaval as emigrating from everything they know and love, they must begin the formidable task of sorting out what to keep and what to let go of. Our immigrants (*if* they are able to articulate their thoughts in English), ask us, "What will help me in this new world, and what will hinder me?" "What choices do I have and what will the consequences of my choices be?" "How will I learn to accept these strange people around me?" "How do I learn to choose a course of action from so many possibilities?" "And if I really have no choice, how do I find a way to cope?" "Where do I find a new sense of identity—who is the 'me' that I am now in this place?" "How do I learn to relate to people with opinions, and experiences, and desires, and skin colour so very different from my own?" And even more specifically: "What kind of car do I need? Do I even need a car?" "Must I really take that degrading job?" "Who should I believe?" "Is this neighbourhood the only one I can live in?" "Would she be a good choice as a new friend, and how do I know?" "Is this the best school for my child?" "These strange clothes—do I have to wear them to fit in?" "Must I eat that disgusting cheese or can I just hide it in my napkin?" And, "If I can cough or sneeze in public in this country, why is it considered rude to belch?"

Foreign visiting students, though their relocation may be temporary, have many of the same questions with the addition of others regarding expectations and norms of the academic institutions in which they find themselves.

These concerns, of course, represent but a few of the common areas of conflict and confusion that our learners deal with on a daily basis. These sorts of questions are the focus of values-based lessons.

LEARNING ENGLISH AS A FOREIGN LANGUAGE

Values Clarification practice has a somewhat different role when English is taught in a setting where it is not used outside of the classroom. We know that students who receive well-balanced input—lessons that provide a combination of 1) mechanical, analytical activity, 2) interactive, contextualized practice, and 3) personalized, relevant content—learn language more quickly. Values Clarification activities make it more possible to provide this well-balanced input in the foreign language classroom. Learners are engaged in collaborative and communicative tasks where their lives, their experiences, and their dreams become the subject matter. These values-related activities can be the prime motivators that remedy the situation mentioned in my opening quote—of a classroom that is " ... irrelevant and remote from the real things that are going on in students' lives ..."

The Values Clarification model, a systematic approach which Sidney Simon began to formulate in the 1970s, generally aims to assist people in emerging, life-changing situations (such as adolescence, divorce, new employment, family crises, etc.), to answer some of their questions for themselves and to realign their own values system and behaviour where necessary. It does not intend to *instill* any particular set of values from the outside, but rather to help individuals clarify their beliefs and goals for themselves and to act on them in a functional, productive, congruent manner.

Simon's personal philosophy of education and the Values Clarification process he helped to develop, while certainly germane to educators in all disciplines, are particularly suited and relevant to ESL/EFL professionals in several ways. Through such creative strategies known by contemporary language teachers as autobiographies, "five years from today," interviews, rank order, choosing from alternatives, "all about me," "daily pie," etc., Simon has provided insightful models for the design and implementation of language lessons that are at once personalized, meaningful, and motivating. [The instructional strategies named above and other well-known values-based examples are included in the Appendix beginning on page 143.] Some of the ways that values-based strategies assist the acculturation and language learning process are presented here.

Some Objectives

Some basic objectives for using the Values Clarification process in the language learning classroom at all proficiency levels, ESL or EFL, include the following:

1) To stimulate relevant and meaningful discussion and reflection in the classroom, drawing upon students' past experiences, current concerns and interests, and future goals and aspirations for lesson subject matter;
2) To build students' cooperative and collaborative group skills and a sense of community;
3) To build students' awareness of the individual and cultural values and beliefs that they bring to their present situation;
4) To enhance their sense of personal and cultural dignity and pride;
5) To create in the classroom an awareness of the basic sublime universalities of the human experience, as well as the ridiculous and often unfathomable disparities;
6) To raise an awareness of, and curiosity about, the customs and lifestyles of other cultural or ethnic groups;
7) To address culture shock issues by eliciting empathetic responses from classmates who may share the same difficulties;
8) To explore new beliefs and behaviours and to freely choose new plans of action, if desired, after having thoughtfully considered the consequences;
9) To give students the opportunity to publicly affirm their beliefs, choices, and behaviours—both past and present—in a "safe" setting;
10) To help students determine if their behaviours or actions match their *stated* beliefs and if not, how to bring the two into congruence.

A Collaborative Classroom Process

In addition to the scores of interactive strategies that Sidney Simon and his colleagues created for educators in general, and upon which our own profession has drawn extensively, Values Clarification has provided models for involving students in classroom *process* as well, such as selecting content, determining objectives, self-monitoring, and self-evaluation.

Regarding selecting content and determining objectives, Bassano and Christison in their book *Community Spirit* (1995) suggest:

> In many cases learners come to class without clear or consistent goals other than a desire to learn another language. It is our task to help them sort out the confusion and give some sort of order to their effort. They may already know some of the essentials according to traditional curricula, but it is our job to guide the students to discover for themselves what is worth learning, worth doing, and worth knowing in their new language.
>
> Although it often remains the property of the teacher as language expert to determine the actual syllabus priorities in the classroom, the students can and should be the selectors of content especially related to the topics of conversation, readings, and writing assignments. They should have a say in what parts of the culture they wish to explore (Bassano and Christison 1995: 38).

In order to help Intensive English Program learners choose specific topics for exploration following a basic Values Clarification model, we can, for example, begin by making a list of possible alternatives on the board, and inviting students to add their own areas of interest to the list to be prioritized or voted on by the group. Or, we could simply invite students to work in groups to come up with 10 areas they would like to learn, talk, read, or write about. The groups might share their lists and vote to prioritize the five most interesting topics to begin with. To get at the core of current critical concerns, some suggested topics of conversation might include such strong values areas as: history, comparative religion, politics, family, cultural differences, current news events, work and money, leisure time, marriage, romance, etc.

On the other hand, for adult immigrant language learners, important life-skills topics to prioritize might include: shopping, getting a driver's licence, renting a house, applying for a job, speaking with the doctor, community services, employment training, etc.

Priorities for content can be established according to a specific set of criteria determined by the students and teacher together, asking, for example: "Is the topic interesting? Informative? Entertaining? Is it valuable for our future? What sorts of resources can be found? Where could we go outside of class to learn more about the topic? Whom could we invite to speak to us? Does the teacher (or anyone else in the classroom) know anything about the topic?" Following are five sample strategies based on Values Clarification models for assisting students to make choices in the content of their lessons. They are reprinted here from *Community Spirit* by permission of the publisher (Bassano and Christison 1995).

Content Selection Strategies

Strategy 1: Picture It
Beginning level students can bring in objects or tear pictures from magazines that tell teachers what words or content areas they want to know about. You could also hang up pictures or signs around the room that depict places in the community where your students need to be able to speak English. As a whole class, have students go and stand by the picture or sign that is the place of highest importance to them for speaking English. Continue moving about having them select a second and third choice. Make a tally so that they are aware of the class's democratic decision.

Strategy 2: Campaign
Have your advanced students bring articles from newspapers or magazines that represent topics they would like to work with in English. Have them campaign to the class giving reasons why that topic would be a good area of exploration. After students have shared their suggestions, have them vote on the most preferred topic.

Strategy 3: Voice Your Choice
Bring a page with several rank order choices on it related to different themes to spark interest. (See Figure 1.) Have your students individually write numbers 1, 2, or 3 according to their first, second, and third choice for each of these questions and take turns discussing each of their choices in small groups. As a homework assignment, ask each student to choose a topic of personal interest (family, employment, sports, music, technology, etc.) and create a rank order sheet similar to the one they just completed. This sheet would have four questions with three answer choices for each question. The teacher duplicates their pages for use in discussion groups over a period of time. Then students could vote on preferred topics from the sheets to focus on in depth during later classes.

Strategy 4: Graffiti
Hang large newsprint sheets on the walls around the room, each sheet having a conversation topic written as a heading—Leisure Time, Friendship and Love, Work and Money, America, Politics, TV and Movies, Travel, etc. Ask students to consider their personal favourite topic of those listed and go stand by the chart to show their interest. (All students move at the same time.) You and your students can immediately see the balance of interests in the group.

Then have them move and stand by a chart that represents a topic they *never* like to talk about. Third, give them each a crayon or watercolour marker and have them move about the room for about 10 minutes just writing comments or questions, or drawing pictures on the charts.

Give them time to go around again to read the charts. This is a low-threat way to get students to begin taking a personal stand—an excellent activity for students

Figure 1

VOICE YOUR CHOICE: LEISURE TIME

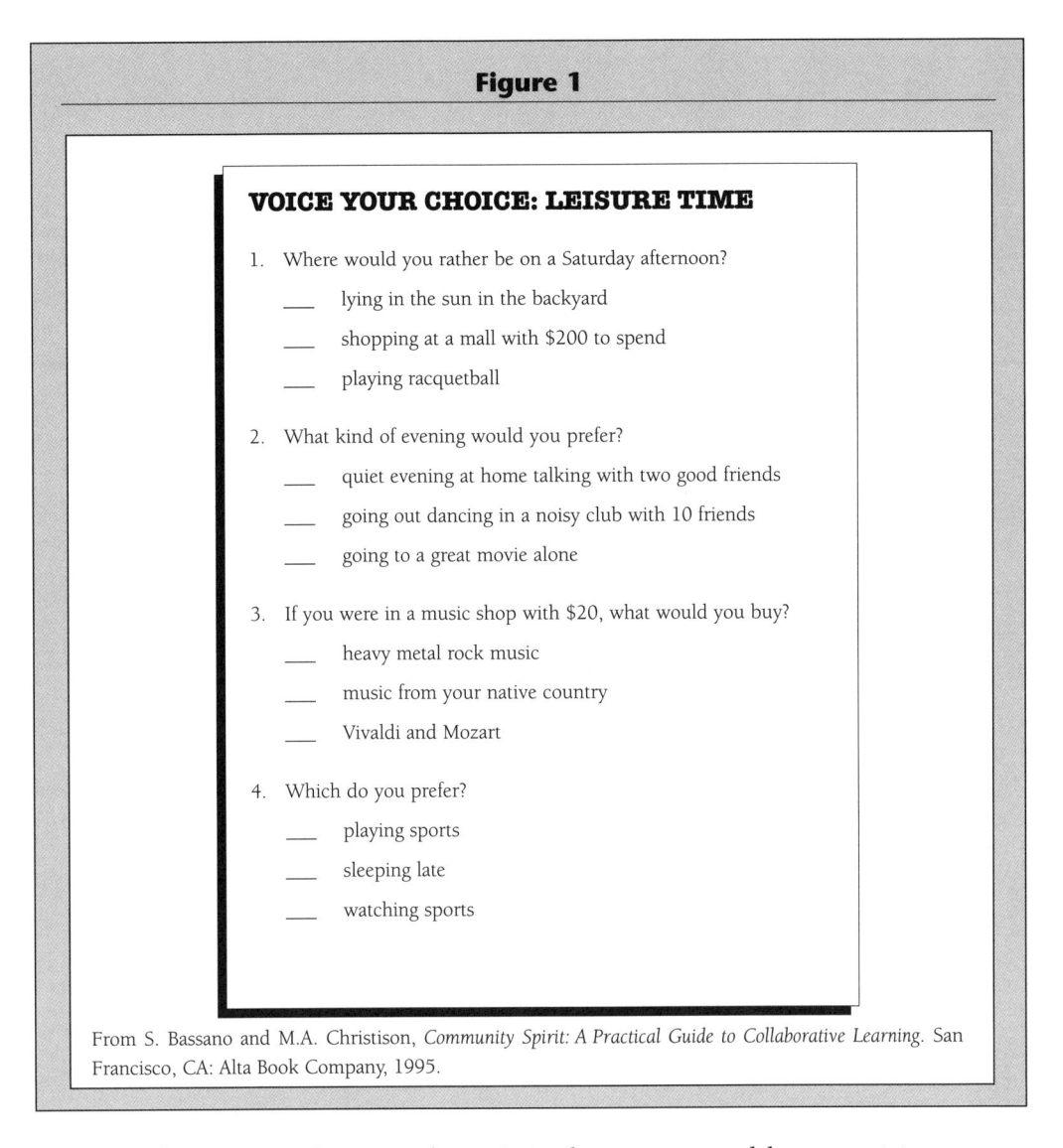

1. Where would you rather be on a Saturday afternoon?
   ___ lying in the sun in the backyard
   ___ shopping at a mall with $200 to spend
   ___ playing racquetball

2. What kind of evening would you prefer?
   ___ quiet evening at home talking with two good friends
   ___ going out dancing in a noisy club with 10 friends
   ___ going to a great movie alone

3. If you were in a music shop with $20, what would you buy?
   ___ heavy metal rock music
   ___ music from your native country
   ___ Vivaldi and Mozart

4. Which do you prefer?
   ___ playing sports
   ___ sleeping late
   ___ watching sports

From S. Bassano and M.A. Christison, *Community Spirit: A Practical Guide to Collaborative Learning.* San Francisco, CA: Alta Book Company, 1995.

who may be nervous about speaking. It is also a structured but energizing way to get them up and out of their seats for a short time, an important consideration in a long class period.

Strategy 5: Surveys

Finally, regarding life skills or adult basic competencies for adult language learners, it is not difficult to do surveys of your group to find out their main concerns and interests. Adolescent or young adult language learners will eagerly respond to surveys about their hobbies, social interests, academic concerns, and career goals.

Students work alone to complete the survey. (See Figure 2 below.) Then as a group they plot their responses on a graph or chart so that they are aware of the wide range of interests (or the similarity of interests) present in the classroom.

Figure 2

INTEREST SURVEY

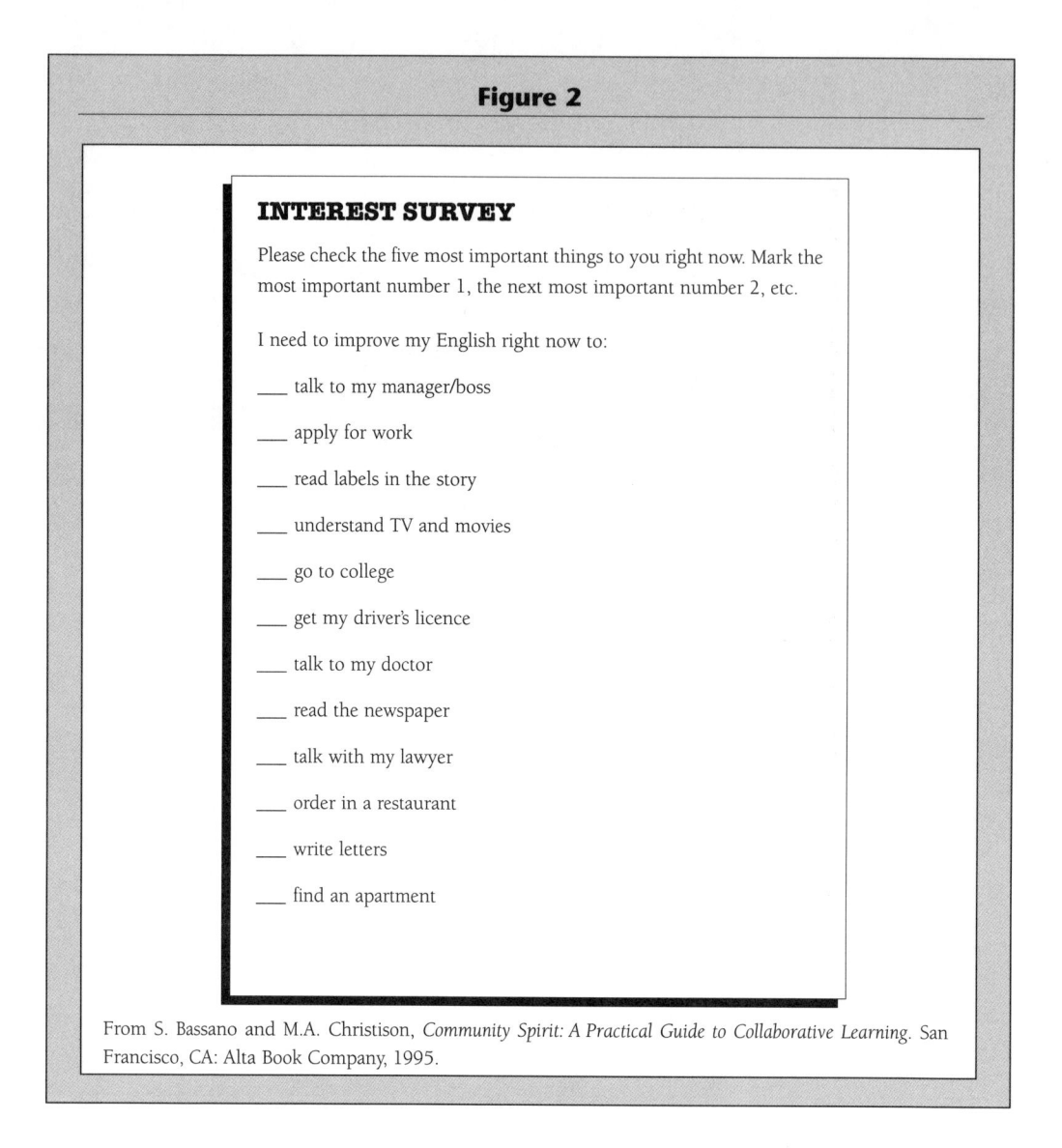

Please check the five most important things to you right now. Mark the most important number 1, the next most important number 2, etc.

I need to improve my English right now to:

___ talk to my manager/boss

___ apply for work

___ read labels in the story

___ understand TV and movies

___ go to college

___ get my driver's licence

___ talk to my doctor

___ read the newspaper

___ talk with my lawyer

___ order in a restaurant

___ write letters

___ find an apartment

From S. Bassano and M.A. Christison, *Community Spirit: A Practical Guide to Collaborative Learning*. San Francisco, CA: Alta Book Company, 1995.

Values Clarification process affirms that monitoring and evaluating progress can be much more than merely testing and assigning grades based on performance. When creatively designed, it can be a very valuable tool to inspire students to learn and provide a basis for formation of positive attitudes toward learning—especially when students are involved in monitoring and assessing their own progress. Values Clarification provides a few easily adaptable models toward meeting this objective, in the way of interviews and conferences with the instructor, monitoring sheets, self-rating forms or rubrics, and student-designed point systems for extra effort. Below, again from *Community Spirit*, are three such strategies to serve as brief examples, followed by sample forms (Bassano and Christison 1995).

Self-Monitoring and Self-Evaluation Strategies

Strategy 1: Progress Conferences
Individual conferences with students let them know how you feel about their progress and participation; any academic problems they may be having are identified and discussed. Conferences can be called by either you or the student as often as necessary to monitor progress and identify problems and solutions. We have found that using a Progress Form with a rating scale as a mediator can help keep the conference focused. (See Figure 3 page 140.) Sometimes only the student fills in a Progress Form and talks about it with you. Other times you both will respond to a Progress Form and compare your perceptions.

Strategy 2: Monitor Sheets
Before you begin group tasks, tell students that at the end of the activity, they will be asked to rate themselves and their groups for active participation by turning in a Monitoring Sheet to the teacher. (See Figure 4 page 141.) If students in a group actively participated in English during the entire task, they could, for example, receive a rating of 10. If they only sat and listened, they could rate themselves a 4 or 5. If they paid no attention and did not participate, they could rate themselves as 1. This evaluation strategy helps students become aware of their own participation patterns as they are being carried out and provides feedback from group members.

Strategy 3: Extra Credit
In addition to points earned for work turned in, for examinations, and for participation, students may earn extra credit for time they spend practising their English outside of the classroom. This system can be set up by the students themselves. Start a list on the board of possible extra credit tasks. Have students brainstorm a list of other possibilities. What do they think will help their English improve? Decide together how many points each activity should earn. Create a checksheet and copy off a large stack of them for students to take and turn in weekly. (See Figure 5 page 141.) Students seem to respond well to these self-determined point systems because they receive instant gratification for the tasks accomplished. They have a greater freedom to pursue the activity that interests them and to choose where, when, and how to carry out their practice. They are able to make up for poor performance in some areas by doing alternative activities.

If highly beneficial language learning activities, such as sustained silent reading and writing of compositions are given a higher point value than watching TV or filling in extra-credit worksheets, there is more incentive to carry out these tasks. Even in a program that doesn't assign grades, students still respond to the points they receive as acknowledgement of their efforts.

Figure 3

Sample Progress Form #1

Student Self-Evaluation Meeting with the Teacher

Name _____ Date _____

I come to school	sometimes	usually	every day
I am learning	a little bit		a lot
I have friends in class. one	two or three	several	many
I study at home never	sometimes	often	always
English is	always difficult	sometimes difficult	easy
I like my class not much	a little bit	most of the time	always

Sample Progress Form #2

Student Self-Evaluation Meeting with the Teacher

Name _____ Date _____

I am	happy with my work	1 2 3 4 5	not happy with my work
My grammar	is improving	1 2 3 4 5	is not improving
My writing	is improving	1 2 3 4 5	is not improving
My speaking ability	is improving	1 2 3 4 5	is not improving
My reading ability	is improving	1 2 3 4 5	is not improving

The thing that was the hardest for me this week was _____
_____

What I can do to learn English more quickly: _____
_____

Sample Progress Form #3

Name _____ Date _____

1 = absolutely yes   8 = absolutely not

	Student self-rating	Teacher rating of student
I always do my best in this class.	1 2 3 4 5 6 7 8	1 2 3 4 5 6 7 8
I study outside of class.	1 2 3 4 5 6 7 8	1 2 3 4 5 6 7 8
I ask for help when I need it.	1 2 3 4 5 6 7 8	1 2 3 4 5 6 7 8
I have made an extra effort to reach goals that are important to me.	1 2 3 4 5 6 7 8	1 2 3 4 5 6 7 8
I am satisfied with my progress.	1 2 3 4 5 6 7 8	1 2 3 4 5 6 7 8
I am working well with my group.	1 2 3 4 5 6 7 8	1 2 3 4 5 6 7 8
I try to contact native speakers outside of class.	1 2 3 4 5 6 7 8	1 2 3 4 5 6 7 8
I am improving in my grammar.	1 2 3 4 5 6 7 8	1 2 3 4 5 6 7 8
I am improving in my speaking ability.	1 2 3 4 5 6 7 8	1 2 3 4 5 6 7 8
I am improving in my writing ability.	1 2 3 4 5 6 7 8	1 2 3 4 5 6 7 8
I am improving in my listening ability.	1 2 3 4 5 6 7 8	1 2 3 4 5 6 7 8
My reading is improving.	1 2 3 4 5 6 7 8	1 2 3 4 5 6 7 8

From S. Bassano and M.A. Christison, *Community Spirit: A Practical Guide to Collaborative Learning.* San Francisco, CA: Alta Book Company, 1995.

Figure 4

GROUP PARTICIPATION RATING SHEET

Date: _____

1. I was an active participant. I talked, I listened, and I assisted my group.
2. I talked and listened most of the time.
3. I talked and listened only a little today.
4. I only listened today.
5. I didn't participate today.

I rate myself today _____

I rate my group today _____

From S. Bassano and M.A. Christison, *Community Spirit: A Practical Guide to Collaborative Learning*. San Francisco, CA: Alta Book Company, 1995.

Figure 5

EXTRA CREDIT FOR EXTRA EFFORT

Name: _____

For the Week of _____ to _____	Points
I watched TV in English for two hours.	(1)
I listened to talk radio in English for two hours.	(1)
I came to class every day this week.	(2)
I asked questions during the interviews.	(3)
I attended listening lab for one hour.	(4)
I completed an extra credit homework assignment.	(4)
I spoke only English during class.	(5)
I was an active group participant in class.	(5)
I turned in a perfect paper.	(10)
I had a conversation with a native speaker in English.	(10)
I read 10 extra pages in English.	(10)
I completed an oral or written book report.	(15)
I wrote an extra full-page paper.	(15)
I talked on the telephone for 5 minutes in English.	(15)
I called a business on the telephone for information.	(15)

From S. Bassano and M.A. Christison, *Community Spirit: A Practical Guide to Collaborative Learning*. San Francisco, CA: Alta Book Company, 1995.

Conclusion

In conclusion, regarding teaching English for Academic Purposes in a setting where the language is not spoken outside of the classroom, students learn to talk by talking. They learn to listen by listening. Both are based in face-to-face interaction. Language teaching techniques based in Values Clarification process encourage students to talk and listen to one another in a real context and provide clear guidelines and structure within which to interact.

Regarding immigrant and visiting student classrooms, in the country where English is the primary language spoken outside the classroom, according to my own mentor, Sidney Simon, only when students develop and clarify their own values, weigh the pros and cons of various alternatives, make their own informed choices, solve their own problems, and critically evaluate the results of their actions may they truly take their place as independent adults in a society. Because this independence and sense of place are primary goals of our immigrants (and visiting students, albeit temporarily), ESL teachers creatively design strategies and use methods, materials, and models adapted from such diverse and timeless sources as Values Clarification to encourage students to consider alternative modes of believing and acting, to think critically, to discover and delight in their new options both in and out of class, and then to take action.

Appendix

Sample Strategies Based in Values Clarification Process

Some of the generic strategies you use (or may choose to use) in your classroom on a daily basis had their origins in Values Clarification strategies developed by Sidney Simon and his colleagues. Following are brief random samples. Some are teacher-designed, values-based activities; others are excerpted by permission of the publishers from a variety of language teaching resources, kindergarten through university, beginning through advanced.

Sample #1

> **ONE-MINUTE AUTOBIOGRAPHY**
>
> In groups of three, you each have one minute to tell "the story of your life." Take turns around the circle. Listen carefully to each other. Listen for the signal bell.
>
> When you have finished, discuss the following:
>
> 1. What makes up a one-minute autobiography?
> 2. Did you and your partners share different kinds of things or were they similar?
> 3. Did you mention your:
>   family?
>   education?
>   work history?
>   accomplishments?
>   _____?
> 4. What sort of "milestones" or special events did you choose to share?
> 5. When you are finished, prepare to report back what you learned in this exercise.

Sample teacher-designed values-based activity, unpublished. Objectives: personal reflection, sharing things about ourselves and our lives with peers, finding common ground, oral fluency building.

Sample #2

FIVE YEARS FROM TODAY

Where do you want to be five years from today? What do you want to be doing? Who do you want to be with? Draw a picture about where you want to be five years from today.

Write about your drawing.

Where do you want to be, with whom, and doing what?

_____
_____
_____
_____

Share your drawing and sentences with your classmates.

INTERVIEW!

Sit down with a partner. Ask your partner the questions and listen carefully. Write your partner's answers on the lines. Your partner will question you the same way and write your answers. If you forget what your partner said, it is okay to ask again! When you are finished, sit down in groups of four. Tell the other group members what you learned about your partner. Trade papers with your partner after the group work.

1. Where do you want to be five years from today?
_____
_____
_____

2. What do you want to be doing?
_____
_____
_____

3. Do you want to be working or going to school? If so, where?
_____
_____
_____

4. Are you making any special plans to help you achieve this goal?
_____
_____
_____

From S. Bassano and M.A. Christison. *Drawing Out.* San Francisco, CA: Alta Book Company, 1995. Objectives: reflecting on, clarifying, and affirming future plans or aspirations; oral fluency building.

Sample #3

INTERVIEW

The Arts

1. Do you feel that the arts are important? In what ways?
2. Do you enjoy art? What kind of art do you prefer?
3. In your opinion, who was/is the greatest artist in the world?
4. Do you enjoy dancing or watching others dance? What kind of dancing do you enjoy the most?
5. What is your opinion of the ballet?
6. How do you feel about opera? Have you seen one? Why?
7. Is it possible to dislike all music or have no sense of rhythm?
8. Do you prefer modern music over classical?
9. What is your favourite instrument?
10. Who are your favourite actors and actresses?
11. Do you enjoy going to the theatre? What kind?
12. What kinds of movies do you prefer? Do you rent movies and play them at home, or do you enjoy going to the cinema?
13. Are you artistic? Why or why not?
14. Have you ever participated in a talent show or play? Were you nervous?
15. Do you have a favourite painter or photographer? Do you enjoy painting or taking photographs?
16. Have you been to a museum in the last year? Why or why not?
17. Do you enjoy going to the circus? Do you think the circus is an art form? What is your favourite circus act?
18. Who was your favourite movie character when you were a child?
19. Do you prefer going to a concert or staying at home and listening to music?
20. Which musical groups are your favourite?
21. Who is your favourite male or female vocalist?
22. What do you think of country music? Rap music? Rock?
23. Who was the greatest musical performer of all time?
24. Would you enjoy the attention you would get being a performer, or would you prefer to have your privacy?

PROCEDURES FOR INTERVIEWS

1. Two students come to the front of the room and speak for three minutes about the question on the card. One student initiates the interview with the question while the second responds. The interviewer can ask any additional questions to elicit more information. The other students listen and monitor the mistakes.
2. Group the students into pairs and have them discuss a card for three to five minutes. Give each pair a different card. Then ask the students to pass the card to the pair on their left. This procedure is repeated until each group has spoken about the question on each card. Circulate around the room, listening in on each pair and marking any mistakes on the mistake cards. After all the interview cards have been completed, the students look at their mistake cards and correct them. Circulate to assist with corrections.

From N.E. Zelman. *Conversation Inspirations*. Brattleboro: Prolingua Associates, 1996.
Objectives: personal reflection, clarifying and publicly expressing individual values and opinions, speaking up in front of a group.

Sample #4

RANK ORDER

Read the choices. Rank order them according to importance to you in your life right now. Number 1 = most important.

In groups of four, share your top three choices and your last choice. Add one of your own if it is missing.

___ personal financial security

___ social recognition or respect

___ close comfortable family ties

___ wisdom or mature understanding

___ true friendship

___ sense of accomplishment

___ peace and quiet

___ self-respect/personal integrity

___ a pleasurable, leisurely life

___ mature love (spiritual or sexual intimacy)

___ personal freedom

___ an exciting, active life

Sample teacher-designed values-based activity, unpublished. Objectives: clarifying, prioritizing and affirming values; expressing desires and opinions; oral fluency building.

Sample #5

INTERVIEW
Talk

> race
> colour
> ethnic group
> discrimination

DISCUSSION
- What makes people different?
- Are there different kinds of people in your neighbourhood?
- How can different kinds of people live and work peacefully together?

MORE QUESTIONS
- Which ethnic groups live in your neighbourhood or work with you?
- Which languages do your neighbours or co-workers speak?
- Do people of different colour live in your neighbourhood or work with you?
- Who do people discriminate against?
- Why do people discriminate against others?
- Has anyone ever discriminated against you? What happened?
- When should you report discrimination to the police or a social worker?

SUMMARY
- What is discrimination?
- When someone discriminates against you, what can you do?

INTERVIEW
Talk

> immigrant
> refugee
> citizen

DISCUSSION
- Why did you leave your country?
- Why did you come to _____?
- What can you and your family do in North America?

MORE QUESTIONS
- Why did you become a refugee or immigrant?
- What is good about life in North America?
- What is bad about life here?
- What do North Americans look like? Eat? Wear?
- What do you enjoy doing the most here?
- Do you miss the most about your country?
- Do you want to become a citizen?
- What do you hope for your own future?
- What do you hope for your family's future?

SUMMARY
- What do you think about living in North America?
- What do you hope for as a new citizen?

From *In print: Beginning Literacy through Cultural Awareness* by Long/Spiegel-Podnecky. Copyright © 1988. Reprinted by permission by Addison Wesley Longman, Inc. Objectives: personal reflection, expressing past and present values, finding commonalities in past experience, critical thinking.

148 EXPANDING OUR VISION

Sample #6

ALL ABOUT ME

Name _____

1. I am a _____

2. I am _____ and _____

3. I have _____

4. I live _____

5. I eat _____

6. I can _____

THIS MAKES ME:
happy, sad, afraid, angry

Name _____

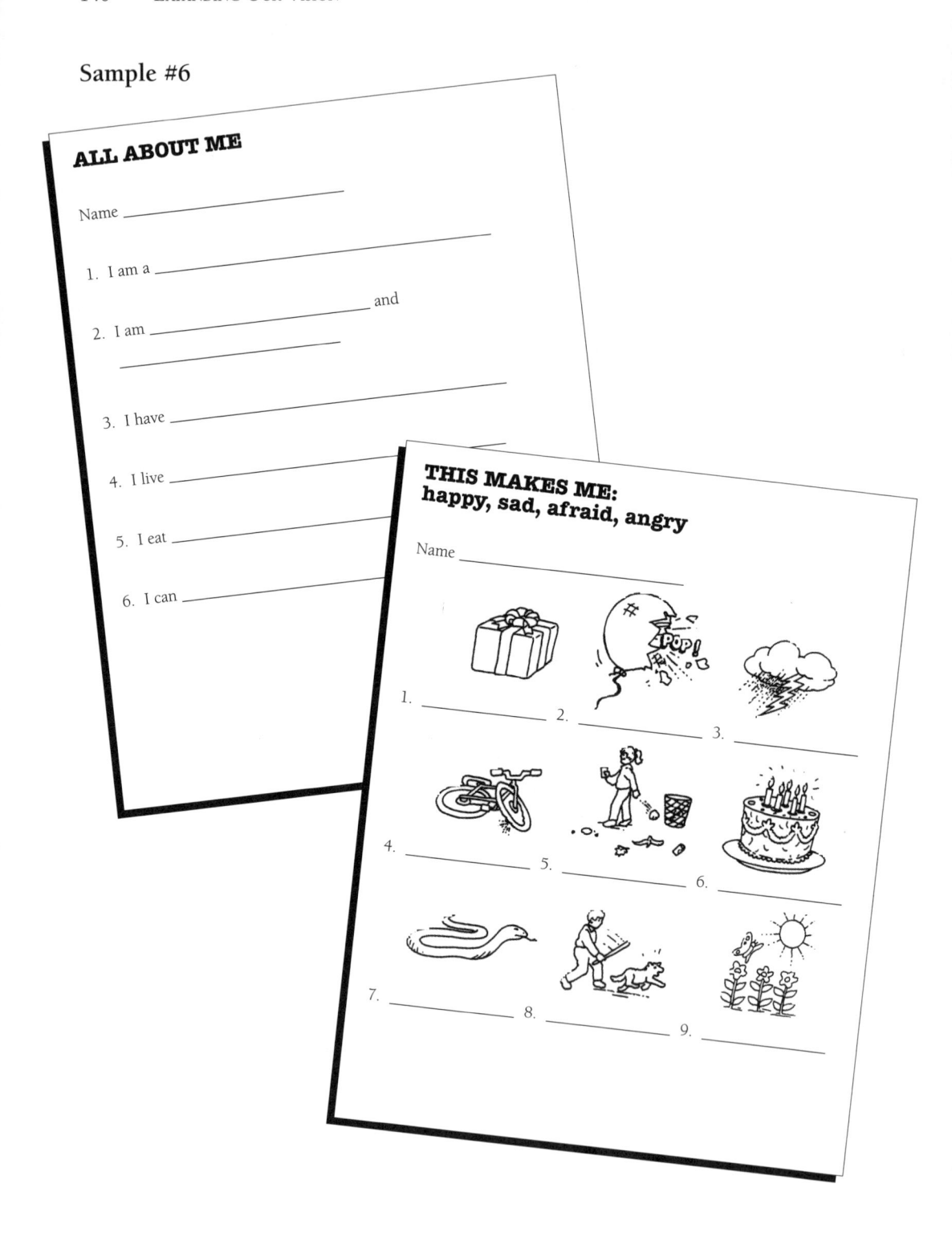

1. _____ 2. _____ 3. _____

4. _____ 5. _____ 6. _____

7. _____ 8. _____ 9. _____

From E. Claire. *Wonder Workbooks*. San Francisco, CA: Alta Book Company, 1991. Objectives: reflection on feelings, affirming values, describing ourselves, oral fluency and literacy development.

Sample #7

DAILY PIE

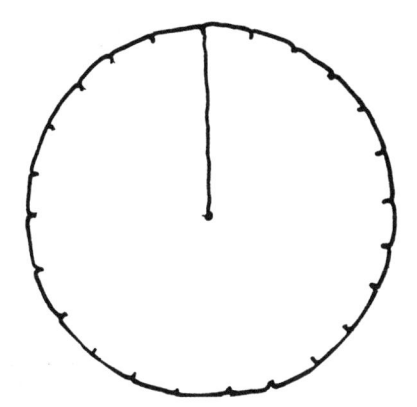

This pie is divided into 24 pieces. Each piece is one hour of your day.

Divide your pie according to how many hours you usually spend in a typical weekday doing the following:

- eating • working at home • watching TV • sleeping
- working for money • bathing and dressing • running errands
- relaxing • talking to your family or friends • studying English

** Do you have extra hours? What else do you do during the day? Finish your pie and label the parts.

** Look at your partner's daily pie. How is it different from yours? How is it the same?

** Write about your daily pie. What do you see? What parts of your pie do you especially like? What parts would you like to change? How could you change your day?

Sample teacher-designed values-based activity, unpublished. Objectives: personal reflection, sharing things about ourselves and our lives with peers, finding common ground, oral fluency building.

Sample #8

MONEY GAME

Directions: *Work with a partner.* Your teacher will bring catalogues and newspaper advertisements to class. With your partner, imagine that you have $250 to spend together. Decide what items you will buy. They should be things you need and want right now. You must agree with your partner on the items. Write the items and their cost on the chart below. (Remember: Don't go over $250.) *Share your list with the rest of the class.*

Item	Cost
1.	
2.	
3.	
4.	
5.	
6.	
7.	
8.	
9.	
10.	
11.	
12.	

PERFECT MATCH

Directions: *Work alone.* Complete each of the statements below by circling a, b, or c. Then listen carefully as your teacher explains what to do next.

1. A perfect Saturday night is
   a. a symphony concert and dessert
   b. a fancy, expensive dinner and a walk in the moonlight
   c. a large combination pizza and a good James Bond movie
2. A perfect movie is
   a. a romantic comedy with lots of rock and roll music
   b. a wild, jungle rescue adventure
   c. a mystery with helicopters, computer wizards, fast cars, and guns
3. A perfect day off is
   a. a long drive in the country
   b. shopping in the big city
   c. cleaning and fixing little things around the house; putting my home in order
4. A perfect vacation is
   a. swimming, sunning, sailing, dancing on a sunny island
   b. sightseeing, shopping, eating at good restaurants in a faraway city
   c. relaxing at home with my family
5. A perfect pet is
   a. a big, old, loving, friendly, playful dog
   b. a quiet, beautiful, independent cat
   c. a large goldfish in an outdoor pond

From M.A. Christison and S. Bassano *Purple Cows and Potato Chips*. San Francisco, CA: Alta Book Company, 1995. Objectives: choosing from alternatives, affirming choices, collaboration, oral fluency building.

Sample #9

WEEKLY REACTION GRID

Something that made me happy this week.	A plan I made this week to do something I want to do.
A compliment I got this week.	How I helped someone this week.
A disagreement I had this week.	How my week could have been better.
Three choices I made this week.	Something new I learned this week.
A compliment I gave to someone else this week.	What I will do to make next week even better.
What I did this week that I was proud of.	The best day of this week.
How this week was different from last week.	What business I had left over this week–something I did not finish.

Sample teacher-designed values-based activity, unpublished. Students write short responses to two or three of these kinds of topics, to be shared and amplified verbally in class. Objectives: personal reflection, clarification and affirmation of experiences and thoughts, critical thinking, finding common ground, building empathy, oral fluency practice.

Sample #10

SILLY INVENTIONS

Directions: Work with a small group (3 to 5 students). Look at the picture below. It is a machine that can do anything you want. With your classmates, decide on *five* things you want this machine to do to help you in your life. Remember, the machine can do *anything* you want, and it can do more than one thing at a time. Explain exactly which part of the machine does what. *Share your information with the class.*

Part of the machine	What it does
1.	
2.	
3.	
4.	
5.	

SENTENCE STARTERS

Directions: Work with the rest of the class. Introduce yourself to a classmate. Then ask that classmate to complete one of the statements below. Write down the person's response and name next to the statement. Ask a different classmate to respond to another statement. Continue interviewing other students until your exercise sheet is complete. Be sure to write down each student's name and share your responses with the rest of the class.

1. My favourite food is _____
2. I like this class because _____
3. My teacher is _____
4. If I had $500, I would _____
5. College is _____
6. The colour I like best is _____ because _____
7. Television is _____
8. My favourite thing to do on weekends is _____
9. The most difficult thing about English is _____
10. People who ride bicycles are _____
11. Studying is _____
12. In five years I want to be _____

From M.A. Christison and S. Bassano *Purple Cows and Potato Chips*. San Francisco, CA: Alta Book Company, 1995. Objectives: reflection, clarifying and affirming values, collaboration, oral fluency building.

REFERENCES CITED

Bassano, S., and M.A. Christison. 1995. *Community Spirit: A Practical Guide to Collaborative Language Learning.* San Francisco, CA: Alta Book Company.

———. 1995. *Drawing Out.* San Francisco, CA: Alta Book Company.

Christison, M.A. and S. Bassano. 1995. *Purple Cows and Potato Chips.* San Francisco, CA: Alta Book Company.

Claire, E. 1991. *Wonder Workbooks.* San Francisco, CA: Alta Book Company.

Long, L., and J. Spiegel-Podnecky. 1988. *In Print: Beginning Literacy Through Cultural Awareness.* Menlo Park: Addison Wesley.

Simon, S. 1990. *Forgiveness.* New York: Warner Books.

———., 1993. *In Search of Values.* New York: Warner Books.

Simon, S., H. Kirschenbaum and L. Howe. 1972. *Values Clarification, A Handbook of Practical Strategies for Teachers and Students.* New York: Hart Publications.

Simon, S., and S. Wendkos-Olds. 1978. *Helping Your Child Find Values to Live By.* New York: Warner Books.

Zelman, N. E. 1996. *Conversation Inspirations.* Brattleboro: Prolingua Associates.

ADDITIONAL BIBLIOGRAPHY

Christison, M.A., and S. Bassano. 1995. *Look Who's Talking.* San Francisco, CA: Alta Book Company.

Genzel, R., and M. Graves-Cummings. 1994. *Culturally Speaking.* Boston: Heinle and Heinle.

Huizenga, J., and M. Thomas-Ruzic. 1992. *All Talk.* Boston: Heinle and Heinle.

Klippel, F. 1985. *Keep Talking.* New York: Cambridge University Press.

Little, L., and I. Greenburg. 1991. *Problem Solving.* Menlo Park: Addison Wesley.

Numrich, C. 1994. *Raise the Issues.* Menlo Park: Addison Wesley.

Rooks, G. 1983. *Can't Stop Talking.* Boston: Heinle and Heinle.

———. 1986. *Non-Stop Discussion Workbook.* Boston: Heinle and Heinle.

———. 1994. *Let's Start Talking.* Boston: Heinle and Heinle.

Schoenberg, I. 1989. *Talk About Values.* Menlo Park: Addison Wesley Publishers.

Simon, S., H. Kirschenbaum and L. Howe. 1995. *Values Clarification: A Practical, Action-Directed Workbook.* New York: Warner Books.

Stevick, E. 1990. *Humanism in Language Teaching*. New York: Oxford University Press.

Tomalin, B., and S. Templeski. 1994. *Cultural Awareness*. New York: Oxford University Press.

Ur, P. 1991. *Discussions That Work: Task-Centered Fluency Practice*. New York: Cambridge University Press.

CHAPTER NINE

GREGORY BATESON

❖

COMMUNICATION AND CONTEXT
An Ecological Perspective of Language Teaching

Mark A. Clarke
University of Colorado at Denver

INTRODUCTION

Gregory Bateson was one of the most original thinkers of the 20th century. The son of William Bateson (the British biologist who coined the term "genetics" in the process of founding that discipline), Bateson grew up among England's intellectual elite. Trained as a biologist and anthropologist, he conducted ground-breaking work in a number of other disciplines as well, including psychiatry, ethology, and ecology. His thinking influenced many social scientists—R.D. Laing, Erving Goffman, and Konrad Lorenz, for example—and he served on the University of California Board of Regents at the request of then Governor Jerry Brown, who valued his views on education. The potential contributions of Bateson to language teachers can be seen as two large and overlapping areas, epistemology and methodology—how we know what we know and how we act on that knowledge. Bateson insisted that we attempt to live in ways that are consistent with the fact that ours is a communicational universe, in which meaning and information are more important than energy and mass. This means, among other things, that we see the world as a swarming bundle of "to whom it may concern" messages, and that we understand that we are communicating all the time through our behaviour, the arrangement of classroom space, the rhythm and pace of our teaching, and through the things that we do not say as well as the things that we do say. It would mean that teaching would be understood as the creating of contexts in which learners experience the relationship between actions, objects, and language, rather than as the didactic presentation of facts or dialogues, situations, or communicative interactions. Successful teaching (by which I mean teacher conduct that results in people learning the language) is the creating of coherent contexts, in which all messages (explicit and implicit) swirl around a core of values, and which contribute to a secure environment in which learners can explore and experiment. The basis of such teaching is communication within relationships, not method or materials, much less curriculum.

This assertion does not provide much comfort for any but the veteran teacher who is happily ensconced in habitual ways of teaching. If teaching is a function of relationship, then it is like all of the rest of life. Each of us has to discover our own truths and make our own way, learning from our mistakes and celebrating our own triumphs. There are no prescriptions or rules to follow. The best way for me to convey the potential contributions of Gregory Bateson to language educators is to tell my own story, and let you decide if there are lessons you can take away for yourself. This is appropriate. Bateson used to tell the story of the computer faced with an insoluble problem, whirring and whizzing, and finally spitting out the message, "That reminds me of a story ..."

Like most of what Bateson wrote, the story resonates with parable-esque ambiguity, so its meaning is not entirely clear. I have always taken it to mean that there are no easy answers to important questions, no direct prescriptions with easy steps to follow. The best way to proceed is to tell stories, and to permit the listeners to make whatever sense they can of them. So, begging your indulgence, I will intersperse my discussion of Bateson with personal anecdote.

Expanding My Vision

I'll begin with my own experience as a language learner. As a ninth grader in first-year Spanish, I found I had a facility for language learning. I enjoyed the drills and dialogues orchestrated by Señor Benevidez, and the class was certainly different from anything I expected. It was conducted entirely in Spanish; we memorized mountains of dialogues, and we were expected to discern grammatical and lexical meaning without the benefit of English explanations—without even a textbook. In fact, we saw no written Spanish at all until halfway through the year. It was not until I got to high school that I was confronted with the request by another teacher to "conjugate the verb *estar.*" I was struck dumb; I had never heard the word "conjugate," nor was I prepared for instruction, conducted principally in English, on Spanish grammar. I did not enjoy these classes much, and it is probably instructive that I cannot remember the teacher's name, but I did learn how to analyze the parts of a sentence. Later in the year, the ebullient Señorita Burrow crashed into our lives with infectious enthusiasm and communicative language learning activities. She did not use drills or require us to memorize dialogues, but the classroom was the scene of riotous conversation and improvisation, and the students did most of the talking. In subsequent years at the University of Colorado, I had a wide range of Spanish teachers, each of whom approached teaching in different ways.

These experiences as a language learner later proved to be instructive. I was not particularly reflective about the teaching I experienced as a schoolboy, but like all learners I had definite preferences for particular teachers, activities, and materials. Without knowing it, I had developed an awareness of differing approaches to language teaching. In my studies at the University of Colorado, the American University in Cairo, and the University of Michigan, I learned that those three teachers were adherents of the "audiolingual method," "grammar translation," and "communicative competence" paradigms, respectively. Thus began my attempts to understand language teaching and learning.

At first, my focus was narrowly instructional; I was searching for teaching methods that would motivate students and provide effective mechanisms for mastering content and skills. It did not take long, however, for me to realize that classrooms are situated in complex relationships with schools, community, and culture, and that any attempt to understand teaching and learning that does not include these will surely fail. I found the work of several social scientists helpful as I sought to forge connections between the classroom and "the world out there." But it is Bateson, with his analysis of systems and system change, who has provided me with the theoretical perspective of human interaction and learning that frames all of my work. Pete Becker, a friend of Bateson's and a professor of linguistics at the University of

Michigan, was the person who suggested I read *Steps to an Ecology of Mind* not long after it came out in 1972.

Steps to an Ecology of Mind struck a chord with me. In subsequent years I read Bateson's other books and countless works by anthropologists, linguists, psychologists, and others who grappled with his ideas, but it is this book that has been my touchstone. The book caused a ripple of excitement on college campuses across the nation when it came out, and it occasioned intense conversations in the teaching assistant cubicles at the English Language Institute. I remember Michelle, a friend and fellow TA, confessing to a certain amount of confusion concerning the little yellow paperback. It seemed to her to be an odd collection of writings that circled topics but never quite addressed them. Indeed, the first seven entries are reports of conversations between a man and his daughter—Gregory and Mary Catherine Bateson, perhaps—with intriguing titles such as "Why do things get in a muddle?" and "Why do Frenchmen?" They are written in such a way that the content and form of the dialogue reflect the problem being explored; in other words, they are examples of themselves, which accounts for their name. Michelle found them entertaining, but she was disappointed when she failed to discover some explanation for them. What did they mean? Bateson doesn't explain; he merely elaborates, and each elaboration moves the topic forward somewhat, but for every riddle solved, another is introduced to take its place.

Bateson characterizes the book as a collection of the most important pieces he had written up to that point in his life, with the exception of items too long to be included or too trivial and ephemeral to merit attention. The pieces cover four broad areas—anthropology, psychiatry, biological evolution, and genetics—and "the new epistemology which comes out of systems theory and ecology" (Bateson 1972: xii). The essays are pleasingly redundant and overlapping. Key concepts—form and content, context, pattern, and information—recur in ways that cause you to adjust conclusions that you had thought comfortably concluded.

Bateson's life work constituted an attempt to understand the pattern that connects all living things and ideas about living things—ferns, crabs, tide pools, school children, definitions of art, understandings of beauty, prejudice, and addiction, just to name some topics that occupied his thinking. He believed that Western approaches to teaching and learning were based on misconceptions about the nature of the world, and that they created divisions between the objects of understanding and the processes by which they were understood.

> *The pattern which connects.* Why do schools teach almost nothing of the pattern which connects? … What pattern connects the crab to the lobster and the orchid to the primrose and all the four of them to you and me? And me to you? And all the six of us to the amoeba in one direction and to the backward schizophrenic in another (Bateson 1979: 8)?

The answer, according to Bateson, was relationships among things—shapes and forms and patterns of messages sent and received. He argued that we need to recognize commonalities across individuals and situations, and he believed that an understanding of systems theory provides the basis for that understanding. He introduces the second part of *Steps to an Ecology of Mind* with the following example.

> The man who studies the arrangement of leaves and branches in the growth of a flowering plant may note an analogy between the formal relations between stems, leaves, and buds, and the formal relations that obtain between different sorts of words in a sentence. He will think of a "leaf" not as something flat and green but as something related in a particular way to the stem from which it grows and to the secondary stem (or bud) which is formed in the angle between leaf and primary stem. Similarly, the modern linguist thinks of a "noun" not as the "name of a person, place, or thing," but as a member of a class of words defined by their relationship in sentence structure to "verbs" and other parts. Those who think first of the "things" which are related (the "*relata*") will dismiss any analogy between grammar and the anatomy of plants as far-fetched. After all, a leaf and a noun do not at all resemble each other in outward appearance. But if we think first of the relationships and consider the *relata* as defined solely by their relationships, then we begin to wonder: Is there a profound analogy between grammar and anatomy? Is there an interdisciplinary science which should concern itself with such analogies? What would such a science claim as its subject matter? And why should we expect such far-flung analogies to have significance (Bateson 1972: 154)?

The answer is deceptively simple—because both plant anatomy and sentence structure are communicational phenomena. This passage provides an example of Bateson's approach to systems thinking.

Systems Thinking

Bateson was a biologist turned anthropologist, and his interests ranged from genetics and the problem of evolution, to patterns of communication in dolphins, to the impact of technological innovation on the ecological system. He was also interested in the interpersonal and institutional dynamics of alcoholism and schizophrenia. One way to summarize his interests is to say that he wanted to understand the relationship between formal theory and human activity, and he wanted his audience to understand that we cannot escape the redundancy of the two. Theory impacts action and action impacts theory.

> … I try to teach my students … that in scientific research you start from two beginnings, each of which has its own kind of authority: the observations can-

not be denied, and the fundamentals must be fitted. You must achieve a sort of pincers maneouver" (Bateson 1972: xxi).

This is a far wider range of phenomena than most of us feel compelled to consider in our work, but an important contribution of Bateson's thinking is precisely this—the pressure to expand our vision, to see the patterns that connect seemingly unconnected phenomena. He would certainly agree on the value of a collection of essays such as this one. Central to his understanding of the world was the construct of system, which he also called "cybernetic system" and "mind." In the following paragraph he defines "system."

> Let me list what seem to me to be those essential minimal characteristics of a system ... (1) The system shall operate with and upon differences. (2) The system shall consist of closed loops or networks of pathways along which differences and transforms of difference shall be transmitted. (What is transmitted on a neuron is not an impulse, it is news of a difference.) (3) Many events within the system shall be energized by the respondent part rather than by impact from the triggering part. (4) The system shall show self-correctiveness in the direction of homeostasis and/or in the direction of runaway (Bateson 1972: 482).

This is a very abstract statement. Perhaps it would be useful if I provided a bit more grounded elaboration. The concept of *difference* is central to Bateson's understanding of all natural phenomena. It is a complex and subtle point, because the notice of difference involves comparison over time. Even the most fundamental act of perception requires this—the saccadic movements of our eyes, or the visually impaired person's fingers moving across the Braille dots, for example. In language teaching, this notice of difference is what happens when a student suddenly sees for the first time the regularity of verb conjugations, or sentence patterns, or cultural phenomena. Once noticed, the point has been learned on some level, even though perhaps not consciously.

The second point, concerning closed loops along which transforms of differences travel, refers to the fact that we experience life as a recursive cycle, and learning occurs as we adjust our understanding, attitude, and behaviour in response to notices of difference. Take the familiar routine of attending language classes, for example. Teachers develop lesson plans that provide new information about language and activities for practising the language in incremental steps, so that students encounter the new in the context of the familiar.

Point number three refers to the fact that living organisms are goal-directed. Events are not entirely predictable because familiar stimuli may produce novel responses, according to the history and current condition of the organisms involved. As language teachers, we know that students bring interests and energy to the class-

room that will influence the course of events. We may arrive with
paraphernalia, but the lesson will develop as a negotiation with the

The last point refers to the fact that living systems function t
whether we are talking about the human body maintaining a body t
37°C [98.6°F] or a language class that seems never to start on time. 1   cor-
rective tendency may be either in the direction of the status quo or in the direction
of "runaway." An example of the latter might be the predictable sequence of escalat-
ing disagreement between two students who compete for the teacher's attention.

All living organisms and aggregates of living organisms are open systems, from single-cell organisms to plants and animals and stable collections of these. The individual human being is the system we are most concerned with, but other systems that require our attention are those in which language teachers play a role—families, schools, classrooms, organizations, businesses, governments, and societies. The elegance of this conception is also its most difficult feature to grasp—that the same set of criteria applies equally to the individual as to all other systems. In other words, Bateson would have us operate on the premise that the task of understanding individuals—even, indeed, understanding ourselves—is the same task we face when we attempt to understand classrooms full of students, school boards, faculty assemblies, or communities. Let me explore in a little more depth some characteristics of systems.

Systems and Environments

Systems interact with their environments. They are both independent of and dependent on the environment in which they exist. This is merely the first of many apparent paradoxes that you will have to keep in mind as you adopt a systems perspective of the world. The exact nature of the tension between this independence and dependence is a source of some controversy in a number of disciplines, but we will not pursue that debate here. The key point is that the unit of analysis is always the individual in context. For example, methods, materials, and lesson plans must be developed with specific individuals in mind, for use in particular circumstances. This aspect of systems accounts for the difficulties school systems have in attempting to standardize curricula and teaching methods.

Control

In open systems, control is distributed throughout the system. The meaning of "control" becomes, in itself, an important issue in systems theory. For our purposes as language teachers, we can define control as the demonstrated ability to influence the functioning of others. We are accustomed to thinking of control in terms of vertical hierarchies—the director or principal is at the top, and the degree of control one exercises diminishes as you move down the hierarchy. And, at least since Rene Descartes, this perspective also applies to the individual. The brain controls the body—"I think, therefore I am." But this is a flawed perception. A moment's reflection convinces us that all control is relative, and power is always negotiated. Even at the level of the individual this is true—witness the struggles we have with ourselves as we attempt to stay on a diet or reduce credit card debt. We believe we are in control, that we are rational beings who set goals, devise plans, and discipline ourselves to accomplish what we have set out to accomplish, but this is an illusion. We must always negotiate with others, and even when others are not involved we find it difficult to accomplish important tasks. If our bodies were controlled by our brains, if parents were the undisputed authority in the family, if the president were in charge of the company, we would not need New Year's resolutions, children would not ignore parents' advice, and production would increase in response to the boss's commands.

The situation is the same in schools; any first-year teacher will tell you that nothing can be more terrifying than a room full of rebellious preschoolers. Systems operate according to discoverable, but non-explicit norms, what we might call thermostatic settings for behaviour. And they function according to these settings in spite of our best efforts to control them. This is not to say that we cannot influence events, but it is important to recognize that we do not have unilateral control over ourselves, our families, our colleagues, our subordinates, or our students.

Constraints

"Cause-and-effect" thinking must be replaced by an understanding of constraints. We are conditioned by experience and the weight of cultural assumption to believe in smooth linear trajectories of cause and effect, but unlike billiard balls, humans are not easily propelled toward a goal. There are always distractions, and people respond differently to different situations. It seems clear that, in order to understand how open systems work, we need a more sophisticated conceptualization than that which permits us to understand billiard balls. Billiard balls are subject to the laws of physics; they respond to physical impact and gravity and the rules of cause and effect. Human beings, on the other hand, are open systems whose response to situations is a function of perception and understanding. Their responses will never be entirely predictable. We must think in terms of probability, rather than predictability. Bateson used the term "restraints" but I use "constraints" because it is the more familiar term in linguistics, and the meaning is the same—any condition that renders an outcome more than randomly predictable (Bateson 1972: 399-410). That is, without constraints the pathways of change would be subject to the laws of probability.

Let's use a common topic of discussion in language teaching circles—student motivation. We typically talk of internal vs. external motivation, and we act as if desire to learn a language were either a relatively stable psychological trait or an attitude subject to direct control by the teacher. However, we must recognize that we cannot make students want to learn. We cannot control them, we can only manipulate the constraints under which they work. A sampling of the constraints we can manipulate to increase student motivation might include the following: interesting and relevant materials, adjustments in the time and the rhythm and pace of class sessions, and variations in the mode of presentation. Other factors, such as peer pressure and family participation also play a role in student motivation but are less directly under the influence of the teacher. All, however, are important constraints in successful language teaching. Notice that "constraint" does not have a negative or positive connotation; it merely refers to conditions which influence student learning.

Information and Meaning

Open systems function on the basis of information. The comparison between humans and billiard balls is an important one, although it may seem that the distinction is obvious. Humans use information and act according to their understanding of the situation, while billiard balls carom around the table according to the impact of the cue ball. The world of billiards is one of physical mass and energy, a Newtonian world where cause and effect are important explanatory devices, and where size and momentum are factors in understanding events and circumstances. When considering open systems, however, we are concerned with meaning, with the receipt of messages and concomitant activity.

Take the notion of leadership, for example. If Newton's perspective were accurate for humans, the best leaders would be the largest and most physically powerful individuals. This is patently not the case, as Napoleon and Gandhi demonstrated, so we need to adjust our thinking about power and leadership. It is common to confuse official titles and organizationally assigned roles with the power that is evident when people follow others. Teachers and directors, for example, are commonly assumed to wield power by virtue of their positions. However, a moment's reflection reveals that their power is largely symbolic; they govern because others permit themselves to be governed. When individuals defy leaders, we see who has the power. This is the basis for the humour in "Home Alone" type movies or films which display ineffectual teachers being terrorized by children. More mundane but far more important are the daily examples of skillful teachers who are able to mold an energetic group of students into a learning community. These teachers are able to govern because they convey information that captures the attention of individual students, not because of the threat of punishments or the promise of rewards.

Survival

Systems function to survive. Systems have no purpose, in the usual sense of the term (Bateson 1972: 426-39). Open systems are alive, and if it were correct to speak of purposes, we would say that their purpose is to continue living. But it is not correct to say this, because this would imply that they have decided to live, that there is some source of unilateral control, and this is inaccurate. We are accustomed to thinking of our own behaviour as being rational, goal-directed, and purposeful. And we are accustomed to thinking of familiar societal institutions—schools, hospitals, courts—as having purposes. But in fact, open systems function merely to survive, and the purposes that we perceive them having are just that—our perceptions of what their purposes are. Another way to state this is to say that systems have as many purposes as there are individuals to perceive them. Take schools, a system with which we all have extensive experience. It is common to hear people complaining about schools. Parents become frustrated with bureaucratic rules and regulations. Administrators fume over the sluggish implementation of mandated reforms. Teachers wonder why they have to waste so much time giving tests when they could be engaged in teaching the skills and knowledge that the tests are designed to measure. At one time or another, everyone concerned with schools might be heard complaining that the purpose of schools has been thwarted by the myopic behaviours of special interest groups. This merely reveals that people have different expectations of schools. Careful observation of people's priorities as revealed by their behaviours on a day-to-day basis shows that everyone involved in schools—children, janitors, teachers, bus drivers, parents, administrators, etc.—has different perceptions of the purpose of schools: to "get an education," earn a paycheque, provide babysitting, prepare workers for the needs of business. Different purposes, same institution, and the system continues to function in spite of differing perceptions of its purpose. The key point here is this: As we teach our classes, and as we work to improve the schools within which we work, we need to keep reminding ourselves that everyone participates according to his or her understanding of relevant purposes, and that changes will not be implemented merely because we deem them necessary.

Flexibility

Open systems require a budget of flexibility to survive. Flexibility is defined as the uncommitted resources available for change (Bateson 1972: 494-504). In environmental terms, this might refer to the ocean's ability to correct itself after massive oil spills. In human terms, the response of societies to war, famine, and overpopulation reveal the amount of flexibility in the system. For example, the human race has always had wars and people have been displaced as a result of these conflicts. The effects of these displacements have always been localized, but now, because of technology, we have less slack in the system. We now have Palestinian children who have no fear of soldiers nor of dying. They face Israeli troops fearlessly, throwing rocks and taking their casualties. The fact that they represent a generation raised in refugee camps, unabsorbed into other Arab cultures, accounts for their sense of hopelessness and their willingness to confront death. In terms of the larger social system, what is significant is that technology permits us to follow events in the Middle East on a day-by-day basis, so that the conflict has become a global affair, rather than a local affair. In addition, technology makes global destruction possible. In this sense, the system has less flexibility: fewer uncommitted resources are available for change.

In terms of our own profession, we have the example of teacher "burnout"—people who are working under such stress, and with so little sense of purpose or accomplishment, that they quit their jobs or suffer breakdowns rather than continue with their work. The pressures on teachers have resulted in a near crisis situation. Teachers have always worked under a certain amount of pressure, and individuals have chosen to quit rather than continue (quitting represents a "resource"—a way of responding to a bad situation to restore equilibrium and health to the individual), but when large numbers of teachers begin to drop out of the schools and competent individuals cannot be found to replace them, the entry into the profession of less qualified, less committed people contributes to more classroom problems and stronger efforts by central administrations to control teachers. And these two trends, among many, further exacerbate the conditions that caused the burnout in the first place. Meanwhile, the increase of diversity—cultural, linguistic, socioeconomic—among students in many schools makes teaching a much more complex phenomenon than it has been in the past. So we witness a downward spiral in the situation—in spite of all the rhetoric, the campaign promises, the money, things just seem to get worse. School systems appear to be losing their budget of flexibility.

Context
Because of the centrality of feedback in a systems perspective of life, an understanding of the importance of context becomes indispensable. In fact, there are bumper stickers that declare, "Context is everything." This is only a slight exaggeration. Bateson defined context as the information we use to make our next move and he asserted that without the ability to predict, to assume that we know what is coming, we cannot learn (Bateson 1972: 279-308). As we attempt to understand teaching and learning, and as we engage in focused change efforts such as language policy and curriculum reform, we need to remember that the unit of analysis is always *individual + context*. While we acknowledge certain consistent characteristics in individuals, we know that situations influence behaviour. In a very important sense, we cannot separate systems from their contexts. In fact, we come to realize that systems are embedded within systems, that distinguishing between systems and their environment is a difficult and ultimately futile task.

This is a complex topic that merits a brief example. Let's consider the contexts of teaching. The most obvious contexts that teachers must consider in making decisions and attempting to change the behaviour, attitude, and skills of students are the classroom and the school. That is, as a teacher I plan activities and gather materials, I take into account the physical constraints of the classroom, the number of learners in the class, and the available furniture and instructional paraphernalia. In addition, I have to consider the rules and regulations of the school, coordination of schedules with colleagues, the schedule of special classes such as gym and music, and the general layout of the building. As the school year gets under way, however, the levels of context that I must take into account multiply. I get to know the students better, and their home situations become part of my image of them. It may turn out that, in addition to the family, I must also consider neighbourhood or peer situations, such as gangs, drugs, violence, etc. In other words, as I examine the options available for instruction, I am attempting to understand the individual learners in the class, but I find that the range and complexity of information required becomes much larger. At some point, of course, I have to act, even though I am aware that I do not have all the information required to understand a situation.

With this broad introduction to systems as background, I will now turn to a discussion of language learning and teaching.

LANGUAGE LEARNING AND TEACHING: ONE LESSON

In the remainder of the chapter I will annotate a lesson from notes I kept during the summer of 1990 when I was teaching an intermediate ESL class at Spring International Language Center in Denver:

> My class that summer was an intermediate-level group of learners from around the world. The class was made up of 13 individuals: 7 Japanese, 6 females and one male, average age about 20; 2 Colombians, both male, about 17 years old; one Russian physician, female, about 40; one Korean male, about 20; one Austrian male, about 19; and one Swiss male, about 19. We met Monday through Thursday from 2:10 to 3:15 p.m. in a large room, which permitted flexible grouping—around a conference table, in small groups around tables, in small groups with chairs pulled into circles, or in one large group circle. Sometimes we used all of these groupings in one class session. It was a lively class composed of individuals who had many reasons for being in the US—to improve their English, to study at American universities, to find political and economic freedom, to relax and enjoy themselves before returning to school. It is not always clear to me which motivation had priority, but I orchestrated events so that the class sessions tended to be opportunities for rambunctious use of the language. I saw my task as focusing the energy without stifling it. At the time I was also working on *Choice Readings,* an intermediate reading text, with colleagues Sandra Silberstein and Barbara Dobson; many of the lessons provided opportunities for classroom testing of readings and exercises from the book (Clarke et al 1996).
>
> I made extensive use of the *Denver Post*, one of two major Denver daily newspapers. I concocted exercises to be done in class and for homework, and I orchestrated group reading and discussion sessions based on what the students and I found of interest on a particular day. We worked on language and literacy skills, and I spent considerable time urging them to be conscious and conscientious in their language learning efforts. They were to keep a journal in which they recorded their efforts, and in which they kept class notes, new vocabulary, etc.

One lesson, which I have come to think of as the "Bug Lesson," involved an article about the noisy invasion of cicadas in the midwestern US that summer. As the students read the newspaper that afternoon, I watched until I noticed a student reading the "Bugs make skin crawl ..." story in the newspaper. I had prepared a lesson around the story that morning. I was ready with some conversational remarks and discussion prompts, and I had prepared a worksheet with comprehension questions and vocabulary work (see Clarke, Dobson, and Silberstein 1996: 153-56). I drew everyone's attention to the story and as they turned to the page in the *Post* I asked scanning questions of the group, encouraging them to shout out answers: "What does the picture show? What are "bugs?" "Which bug is causing the problem?" People chimed in with answers as they focused on the picture and the text. I asked a skimming question: "What is the problem?" They took a few minutes to read, but I was leaning forward in anticipation of their answers, hoping to convey the need to hurry. The discussion of the problem was speculative and somewhat contentious—several students had opinions and they defended them using portions of the text. This was fast-paced and conversational; the idea was to get them to behave in ways typical for newspaper readers—looking quickly at headlines and pictures; asking questions of themselves and reading to answer them; talking among friends about the news of the day.

I noticed that we had about 30 minutes left in the class. I read the story aloud while they followed along. This forced them to read more quickly than they might have wanted to read, emphasizing the psycholinguistic principle that good readers are not word-by-word readers, but rather predictors, skimmers, and scanners who can tolerate ambiguity and partial understanding. Then I gave them time to reread portions as they desired. I passed out the questions I had prepared and told them to work for 10 minutes on their own. After most students had had a chance to answer the questions, I had them get into small groups or pairs. They were to compare answers using the paper to confirm/reject their answers. There was no stated time limit at this point, but I gave them about 15 minutes. The class time ended. The homework was to finish questions if they had not already done so. I called their attention to the last question, which required them to write a paragraph as if it were part of a letter to a friend. I told them to be thinking about this, because we would work on it the next day and it would be the homework assignment for Wednesday. They were to begin imagining what they would say in their letters.

The question now is how to proceed with the remainder of this chapter. I have tried your patience by careening from the dense abstractions of systems theory to the mundane descriptions of a language lesson, and I am aware that I now run the danger of having two sections which do not connect with each other. I would like to try to tie them together, but I want to avoid giving the impression that particular systems concepts can be directly connected to specific teaching techniques. As I implied in the beginning, this view of language teaching—which I refer to in the title of the chapter as an ecological perspective, but which we could just as easily call a systems perspective—is one which does not require lines to be drawn between spheres of thinking or acting. That is, there is just one thing—life—and the healthy conduct of one's life depends, to a certain extent, on being able to make connections between the various parts. Or, more accurately, it means being able to see that as we move through time and space we may use different labels for our behaviour, but we are essentially doing the same things—that, for example, relating the events of the day to one's significant other is essentially the same as explaining a concept to a student. So, I would like to return to the definition of system as I attempt to connect "Bugs" and "Bateson."

> Let me list what seem to me to be those essential minimal characteristics of a system ... (1) The system shall operate with and upon differences. (2) The system shall consist of closed loops or networks of pathways along which differences and transforms of difference shall be transmitted. (What is transmitted on a neuron is not an impulse, it is news of a difference.) (3) Many events within the system shall be energized by the respondent part rather than by impact from the triggering part. (4) The system shall show self-correctiveness in the direction of homeostasis and/or in the direction of runaway (Bateson 1972: 482).

Operating with and upon differences. I know that I need to get students to focus, to see the language the way I see it, and to pay attention to the sorts of details that English speakers notice. At a very fundamental level, students must recognize the particular configuration of print on the page as words, and these words need to convey meanings that we can talk about. On another level, they must learn to recognize the conversational signals used in the culture to indicate turn-taking, questioning, confusion, disagreement, etc. Even the lesson must be recognized for what it is, lest they think we are just sitting around having a pleasant chat.

Closed loops of pathways. Our experience together in this class is a recursive phenomenon—we observe certain routines and rituals, we operate within predictable cycles of activity within which small variations of language use, encounters with new words, and grammatical structures provide opportunities for learning. By the time of the "Bugs" lesson, we had an established routine that included a preliminary time of greetings, followed by focused reading and discussion punctuated by grammar and vocabulary work, and ending with assignments for the next day.

Events within the system energized by the respondent. I put events in motion by presenting the newspaper as the focus of attention, and I orchestrated events as we got rolling, but the direction of the session and the content covered was largely a function of the responses of the students. Their interests provided the energy for the class.

Self-correctiveness in the direction of homeostasis and/or of runaway. All of us, as individuals and as a group, tend to develop comfortable routines and habitual ways of responding to events. This can be a source of resistance to learning, as occurs when students continue to speak their native language or sit back and let others do the work of participating. At the other extreme are cases of student/teacher or student/student interaction characterized by competitive exchanges or challenges to authority. Language classes often develop personalities of their own, and teaching becomes a struggle to move them beyond their homeostatic setting.

I do not claim that the "Bugs" lesson is unique. Indeed, I imagine that it appears much like many communicative-focused language lessons that one might see in intensive English centres around North America on any given day. However, my understanding of what I was doing at the time, and my analysis, now, eight years later, of what was being learned and how that lesson fits into larger patterns of language and identity development for these students are very much influenced by my understanding of systems and system change as developed by Bateson.

This session occurred after several weeks of class, so the students were fairly relaxed and comfortable about classroom procedures and activities. I had worked to create an informal atmosphere in which I exercised control through friendly pressure rather than strong authoritative measures (i.e., quizzes, grade pressure, furrowed brow, etc.). I was only moderately happy with the results, because the two Colombians and the Japanese male were serious party animals who tended to influence the class in ways I viewed as frivolous. I would have liked them to be more serious in their approach to activities, but I would have had to abandon the informal approach to accomplish it, and I was not willing to do this. This is consistent with the view that the only way to change people is to create the conditions for them to change themselves, and while more coercive measures might have resulted in their conforming to my expectations for a short period, I think the changes in attitude and study habits would have been short-lived.

The "Bugs" lesson also reflects my conviction that improvements in language learning attitudes and strategies can only occur when students are given opportunities for authentic language experiences—opportunities to seek information and ideas that they are interested in, and to read for their own purposes. By reading the newspaper and talking in a conversational manner, I modelled the behaviour I would like them to adopt. I tried to maintain a low profile as teacher during this time. However, I also believe that ESL students need focused input—in this case literacy and language practice that is transparently organized to improve their skills. I therefore got up at the crack of dawn and read through the paper in search of appropriate material for class work. I prepared the questions with students' abilities and interests in mind, and with an awareness of the language and reading skills I wanted to develop.

Bateson identified levels of learning from the relatively simple act of noticing the clock and "learning" that it is lunch time, to the subtle and complex insight that occurs when one learns how to learn, i.e., that one can adopt different strategies for learning (Bateson 1972: 279-308). Because learning is occurring all the time, and because each learner brings his or her own experiences to bear on the current situation, I do not try to control what is being learned. In this lesson, there were some items being learned by everyone—vocabulary pertinent to the situation with the cicadas, for example. But there were other, more subtle learnings that were occurring as well. For example, I suspect that for most of the students, a fairly significant insight acquired that summer came gradually as they learned about me and my approach to teaching. The dawning awareness that, in spite of my informal demeanour, I had high standards for the time and energy they were to devote to their studies, came as I quietly but insistently pushed them to answer questions, waited while they struggled, and followed up with additional homework or individualized assignments when I discovered gaps in their understanding. As a result of this experience, they may have also concluded that school in North America differs significantly from school in their countries.

This is an example of apperceptive learning, learning that occurs on the periphery of consciousness as a result of day-in-day-out participation in the rhythms and routines of my classroom. I organized lessons so that students would learn, not only English, but also the values of what might be called democratic interaction—respect for others, freedom of choice, opportunities to fail or succeed on one's own terms. These are not lessons that can be learned from didactic instruction (there were no lectures on how to work independently), they have to be experienced, so that the insights and understandings seep in around the edges of consciousness and become habits of mind.

It was my intention to conduct English lessons that modelled these values and that provided guidance for students on how they might conduct themselves, both as language learners and responsible classmates. Bateson, elaborating on a phrase used by Margaret Mead, referred to this as conduct whose immediate implicit value provided the basis for learning. Mead had presented a paper in which she argued that democracy could not be achieved by totalitarian means. Bateson wrote a response that supported her analysis, arguing that social scientists cannot treat humans as if they were mere tools (Bateson 1972: 159-76). Although his remarks were intended for social scientists who had convened to address the threat of Nazism, the remarks also apply directly to the work of all teachers.

> We can, for example, put our finger very simply on the process which leads to tragedy and disillusionment whenever men decide that the "end justifies the means" in their efforts to achieve either a Christian or a blueprinted heaven-on-

earth. They ignore the fact that in social manipulation, the tools are not hammers and screwdrivers. A screwdriver is not seriously affected when, in an emergency, we use it as a wedge; and a hammer's outlook on life is not affected because we sometimes use its handle as a simple lever. But in social manipulation, our tools are people, and people learn, and they acquire habits which are more subtle and pervasive than the tricks which the blueprinter teaches them. With the best of intentions in the world, he or she may train children to spy upon their parents in order to eradicate some tendency prejudicial to the success of the blueprint, but because the children are people, they will do more than learn this simple trick. They will build this experience into their whole philosophy of life; it will colour all their attitudes toward authority (Bateson 1972: 163-64).

In other words, just as we cannot force people to behave democratically, we cannot achieve communicative classrooms through drill and lecture. If we want students to acquire conversational control of the language, they have to not only learn the language, but participate in class activities that permit them to experience the freedoms of conversation. This is not a novel assertion, but it is made, not from an ideological commitment to a particular method, but from an understanding of humans and human interaction derived from Batesonian premises of communication, context, and control.

Conclusion

In conclusion, I would like to elaborate on the use of the term "ecology" in the title of the chapter. In my effort to develop a unifying framework for my work, one that provides a way of organizing my understanding of the complexity of learning and teaching, I have settled on ecology. As areas of professional conduct, ecology and education share a number of similarities. Both deal with the everyday world familiar to everyone, and both utilize insights from many disciplines. Both are concerned, not merely with the material world, but with recursive cycles and patterns of relationships among phenomena of different size and scope in that world. So, for example, ecologists study, not foxes and rabbits, but the cyclical fluctuation of fox and rabbit populations in relationship to the specific flora and fauna of their habitat. Likewise, we language educators are concerned, not merely with the educational gains of particular students, but with the complex environments of classrooms, schools, and communities and the conditions that promote such gains. Like ecology, education is a science of practice, and while there is certainly much more to teaching than what can be observed in the classroom, teaching is always and ultimately a practical endeavour. And finally, like the ecologist, we must take pains to assure that there is a fit between our ideas about the world, our observations of it, and our attempts to work in it on a day-by-day basis.

As I hope this chapter makes clear, Bateson has provided an important foundation for my efforts at developing an ecological perspective of language teaching. But for me, the task is much more fundamental than that. In this chapter, I have attempted to show how one might take a view of the world and bring it to bear on the teaching of languages. I have said that "it is all one thing," referring to language learning and teaching and all other aspects of life. I took this attitude first from Gregory Bateson and then later from Earl Stevick. Bateson said that he had "worked to practise living in the world of truth instead of the world of epistemological fantasy" (Bateson 1972: 480). He was referring to the need for modern humans to live their lives in such a way that they understand ours is a world of finite resources. Stevick had originally chosen a different title for his classic *Teaching Languages: A Way and Ways* (Stevick 1980). He wanted to call it, *Teaching Languages: A Matter of Life and Death,* but his editor said this was too much—too heavy a title for a language text. I think he had the same sorts of commitments in mind when he suggested that title as Bateson did when he asserted the need to live in a world of truth.

When we get to the point, as teachers, that we enter the classroom feeling, not just confident that we have a good lesson to give, but that we are engaged in an authentic activity, that who we are as teachers is who we are as human beings, and that our efforts contribute to the greater good, then we will have arrived at the goal envisioned by Bateson and Stevick.

REFERENCES CITED

Bateson, G. 1972. *Steps to an Ecology of Mind.* New York: Ballantine Books.

———. 1979. *Mind and Nature.* New York: E.P. Dutton.

Clarke, M.A., B.K. Dobson, and S. Silberstein. 1996. *Choice Readings.* Ann Arbor: University of Michigan Press.

Stevick, E.W. 1980. *Teaching Languages: A Way and Ways.* Rowley, MA: Newbury House.

CHAPTER TEN

JANUSZ KORCZAK

❋

UNTUNNELLING OUR VISION
Lessons From a Great Educator

David J. Mendelsohn
York University, Toronto

Introduction

The "information revolution" that has accompanied the astounding technological developments of the latter half of this century has enabled academics and teachers to have easy and immediate access to vast quantities of information. This has, however, had a negative impact as well: it has resulted in the fact that our profession has become somewhat inward looking. Flooded with information in our own field, we sometimes fail to benefit from the wealth of knowledge and ideas in other fields—we are suffering from "tunnel vision."

This chapter describes the ideas and life of a great man, Janusz Korczak, who had nothing to do with language education, but whose thinking and values have had a profound effect on my ideas about language teaching, and who had something very valuable to say to all of us. My goal is to apply these ideas to the second/foreign language (ESOL) classroom. Interestingly Korczak himself built his ideas from his knowledge in very disparate fields: medicine, sociology, socialist thought, and humanism. It is to this great man, his orphanage children, and his staff, that I dedicate this paper.

The following story had a profound impact on me as a young graduate student, and shaped the way I try to relate to my students. In 1964, when I was a young graduate student, Professor A.E. Simon in one of his lectures recounted the following story about Korczak:

> In the 1920s, an eminent humanist educator of Polish nationality and Jewish origins, Janusz Korczak, gave a large group of prospective teachers their first lecture. His lecture was entitled, "The Heart of the Child." He came into the lecture hall accompanied by a very small boy clutching his hand. Without speaking, he stood the boy behind a fluoroscope, which enabled the audience to see the rapidly beating heart of the nervous child. After a few moments, he said: 'Don't ever forget this sight. Before you raise a hand to a child, before you administer any kind of punishment, remember what this frightened heart looks like. That is all for today.' And he left the room, still holding the little boy by the hand.

Ever since I heard about this remarkable and dramatic demonstration, Korczak's ideas have guided the way I function as a teacher, whether teaching ESOL to beginners or to advanced students, teaching children or adults, or lecturing to inexperienced pre-service teachers or to experienced in-service teachers. Korczak epitomizes the dedicated, humanistic educator—a man with a very deep love for his students, children in the orphanages he ran. Korczak's work was all with children, and this will be reflected in many of the quotes that are cited. However, if we replace the word "child" with the word "student," then virtually everything he wrote will be meaningful to us, regardless of whom we teach. This does not imply that I am equating second/foreign language students, many of whom are adults, with children. On the contrary, it is precisely because I believe that our students, like children, are often treated with less respect than is due to them, particularly when they are immigrants or refugees, that Korczak's call for respect and love for his students is so poignant for us.

WHO WAS JANUSZ KORCZAK?

Janusz Korczak (1878-1942) was an extremely important figure in European education. He was especially prominent and influential in educational circles in Poland and throughout Eastern and Central Europe in the period up to World War II. Unfortunately, his work is not well known in the English-speaking world, largely because he preferred to present his ideas not as "educational theories" in academic publications, but rather as thoughts expressed in anecdotes and fictional stories.

Korczak was born Henryk Goldszmit in Poland in 1878. Because of the rampant anti-Semitism in Poland at that time, he wrote under the non-Jewish sounding pseudonym Janusz Korczak, by which he is best known. His parents were very assimilated, non-religious Jews, who stressed the ethical rather than the ritualistic aspects of Judaism.

Korczak did not have a very easy childhood. His father was mentally ill, suffering a nervous breakdown when Korczak was 11 years old, and ended his life in an asylum. As a result, Korczak had to contribute to the family income. In his teens he began tutoring children, and discovered he liked this work. By this stage, although he already was a very successful writer of children's and adult fiction, he decided to become a pediatrician and not a full-time author. He did, however, continue to write fictional works. As he wrote: "Literature is just words, while medicine is deeds." He wrote that medicine would give him insights into human personality. He wanted to understand children in general and why each one was different.

While a medical student, Korczak became part of the "Flying University"— Poland's flourishing underground college, where the greatest minds in the country had to meet secretly because of their democratic, socialist leanings. It was there that he met and came under the influence of Jan Wladslaw Dawid, Poland's first experimental psychologist. Dawid, greatly influenced by the work of Rousseau, advocated radical change in education, liberating the child from traditional restraints. Korczak was also greatly influenced, as can be seen especially in his later writings, by the educational theories of the Swiss educator, Pestalozzi. He was to carry the lessons he learned from Dawid and subsequently Pestalozzi throughout his life as a teacher and orphanage director—evidenced by his meticulous recording of scientific data such as the children's weight and height, and his insistence on teachers carrying out extensive observations on each of their students.

Korczak became a highly successful pediatrician and served as a medical officer in 1905 in the Russo-Japanese war. The suffering of soldiers and civilians that he witnessed served to strengthen his interest in children. In 1910 he gave up his medical practice to work in an orphanage and summer camp for Jewish children, which he became head of in 1912. By this time, his fame was spreading as a result of his fictional writing, for which he received many prizes. In the orphanage and the summer camps, his educational ideas were put into practice: he established a children's newspaper and a children's court, which insured the fair administration of the orphanage.

In these years, we see Korczak beginning to champion the rights of the child. He saw children as the salvation of the world and built his ideas on a genuine and sincere affection for children—both for what they are, and a respect for what they can become. This did not, however, mean that he believed in giving children complete freedom or never punishing them.

After four years of working in the Jewish orphanage, Korczak was conscripted into the Czar's army for World War I. It was while in the army that he wrote his seminal work, "How to Love a Child" (in Wolins 1967). This, together with "The Child's Right to Respect," provide the clearest statement of his educational values and beliefs (in Wolins 1967).

On returning to an independent Poland, he was asked to head a Catholic orphanage, but, since Jewish children were barred from attending this institution, Korczak agreed to become the head of this orphanage while maintaining his position at the Jewish orphanage that he already headed.

During the period from the end of World War I to Hitler's rise to power in the 1930s, Korczak became a very prominent educator, and was known in many parts of Europe. He gave many talks to educators, had a regular radio show called "The Old Doctor," and always stressed the notion of humane, moral, loving education.

KORCZAK'S EDUCATIONAL PRINCIPLES

Janusz Korczak was a great educator and a great teacher. He was never a theorist, and despite his extensive writings on education, he never claimed to offer a unified educational theory—or, indeed, one that was suitable for all settings at all times. What made him an outstanding and unique educator was his most unusual correlation between rhetoric and reality. Korczak rarely preached what he didn't practise, and rarely practised what he didn't preach. Korczak's ideas took shape over 70 years ago in a very different part of the world, and with no thoughts whatsoever concerning language education. Hence, the most exciting and fascinating part about researching Korczak's educational principles is that this man's ideas and writings on education are extremely valuable and relevant to us in TESOL today. As his friend Igor Newerly stated, what is so very important in Korczak's writing is the "climate of his words, and his life, the regenerating power of thinking in the categories of humanism." He said, "From a conversation with Korczak one may emerge ... a slightly better man, slightly more complete" (Newerly "Introduction" in Wolins 1967: xiv).

Underlying everything Korczak wrote about and did in education is the fact that he cared about his students. He always treated them with respect, and pioneered what today we call "moral education" (Lifton 1988: 62). Korczak came to education as a humanist and social reformer. He saw education as a form of social engineering. For Korczak, "the reform of educational goals was therefore nothing less than the reconstruction of the world to better, more humane values" (Frost Incomplete: 39).

He created what he called a "children's republic," built on the premise that our students are not the people of tomorrow, but they are people today, thus entitled to be taken seriously and treated as equals, with respect. This notion has very important implications for us in ESOL. All too often, we forget that our students, particularly those with a very low proficiency level, are highly intelligent people to be respected and valued. Sadly, I have many times seen jaded teachers of ESOL who have forgotten this and treat their students as mentally deficient. This also has implications for our choice of ESOL teaching materials. Particularly when we need low level materials, it is easy for us to fall into the trap of selecting more childish materials on the premise that they will be simpler, when, in fact, this is not necessarily the case. Instead, they may be downright patronizing.

In "How to Love a Child," Korczak wrote extensively about the necessity for teachers to love and to accept their students, never abusing the teachers' authority. Korczak uses the term "love" to mean what he called "pedagogic love," which he defines as true giving of self. It is a term I think we should all adopt. This is what the Greeks called *agape*—selfless love—to distinguish it from *eros*—selfish and carnal love. Korczak offers a rather surprising model for the school or educational institution. His model is the hospital. His reason for this analogy is that the hospital and its staff neither accuse nor judge, but rather examine and treat ("The Special School" in Wolins 1976: 540-41). I believe it would be a healthy shift in mind-set for most of us to relate to a school or any educational institution in these terms. He defines one of the main goals of educators as raising students to a state of self-reliance and autonomy—identical to one of our goals in ESOL.

He believed that teachers' power exceeds their competence—as he put it, *sic volo, sic jubeo*—paraphrased as "so I want, and so I order" ("How to Love a Child" in Wolins 1967: 449). Or, as he put it, "We must end despotism [by teachers]" (in Wolins 1967: 405). As a result, he established a very effective "Children's Court," with rules and regulations for students and staff alike. It sat in judgment over the offenders regardless of whether they were students or staff members. This guaranteed accountability by everyone, it established equality, and it provided recourse. And at the same time, it taught the children about self-government.

Korczak also believed very strongly in the importance of a school newspaper. He argued that it fosters a sense of importance and independence, helps the shy students to express themselves, and helps the students to learn to express themselves logically. We in ESOL programs often have institutional newspapers, but they tend more to be showpieces of our student's progress in writing, rather than an important binding force for the whole institution. Maybe we should modify our newspapers accordingly, and perhaps use computer-mediated communication as well.

In a talk entitled, "Principles of Education: Conversations with Tutors," Korczak offered five basic principles of education:

1. We need to respect the bad child as well as the good child. If we begin by loving the good child, he says, somehow ultimately we will also love the bad child. He also warns us against being drawn to the nice students ("How to Love a Child" in Wolins 1967: 306).

2. We must acknowledge that equality is a myth—all students are different. Acknowledgement of this inequality is of vital importance if we are to treat our students fairly, despite huge cultural, cognitive, social, and affective differences between them. True educators need to relate to each child as an individual, as a unique case, adapting their behaviour to suit the different personalities in their classes (Frost 1983:17). For example, we have to be sensitive to the socially awkward student, for whom group work or pair work is truly painful. In fact, such a student might refuse to participate, making it necessary to devise individual tasks for when the rest of the class is working in groups. What is more, this has to be handled with great tact. Happily, recent work on differences in learning styles is raising our consciousness on this matter significantly, thereby bringing us closer to this acknowledgement of the uniqueness of our students that Korczak is calling for.

Building on this notion of acknowledging the uniqueness of every student, Korczak advocates exceptional laws for exceptional children, "with the consent of the community" ("How to Love a Child" in Wolins 1967: 170). Korczak's ideas call for us to change the sense of our task—not to mold the students, but to work on what they can become. Frost, translating Korczak's own words, says: "Not, 'I shall make of you a man,' but 'What could you become—Oh man!'" (Frost Incomplete: 72).

3. We can strike a balance between freedom and discipline. If you want to be able to teach, says Korczak, there has to be order and discipline, however much we believe in giving children as much freedom as possible. He writes how he began as a young educator believing in complete freedom, and what a disaster that had been. There have to be rules. But the rules must be thoughtful, sensitive, and rational. Interestingly, for Korczak, the opposite of "total freedom" is not "rules" or "oppressive regulations," but "cooperation" by the students. In our communicative teaching model, we sometimes send our students the wrong message—that anything goes, and that there are no rules or requirements. Korczak believed that students expect and deserve the teacher-provided structure, order, and efficient classroom manage-

ment within which to carry out their work—and the same would surely be true for a communication-based lesson. Unclear instructions or careless grouping of students for group work is sufficient for excellent activities to be a dismal failure.

4. Korczak says that educators should not become genuinely angry. He says, "If the students do not do what I say, ask why." We can act as if we are angry, but this should never be real anger. In this way, the reaction will always be rational. However, if we are genuinely angry with a student, he recommends that we do not react immediately, but rather wait a day because we can cause wounds with our words. As well, he says that we should try not to raise our voice, because when we do, students stop understanding and begin to fear.

When we have an impossible student, we need to think about their background and what has made them the way they are. He tells about an impossible child in the orphanage, who he could no longer keep and "returned" to his grandfather. On doing so, he said, "Don't hit him." The grandfather replied, "Why should I hit him? Life will do all the hitting that is needed."

5. Korczak also believed that we must teach students to set realistic goals. He did this through a system of "wagers" or bets between himself and a student. For example, a student who had a fight on average five times a week, bet that he would only have one fight in the following week. Korczak would then negotiate a more realistic target for the week, since for that child to go down to only one fight per week from his usual five, was not realistic. The children involved in wagers reported back the following week, and if they had kept to what was wagered, they received a reward in candies.

This idea translates very nicely for us in ESOL teaching into the negotiation and setting of realistic goals for each of our students. By individualizing these, ensuring that the goals are realistic, and constantly reviewing the students' progress, we can provide ongoing feedback, and, hopefully, a very positive sense of progress.

How to Treat Students

Korczak had very clear opinions as to how to treat students. Korczak told how at first, he used to speak to children rather patronizingly and condescendingly, and how he changed this ("How to Love a Child" in Wolins 1967: 401). This is a healthy reminder to us in ESOL. All too often, especially when explaining complex ideas to low-level students, we speak in a patronizing way, which is unacceptable, regardless of the students' level of proficiency.

Korczak also comes out very strongly against sarcasm in the classroom. He sees this as an example of teachers hurting their students with words, and forgetting the enormous power that they wield. As he wrote: "By jeering at a child for not knowing, you kill the desire to learn, to know" ("Educational Factors" in Wolins 1967:

38). As the late Professor Simon, a dedicated follower of Korczak, said, there is absolutely no place for sarcasm ever in the classroom. Sarcasm is revenge when the teacher has been hurt. Besides, it doesn't usually work in the ESOL class because sarcasm relies on a level of linguistic sophistication that many ESOL students do not yet have. Whenever I am tempted to be sarcastic, I remember Professor Simon's words.

Students have the right to be taken seriously, to be treated with respect, and to be addressed respectfully. I see this as being related, for us, to the fact that many ESL teachers do not ever succeed, or do not even try to master the names of their students. To fail to learn the names of students, or even worse, to arbitrarily assign them Western names, as I have seen some teachers do, is, I believe, to demean the individual in a very serious way.

We may believe that we do not punish our ESL students, and that is why Korczak's words are so important to us: "Constant slighting and humiliating withdrawal ... a reproachful glance, a gesture of resignation, a sigh of exasperation ... an unfulfilled threat, ... is a severe and painful punishment" because it discourages the student, and leads to him or her giving up and losing self-confidence ("How to Love a Child" in Wolins 1967: 276, 279).

Korczak is also very critical of collective punishment or collective blame. It leads to stereotyping, which we have to guard against so carefully in our field. As Korczak says, we must avoid resorting to comments or attitudes such as, "That's what they are like" or, "[It's] all they can do" ("The Child's Right to Respect" in Wolins 1967: 496).

Establishing the right rapport in the classroom is very important. He states that students have to be treated with sensitivity by the teacher and, more importantly, by their peers. The students have to know, for example, that it is never acceptable to laugh at anyone, and that when giving another student negative feedback on his or her efforts, it must be suitably softened. We know how true that is for us, particularly teaching within a communicative model, since we want our students to take risks and to try things without danger of reprimand or embarrassment.

Finally, Korczak makes the very important point that students have the right to make mistakes and to fail. "There are no more fools among children than among adults" (quoted in Lifton 1988: 356-57).

The Good Educator

Korczak liked to talk about being an educator rather than being a teacher. He wrote that a teacher is paid to drill something into the student, while an educator draws something out—strives to achieve not what ought to be, but what is possible from every student.

Korczak spells out seven basic requirements of good educators, and each and every one is as relevant for us today in our world, in our field, as they were for him in his.

1. To be good educators, Korczak demanded, first and foremost, a commitment as deep as his own, a boundless love for the students, and the clear goal of helping and improving them.

2. A good educator is not one with the greatest amount of knowledge, or with the clearest philosophy, but one who asks questions, and knows how to go about getting the answers—hence the requirement never to laugh at a student's questions (Cohen 1988: 177). He wrote that teachers should keep diaries of their own endeavours. This leads to a taking stock of one's successes and failures, and learning from them. In short, translated into our terms, Korczak was calling for what Richards and Lockhart call "reflective teaching" (Richards and Lockhart 1994).

3. Good educators, says Korczak, are modest and acknowledge the limits of their knowledge, never pretend to be all-knowing, and are always willing to find out more. In addition, they are very critical of what they are doing and admit their mistakes. Good educators know themselves and are true to themselves. They know their strengths and their weaknesses, and admit the weaknesses. Korczak distinguishes the "good" from the "bad" educator by saying that the good educators learn from their mistakes while the bad educators blame their students. Part of the appeal of Korczak is that he is incredibly honest about his failures. Many of us suffer from what I cynically call the "Genesis Syndrome." In *Genesis*, it says, "And God looked on His work and saw that it was good." We tend to do the same, particularly when we have invested a lot of time and effort in preparation. If something, some activity is not working, hard as it is, surely we are best off to admit this, to abandon it, and to move on.

4. The good educator is a doer, not merely a talker. Korczak wrote: "Keep your mouth shut if you are not helping. Don't criticize if you don't know a better way" (quoted in Lifton 1988: 47). Korczak lived up to his own demand that an educator must be a doer, in everything he did, even in the horror of the Warsaw Ghetto. After describing in graphic detail the lack of funds from which his orphanage was suffering in the Ghetto, he continued: "I demand that you remit one hundred zloty for the support of the orphanage. I demand—I do not ask. I shall personally call within the next few days for the funds" (cited in Frost 1983: 9). This is a drastic example, called for in drastic times. However, it is not different in spirit from the call made by Mary Ashworth in her excellent book *Beyond Methodology* (1985), in which she says that teachers must be active doers and not just complainers.

5. Good educators motivate their students and make learning pleasurable. We sometimes make the mistake of taking motivation for granted, and assume, particularly if we are teaching adults, that our students will automatically be highly motivated. This is not necessarily the case, and motivation is something that has to be worked at at all times in all programs. Korczak is also very critical of rote learning. He sees it as pointless, and in fact damaging because it can lead to cheating to avoid failure. What is more, rote learning does not encourage inquiry and investigation, and leads to unhealthy competition instead of cooperation.

6. Good educators are constantly trying new things, and, what is more, this is a way of avoiding burnout. Falling into a routine can lead to burnout, says Korczak. Interestingly, he says one of the ways to avoid burnout is by focusing a lot of attention and effort on the students who are problematic.

7. Good educators involve their students by explaining to them what they are doing and why. This is particularly relevant in a field like ESOL, where we often teach students who are used to a very different approach to learning and teaching from the seemingly unstructured communicative approach. It is not sufficient to say to students, "I know what I am doing—trust me." Surely it is more effective if their consciousness is raised, and they understand fully what is going on and why. When students are involved in this way, I have found that they are much more likely to "buy into" what is being done and to cooperate. It shows that the teacher respects them and their abilities.

Teacher Education

With regard to teacher education, I would like to begin with a generalized observation. As I did the research for this chapter, it became very clear to me that what is missing in many TESOL teacher education courses is a course on "theories and principles of education." A course of this type has a very definite place, in my opinion, if we are truly committed to educating our prospective teachers rather than merely training them. The course could present different educational thinkers and their ideas, as they apply to language education, and could explore basic humanistic values and principles such as those of Korczak. This would help to expand the vision of the prospective teachers whom we educate, and space should be made for such a course in our TESOL programs. After all, we spend a great deal of time teaching about different methodologies. But methodologies come and methodologies go, while the validity and importance of these values is forever.

In his writings on education, Korczak had some very valuable comments to make specifically about teacher education. In a section of one of his essays, "The Special School," Korczak describes the relationship between theory and practice. He sees theory merely as a starting point to be built on by practice. As he says, "I make a start from what others know" ("The Special School" in Wolins 1967: 525). But then practice must validate theory as follows: "Theory enhances the intellect, ... [but] 'I know' does not mean that I act in accordance with what I know." Good educators must recognize that theory without practice is meaningless. To quote Korczak: "Practice is the soul of theory," and teachers should never enslave themselves to a theory or a book (cited in Cohen 1988: 172).

Korczak describes teacher education as an education in what to ask and how to seek answers, rather than as a transmission of information and recipes. This fits extremely well with current thinking on TESOL teacher preparation. His approach, in effect, goes further, and demands lifelong in-service learning and reflection by teachers.

Korczak believed that teachers should do precise and extensive observation of their students (cited in Cohen 1988: 184). In TESOL, we aim for prospective teachers to observe a lot of classes, mainly in order to observe the teacher. But what Korczak is calling for is very close observation and note-taking on our students in order to get to know their backgrounds, personalities, likes and dislikes, and learning styles. It is particularly important for us in ESOL to know about our students' backgrounds, as some of them are refugees who have suffered terrible trauma, while others may be unemployed and/or very short of money. It is imperative that we be sensitive to this.

Korczak drafted a very intriguing six-year teacher education program. The first year is devoted to a study of self, the second year to observation of children, and only then do they get three years of theory, and finally, in their sixth year, they work with teachers in schools. This model may be clumsy and impossible for today's world, but what is really interesting is the approach, and the order in which he handles theory and practice. He even went so far as to design a subsequent 30-year "period of reflection"—in-service teacher education for the practising teacher, divided into six blocks of five years (Cohen 1988: 171-75).

KORCZAK AND THE HOLOCAUST

On 1 September 1939, Hitler invaded Poland and one year later, on Yom Kippur, 12 October 1940, the Warsaw Ghetto was established and all of Warsaw's Jews were forced to move into that part of the city. This included Korczak and his orphanage. From the Ghetto, the Jews were sent to their deaths in one of the Nazi extermination camps.

In the Warsaw Ghetto, under the Nazis, Korczak did not compromise his values and principles, even against all odds, as the walls of sanity and humanity crumbled around him. He wanted the children to remain with a positive disposition, and so when they were forced to move within the Ghetto walls, into truly terrible conditions, he organized this tragic move as if it was a circus parade coming into town. The parade was headed by Korczak, carrying the banner of their orphanage, which was the flag of Korczak's fictional child-king, Matt the First, in his famous children's story of the same name.

Korczak was determined that his orphanage would continue to be a just and positive place, and he succeeded right to the very end. His orphanage was decorated with paper flowers, it was governed by the children according to Korczak's principles, and, according to eyewitnesses, it was the envy of the Ghetto for its humanity. Educational and cultural programs continued until the day before their deportation.

Despite this, the children were extremely undernourished and sickly, and they lived in fear, with bestiality and death all around them. The conditions were appalling—it is only that their conditions were slightly less appalling than that of the rest of the children in the Ghetto. Part of the reason that Korczak, ever the "doer," managed to feed the children a little more than some, was that he devoted his entire day, every day, to begging, scrounging, and negotiating for food.

Korczak's heroism manifested itself in his acts of bravery and defiance when trying to get food for the children, even when it meant going to the Gestapo Headquarters and demanding back a wagonload of potatoes that an SS guard had stolen from the orphanage. This cost him a month in the Gestapo prison, and very nearly cost him his life.

In the face of all this evil and hatred, Korczak continued to see the good in people: In response to a friend's outburst about Poles who informed on Jews in hiding and handed them over to the Gestapo, Korczak said: "Remember, for each one who acts like that, there are many who behave decently. Basically, people are good."

But his true altruism and heroism, because it was both, was in his dedication to the children and his refusal to abandon them. Three times in those terrible years, Korczak could have saved his own life, and three times he opted, instead, to stay with the children. First, when they were due to move into the Ghetto, his non-Jewish friends offered to hide him in the Aryan sector. He refused. Then, about a month before his death, his non-Jewish friend Igor Newerly smuggled himself into the Ghetto in a garbage truck, with forged papers for Korczak, and again Korczak refused to leave. And finally, at the railway siding, while the children were being loaded into cattle cars for "resettlement," a Nazi official called him aside, and eyewitnesses are almost certain that again an offer was made to him, but once again he refused, and instead he went with the children. When Newerly came into the Ghetto with the forged papers and pleaded with Korczak to save his own life, given that there was no hope of him saving the children by staying with them, Korczak's reply to Newerly was simple and yet monumental: "You do not leave a sick child in the night, and you do not leave children at a time like this."

On the evening of 5 August 1942, 22 months after entering the Warsaw Ghetto, Korczak was informed that the following morning all the members of his orphanage were to go to the square from which the "resettlement trains" left.

Korczak knew what this meant, and the following morning the children were told to dress in the best clothes they had, and he lined them up in front of the orphanage and led them to the square. Korczak led the children, and at the head of the column marched one of the children with King Matt's flag—their flag, held high.

Nahum Remba, the secretary of the Jewish Council of the Warsaw Ghetto and an eyewitness, described the scene as follows:

> Korczak led the procession. This was not an ordinary boarding of a train for a journey; it was a march of mute protest against barbarism, a scene never to be forgotten. The children marched in groups with Korczak in the lead holding two little ones by the hand ... They marched to their death with dignity and with looks of utter contempt at the barbarians, their eyes crying out for someone to avenge their tragedy—and ours. Even the Ghetto police stood at attention and saluted as they passed. Germans who witnessed the scene asked, "Wer ist dieser Mann?" (Who is that man?) (Korczak *Ghetto Diary* 1978: dust cover).

Korczak's life ended tragically, yet heroically on 6 August 1942 when, under Nazi machine guns, he walked ahead of his 192 students and 10 orphanage staff to the railway siding in the Warsaw Ghetto, into the box cars, and from the box cars directly to the gas chambers at Treblinka concentration camp. Not one of them survived.

This is the compelling, uplifting, and tragic story of a great educator. Without knowing the background, an analysis of his educational ideas would not be complete. Here was a man who truly loved children and who believed fervently in the importance of providing them with a sound education. A man who describes in his fictional play, *Senate of Madmen* (1931), a very bleak and Kafkaesque view of the world of adults. A man who saw the only hope lying with the children. He describes how God exploded himself into millions of drops of water and penetrated into the heart of every child.

I would like to close with the words of Adir Cohen:

> Korczak was an enlightened and loving educator who gave his whole life to the education of his children. He carried the "flag of life" through the "gates of death" to eternity. His name will continue to be a beacon of light for those dreamers who dream of a better world (Cohen 1988: 339).

My thanks to my friends and colleagues Marc Silverman, Rena Helms-Park and Robert Fisher for their comments on various drafts of this paper.

REFERENCES CITED

Ashworth, M. 1985. *Beyond Methodology*. Cambridge: Cambridge University Press.

Cohen, A. 1988. *Education as Love: Janusz Korczak the Educator* (in Hebrew). (Hebrew title: *Lihyot Shemesh, Lihyot Or: Hachinuch Ke Ahava—Dugmato shel Janusz Korczak*.) Haifa: Ach Publishers.

Frost, S. Incomplete manuscript. *Janusz Korczak: Believer in Goodness in a World of Evil*.

———. 1983. 'Janusz Korczak: Friend of Children.' *Moral Education Forum*: 4-22.

Korczak, J. 1931. *Senate of Madmen*. Warsaw.

———. 1962. 'Principles of Education: Conversations with Tutors' (In Hebrew). (Hebrew title: '*Klalei Chinuch: Sichot im Madrichim*'). *Mibifnim* (Sept.): 417-19.

———. 1967. 'The Child's Right to Respect'. In *Selected Works of Janusz Korczak*, edited by M. Wolins, 463-500. Washington DC: National Science Foundation.

———. 1967. 'Educational Factors.' In *Selected Works of Janusz Korczak*, edited by M. Wolins, 1-80. Washington DC: National Science Foundation.

———. 1967. 'How to Love a Child.' In *Selected Works of Janusz Korczak*, edited by M. Wolins, 81-462. Washington DC: National Science Foundation.

———. 1967. 'The Special School.' In *Selected Works of Janusz Korczak*, edited by M. Wolins, 524-54. Washington DC: National Science Foundation.

———. 1978. *Ghetto Diary*. New York: Holocaust Library.

Lifton, B.J. 1988. *The King of Children: A Biography of Janusz Korczak*. New York: Schocken Books.

Newerly, I. 1967. 'Introduction.' In *Selected Works of Janusz Korczak*, edited by M. Wolins, xvii-xlvi. Washington DC: National Science Foundation.

Richards, J.C. and C. Lockhart. 1994. *Reflective Teaching in Second Language Classrooms*. New York: Cambridge University Press.

Wolins, M., ed. 1967. *Selected Works of Janusz Korczak*. Washington DC: National Science Foundation.

Notes on Contributors

Editor

David J. Mendelsohn is associate professor of ESL, Director of the MA program in theoretical and applied linguistics, and Co-ordinator of the ESL Tutoring Centre at York University in Toronto. He has also held teaching appointments at the University of Toronto and the Hebrew University of Jerusalem. He has published five books (as author or principal author): two theoretical books on listening comprehension, a classroom text and teacher's manual for the speaking class, and a classroom text for the writing class. His research is concerned with bridging the gap between theories and classroom practice. He has been an invited speaker at numerous conferences and universities in Canada, the US, Israel, Britain, Mexico, South Africa, Singapore, Malaysia, Thailand, and the Czech Republic.

Contributors

Sharron Bassano is a teacher trainer and consultant in ESL methods and materials and in English Language development in the content areas. She currently conducts teacher preparation courses for TESL Certificate programs at the University of California at Berkeley, Santa Cruz, and Santa Barbara. An ESL instructor and coordinator for over 21 years, she has authored and co-authored many student texts and resource books for teachers including *Look Who's Talking!*, *Drawing Out*, *First Class Reader*, *Purple Cows and Potato Chips*, *Community Spirit* (Alta Book Company), the *Sounds Easy* series (Prentice-Hall), and the *STAR Series: Life Science*, *Earth Science*, and *Social Studies Topics* (Addison-Wesley) for ESL students.

Robert Burden is a Professor in Applied Educational Psychology at the University of Exeter where he has worked for 25 years training teachers and school psychologists. He has been president of the International School Psychology Association where his particular interests have been in the development of whole school consultancy approaches in implementing school psychology and in students' perceptions of their learning experiences. He is the co-author with Marion Williams (see below) of *Psychology for Language Teachers* (Cambridge University Press).

Mary Ann Christison is a professor of ESL/English and Director of the International Center at Snow College in Utah. She also teaches courses in the Linguistics Program at the University of Utah as an adjunct professor. She is co-author with Sharron Bassano of seven books including *Look Who's Talking*, *Drawing Out*, *Community Spirit*, and *Purple Cows and Potato Chips*. A popular workshop presenter and speaker, she has consulted for more than 60 organizations in the United States and worked as a TEFL educator in more than 20 countries.

Mark A. Clarke is a professor of Education at the University of Colorado at Denver, where he directs the doctoral program and teaches in the Division of Language, Literacy, and Culture. He has written extensively on language learning and teaching, with a particular interest in issues surrounding the relationship between theory and practice. With Barbara Dobson and Sandra Silberstein, he is a co-author of *Reader's Choice*, *Choice Readings*, and the forthcoming *First Choices*, all published by the University of Michigan Press.

Judy B. Gilbert teaches pronunciation methods in the TESL Certificate program in the Education Department (Ext.) at the University of California at Berkeley. Her special interest is in enhancing pronunciation learning through the use of visual and kinesthetic aids. She has written many articles in technical and non-technical books and journals, is the author of two textbooks: *Clear Speech* (North American English) and *Clear Speech from the Start* (forthcoming book for beginners), and she is co-author of *Speaking Clearly* (British English).

Carol Hosenfeld is associate professor in the Department of Learning and Instruction and a member of the Center for Cognitive Science, State University of New York at Buffalo. Her research interests include literacy in English as a second language, cognition and second language acquisition, and developing frameworks for teaching cognitive and metacognitive processes. Her current publications include two book chapters in *Deixis in Narrative: A Cognitive Science Perspective* (Lawrence Erlbaum Associates) and articles on person and tense in *Discourse Processes* and on vocabulary development in *Foreign Language Annals*. Her recent conference presentations were on such topics as "Theories of Mind: Metacognition" and "A Crisis of Representation in Anthropology and Education" presented at the American Association for Applied Linguistics.

David J. Mendelsohn (see above)

Robert Oprandy is associate professor in the TESOL/TFL Program at the Monterey Institute of International Studies in Monterey, California. He has worked as a teacher or teacher educator on five continents and served on the TESOL Board of Directors from 1991-1994. His book, *Language Teaching Awareness* (Cambridge), co-authored with Jerry Gebhard, is being published in 1999. His scholarly interests are in the areas of teacher education, the development of listening skills (the subject of his next book), and humanistic approaches to education.

Adrian S. Palmer is an associate professor of English at the University of Utah, where he directs the TESOL training program. His main areas of interest include language testing research and test development, teacher training and professional development, and language teaching methodology. He is the author of nine books in the areas of language teaching methodology, testing research, communicative language teaching, language for special purposes, language teaching games, and professional development resources for teachers. His most recent book is *Language Testing in Practice: Designing and Developing Useful Language Tests* with Lyle F. Bachman (Oxford University Press).

Thomas Scovel is currently professor of Applied Linguistics at San Francisco State University. He has taught at over 20 universities in North America and around the world at summer institutes, as a USIS lecturer, and as a visiting scholar. He has published about 50 articles and reviews on linguistics, second language acquisition, TESOL methodology, and psycholinguistics. His 1988 book, *A Time to Speak*, is often cited as an important summary of the biological basis for a critical period of human speech. Two recent books include one on psycholinguistics for Oxford University Press and another on second language acquisition for Heinle and Heinle.

Marion Williams is a senior lecturer in Applied Linguistics at the University of Exeter. She has been involved in teaching English as a Foreign Language and teacher training for the last 25 years in the UK, Nigeria, Hong Kong, and Singapore. She now coordinates all the postgraduate TEFL courses at The School of Education. She is co-author with Robert Burden of *Psychology for Language Teachers* (Cambridge University Press).